Skills in

Cognitive Behaviour Counselling & Psychotherapy

Series Editor
Francesca Inskipp

Skills in Counselling & Psychotherapy Series
Series editor: Francesca Inskipp

Skills in Counselling & Psychotherapy is a series of practical guides for trainees and practitioners. Each book takes one of the main approaches to therapeutic work and describes the core skills and techniques used within that approach.

Topics covered include

- how to establish and develop the therapeutic relationship
- how to help the client change
- how to assess the suitability of the approach for the client.

This is the first series of books to look at skills specific to the different theoretical approaches, making it ideal for use on a range of courses which prepare the trainees to work directly with clients.

Books in the series:

Skills in Gestalt Counselling & Psychotherapy
Phil Joyce & Charlotte Sills

Skills in Transactional Analysis Counselling & Psychotherapy
Christine Lister-Ford

Skills in Person-Centred Counselling & Psychotherapy
Janet Tolan

Skills in

Cognitive Behaviour Counselling & Psychotherapy

Frank **Wills**

Los Angeles • London • New Delhi • Singapore

SAGE Publications Ltd
1 Oliver's Yard
55 City Road
London EC1Y 1SP

SAGE Publications Inc.
2455 Teller Road
Thousand Oaks, California 91320

SAGE Publications India Pvt Ltd
B 1/I 1 Mohan Cooperative Industrial Area
Mathura Road
New Delhi 110 044

SAGE Publications Asia-Pacific Pte Ltd
33 Pekin Street #02-01
Far East Square
Singapore 048763

Library of Congress Control Number: 2007936066

British Library Cataloguing in Publication data

A catalogue record for this book is available from the British Library

ISBN 978-1-4129-2167-1
ISBN 978-1-4129-2168-8 (pbk)

Typeset by C&M Digitals (P) Ltd., Chennai, India
Printed in Great Britain by The Cromwell Press Ltd, Trowbridge, Wiltshire
Printed on paper from sustainable resources

CONTENTS

FOREWORD

Frank and I met in 1994 on the Cognitive Therapy course in Oxford. We sat next to each other on the first day, and, like many group participants, continued to sit in exactly the same seats for the entire year. The trainees came from mixed backgrounds – nursing, social work, counselling and psychiatry – but the majority were clinical psychologists. At that time the main practitioners of CBT were psychologists and psychiatrists and 'non-psychologists' who were interested in the approach were regarded with suspicion. Most of the literature and research in CBT had a definite psychiatric bias, in its language and use of diagnostic categories, and as such was off-putting to many counsellors and psychotherapists. Frank and I were struck by the value and pragmatism of CBT, how it made good sense to clinicians and clients as a portable, educational and effective model. We'd come across a hostile response from counsellors, who accused CBT of reinforcing the medical model, being over-simplistic, dealing with symptoms rather than causes and lacking the weight and depth of other therapies. To give a flavour of old hostilities, an information booklet published by a local branch of a mental health charity described CBT as 'an argument between therapist and patient'. Cognitive therapy seemed to have a huge amount to offer, but definitely had an image problem.

Since completing our training in 1994, Frank and I have been on a mission to make CBT more rounded and accessible to people from traditions other than psychology and psychiatry – and hence the birth of our first book, *Cognitive Therapy: Transforming the Image* and the start of a long writing career together. *Skills in Cognitive Behaviour Counselling & Psychotherapy* is Frank's first solo book, and I am delighted to have a token presence in writing the foreword.

The tables have turned in many ways, and CBT is now the primary model for clinicians, counsellors and therapists from many backgrounds. The Layard Report is encouraging CBT training for an army of mental health workers with minimal clinical experience. Alongside the explosion of interest, CBT has moved on immensely since Frank and I trained. Concepts of compassion, mindfulness, acceptance and the centrality of emotion are coming alongside CBT's traditional focus on change, challenge and problems. We now talk about coming alongside our experience, watching it, letting it go, as well as writing it down and looking for alternatives. Process is as important as method. The therapeutic relationship has come centre stage.

The challenge for trainers and practitioners in the field is to know when to use different approaches, and not get swept away in the excitement of the 'third wave' of CBT. Practitioners from counselling and psychotherapy often make a beeline for the newer developments – concentrating on past experiences, taking a developmental perspective, schema focused work – which may risk losing the effective ingredients in traditional CBT. At the other end are new CBT converts, who chuck out all they have learned about being therapists and dive in with methods and techniques, anxious to practise thought records and behavioural experiments, leaving the poor client awash in a sea of activity. The art of CBT is to balance all these goodies, with a time and a place for everything. *Skills in Cognitive Behaviour Counselling & Psychotherapy* weaves an elegant tapestry of the old and new. The book covers all the key ingredients of CBT – a collaborative therapeutic relationship, maintaining structure and focus, formulation – and a range of methods and techniques, while also introducing the newer approaches of mindfulness, compassion and therapeutic process.

Therapy is a messy and unpredictable business. At times it goes to plan, but at other times we enter the murk and mire of human psyches and find ourselves in deep water. Frank has a wealth of experience of working as a CBT therapist and trainer, his students coming from a wide range of backgrounds. He has his own inimitable style, bringing in case studies and anecdotes to illuminate the practice of CBT. He shares the mess of his experience, good and difficult, which makes this book such a useful as well as entertaining read. He is not afraid to describe the times when he could have done things differently. He is not afraid, too, to talk about his personal thoughts and experience, and how he has used CBT for himself. Most importantly, Frank's description of CBT is grounded in emotion and interpersonally informed, and always holds the therapeutic relationship centre-stage. There are rich pickings to be had in this book, whether the reader dips in for a quick brush-up of a skill, or reads cover to cover.

Diana Sanders
Oxford
February 2008

INTRODUCTION

Two minor professional experiences in the mid-1990s seem to me to capture my approach to the skills of cognitive behaviour therapy. Firstly, I was asked to participate in a national attempt to establish NVQ competencies for psychotherapy in general and cognitive behaviour therapy in particular. This involved an extended series of meetings in London, sometimes in a smaller CBT group and sometimes in a larger group for all models. On day one, the CBT group quietly set about its task and by mid-afternoon had written a pretty fair first draft document containing the full range of CBT competencies. Before departing the metropolis, all the groups were called together for the final hour to compare notes. Clutching our nearly finished work, the CBT group was surprised to find that few other groups had got anywhere near so far. One group, I remember, was still having an unresolved argument about the exact definitions of 'therapist' and 'client'. I came away from this event believing that CBT had an unusually clearly and consensually defined set of skills and competencies. CBT people are generally quite pragmatic and inclined to get on with the job in hand. Nagging doubts, however, remained in my mind: are we too linear in our thinking and have we been missing something here?

A second incident happened at a conference in which I was giving a research paper on training counsellors in CBT. With my tongue somewhat in my cheek, I observed that, from a CBT perspective, counsellors sometimes 'listened too much'. By this I meant that some counsellors seem to want to reflect virtually anything the client says and thereby find it hard to achieve the kind of focus needed for the parsimony ('maximum gain for minimum effort') of CBT. Afterwards another trainer, who trained staff in the National Health Service, approached me with the remark, 'I was interested in that because I have a real struggle to get my trainees to listen at all.' I am sure that we were both exaggerating somewhat to make clear our respective predicaments (see Chapter 6 on working with emotions), yet there was also a grain of truth of our difference. I thought then, as I do now, that, on balance, I'd rather have my training problem than his.

Reflecting back now, I believe that these two incidents crystallised ideas that became and remain my main professional driving forces. In my practice, I have striven to combine careful and respectful listening to clients with focusing and clarifying key issues in ways that raise hope and signal realistic markers for change (Wills & Sanders, 1997; Wills, 1998; Sanders & Wills, 1999, 2003, 2005).

In my training work, I have tried to find ways of helping others to develop these same skills and qualities (Wills, 2006b). It is encouraging to note that there is now solid research evidence to suggest that it is possible to develop such effective balances of a range of skills and that CB therapists are as good as anybody in doing so (Keijsers et al., 2000).

In doing this training work, I have sometimes had to run the gauntlet of trainee reservations. While not always a comfortable experience, it has been helpful in making me keep rethinking my assumptions. I have worked with different professional groups, including counsellors, community justice workers, social workers, teachers and youth workers. One of the main reservations articulated by counsellors has been the alleged directiveness of CBT. As a matter of fact, I do believe that all therapies have their characteristic faults (Wills, 1998): often their faults are closely linked to their virtues. The characteristic sin of CBT is, I believe, the tendency to be overly directive and persuasive. Developing finely grained collaboration with the client offers the most effective safeguard against these tendencies. Initiating and developing such collaboration will be heavily emphasised throughout this book. The collaboration process itself is best safeguarded by subtle use of certain aspects of structuring the therapy process.

Other helping professions perhaps have fewer problems with the idea of direction in therapy but are often concerned about the 'disempowering' effect of highly technique-driven CBT. In this regard, it is important that CB therapists adopt methods to 'guide discovery' rather than to 'change minds' (Padesky, 1996). Creative ways of guiding discovery will infuse all aspects of the CB skills in this book and will constitute its second main pillar alongside collaboration.

Each chapter therefore assumes a stance of collaborative discovery in each practice area. Chapter 1 will describe and analyse some main theoretical underpinnings for different skills. It will also offer brief overviews on the CB perspective on interpersonal, cognitive, behavioural and emotional change. Chapter 2 will consider the skills of assessment and issue mapping (formulation). Chapter 3 will cover interpersonal skills from a CB perspective. Chapters 4, 5 and 6 will consider working to achieve therapeutic change in the areas of thinking, behaviour and feeling respectively. Chapter 7 will describe working to achieve changes in deeper seated and longer established 'patterns' ('schema change'). The final chapter, Chapter 8, will take a leaf from the excellent book of this series on Gestalt skills by Joyce & Sills (2001) and reflect on what it means to be a CB therapist in the wider field of the helping professions today.

I have noted before that it is hard for a writer to keep up with CBT because it is developing so quickly. I did not want this book to be too long so it has been hard at times to know what to put in and what to leave out. I have been helped immensely by various colleagues who have looked at my work: my thanks go out to my style consultants, Diana Sanders, Janet Grey and Annie Wills. Francesca Inskipp has been an inspirational and supportive series editor, going well beyond the extra mile on many occasions.

Francesca has edited this series of books on skills in the different therapeutic traditions. I have recently had the pleasure of interviewing Francesca as part of a series of recorded interviews with significant contributors to the development of counselling (School of Social Studies, University of Wales Newport). Francesca's work was seminal in the skills development area (Inskipp, 1986, 1996). I have always found the exercises in her various handbooks to be exceptionally clear, effective and (in one of the favourite words of CB therapists) parsimonious. Taking inspiration from her exercises, each chapter has included suggestions for exercises and reflections.

I must also say a very big thank you to Alison Poyner and her team at SAGE for their skilled help and forbearance.

I wanted to keep the book reasonably short, imagining that it could be taken into action, rather than left back at base. I sometimes feel that therapy books need the equivalent of the *Guardian* 'digested read' service. The *Guardian* now has a 'digested, digested read' feature. If this book is ever included there, I hope it will read: *CBT: once more but this time with more feeling!*

There is a companion website accompanying this book. This can be found on the SAGE website at: www.sagepub.co.uk/wills.

Note

CBT theory, practice and skills are intimately related. Competent practice requires that skill use is underpinned by theoretical knowledge. This SAGE series is firmly centred on skill use. In order that this book stays within reasonable length, it is necessary to assume that the reader will have a certain familiarity with basic CBT theory so that it does not always need to be fully described here. Some such knowledge is assumed about:

- the basic relationship between thoughts, feelings and behaviour,
- the nature of and relationship between negative automatic thoughts, dysfunctional assumptions, core beliefs and early maladaptive schemas,
- the nature of avoidance,
- the basic CBT models of depression and anxiety,
- the collaborative therapeutic relationship.

Further references and reading on these concepts are listed throughout the book and on the SAGE website connected to this book.

On the other hand, understanding the knowledge base is so crucial to some types of skill use that a fuller account is necessary even here (for example, the discussion of 'cognitive processing' in Chapters 4 and 6). There are, however, also some instances of helpful concepts related to use of skills that are not widely described in the CBT literature: for example, Seymour Epstein's work on the relationship between cognition and emotion (see Chapter 6).

1

COGNITIVE BEHAVIOUR SKILLS AND THEIR UNDERPINNING KNOWLEDGE BASE

*In the management of your principles, take
example by the pugilist, not the swordsman.
One puts down his blade and has to pick it
up again; the other is never without his
hand, and so needs only to clench it.*

Marcus Antoninus Aurelius (1989: 181–2)

This book is cognitive and behavioural. It will suggest ways of developing knowledge about CBT that may influence your thoughts about psychological therapy. In turn, this knowledge may influence how you behave as a therapist. The book will make suggestions about skills and techniques that will help you to apply CBT knowledge in an artful way. The book also aims to influence how you feel about doing CBT, hoping to foster confidence and, most of all, a sense of self-efficacy: to feel in your head and think in your heart 'I can do this.'

The balance between knowledge and skills is extremely important. Knowledge without skill can make us able to understand but not help clients. Skill without knowledge can lead us into shallow work and therapeutic dead ends.

This chapter will therefore begin by describing a set of simple principles that underpin the skills, techniques and strategies described throughout the rest of the book. As the consumer of Blackpool Rock should find the name 'Blackpool' embedded into his rock after every bite, so should the reader find the principles described in this chapter embedded in the skills described throughout the book. I will use the template of CBT principles, first described by Aaron Beck (1976: Beck et al., 1985) and further developed by his daughter, Judith Beck (1995) – see Figure 1.1.

CBT has changed and developed over the years. The development has been rich and international in its dimensions. Some therapists have been taught only basic and early versions of the model so that a rather stereotyped and impoverished view of CBT has persisted in some parts of the therapy world. This stereotype and attendant fears about CBT 'taking over' the therapy profession have resulted in a debate more characterised by heat than light (Wills, 2006b). We should all welcome critical debate but debate based on stereotyping does not help.

First, some terms need to be explained. As already hinted at, this book will particularly focus on Beck's cognitive therapy model. Beck's model should be

A way of understanding clients and their problems:
CBT is based on a cognitive behavioural formulation.

A base from which to help clients:
CBT requires a sound therapeutic relationship.
CBT is collaborative.

A strategic posture for our helping efforts:
CBT is relatively short-term.
CBT is problem-focused and goal-orientated.
CBT is initially focused on present-time issues.
CBT is structured and directional.
CBT is educational.

A skills base for implementing such strategies:
CBT methods are inductive and Socratic.
CBT makes regular use of homework tasks.
CBT uses a variety of techniques to change thinking, mood and behaviour.

FIGURE 1.1   *The principles of CBT (adapted from Beck, 1976; Beck et al., 1985; J. Beck, 1995)*

regarded as one of the more influential models that make up the cognitive behavioural family of models. The cognitive therapy model has strongly emphasised the role of behavioural methods so that the terms 'cognitive therapy' and 'CBT' can be used interchangeably without much harm to either term. Other vibrant CBT traditions, such as behaviour therapy and rational emotive behaviour therapy (REBT), will also be drawn from. I make no apology for the fact that cognitive therapy is simply the model that I know the best. More generally, I think that all models of therapy have much to teach each other and I favour an assimilative integrative form of practice. The reader will find many references to psychodynamic and humanistic thinking in this book. Later, however, I will argue that for most of us there are limits to the amount of other knowledge and skills that can be integrated tidily into everyday practice, a factor that means that the broad highway of my practice is solidly based on CBT.

The underpinning principles that will be described here aim to offer:

- a way of understanding clients and their problems,
- a therapeutic relationship with clients,
- a strategic posture for therapeutic interventions,
- a skills base for implementing such strategies.

Understanding clients: cognitive-behavioural formulation

At the heart of the CBT paradigm there is a very simple yet effective working model: the way people think about their situations influences the way they feel and behave. It may be helpful to see how quickly a client may be able to work with this notion by using a dialogue such as the following to give a rationale for CBT:

Therapist: I sometimes explain how CBT can work by telling a story about two people I knew. They both worked in the same factory and were of a similar age and family set-up. Sadly, one day they heard that they were both on a list of people to be made redundant. One of them thought to himself 'This is terrible – I might never work again. What will my wife think? She might even leave me.' Thinking like that, how would you say he felt?

Client: Desperate, I should think. You know, really low and depressed.

Therapist: Yes, that's right, he did. Now the other fellow thought, 'Well, this is bad. It's a scary situation. On the other hand, I'm not so happy working there: maybe this could be a chance to try out some other things I'm interested in.' How do you think he felt?

Client: Well, better. He'd still be worried but he seems to have a bit more hope.

Therapist: And if a job did come up, who would be most likely to go for it?

Client: The second bloke. The first one might just give up: maybe not even apply?

Therapist: That's right and that's exactly what did happen.

This kind of rationale story works because it shows two people reacting differently to pretty much the same situation. This stresses the importance of the way the event is appraised. We might represent the appraisals and their effects by diagrams (see Figure 1.2).

Some important points emerge from this example. Firstly, the person who shows a more adaptive response is still concerned about his situation: he is not phlegmatic and certainly not happy. Concern is appropriate in this context and would be more likely to motivate a person to engage actively in surmounting the crisis of redundancy, though of course sometimes a period of mourning loss may be necessary. Secondly, the diagrams in Figure 1.2 constitute examples of 'cycles' – one 'vicious', the other 'positive'. In the 'vicious cycle', that is the negative example, the emotional and behavioural responses may well confirm the initial cognitive appraisal in what can also be termed a 'self-fulfilling prophecy'. In contrast, the positive cycle is helpful and takes the client out of the problem. Finally, the separate elements of the 'vicious cycle' diagram can each be regarded as potential targets for a series of change strategies: thoughts can be modified; emotions can be worked through and behavioural experiments (page 90) can be tried. Vicious cycle diagrams are omnipresent in CBT practice – sometimes drawn on a pad or on a white board. They should be regarded as provisional, not set in stone: the client can draw them into her therapy notebook and take them home to study, play with and customise (see Chapter 2). It can be a powerful moment in therapy when clients first begin to hear their own negative thoughts and this can be initiated and/or strengthened by seeing them written down.

The factory workers' story is one that can speak to many people but the context can also be varied to their own experiences, that is, situations in offices, schools and other places. Despite the modern setting of the example, it also carries an echo of the wisdom of the Socratic and Stoic traditions, most famously stated by Epictetus (1995), who said: 'People are disturbed not by events alone but by the view they take of them' (*Enchiridion*, V).

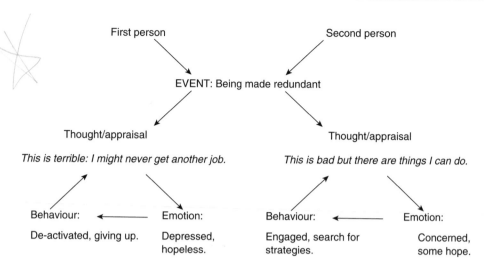

FIGURE 1.2   *The 'vicious cycle' concept*

Suggestion

If you are working in pairs, role-play giving a client a rationale for therapy: (perhaps along the lines of the 'factory' story above). Try to adapt the story to the situation of the person you are speaking to. This could be by changing the employment focus or shifting the scene to some other context that you think might speak to them. For example, if the person is interested in party politics, the example of how two different people might react to defeat in an election could be used.

If you are working by yourself, try to think of a story that would appeal to a recent client.

The simple 'vicious cycle' diagram is really the first part of a formulation (also termed 'conceptualisation') of the client's situation in CBT. Second and third stages are 'recognising cognitive distortions' and 'applying cognitive specificity' respectively. Drawing up a full longitudinal formulation completes the conceptualisation. These concepts are more fully described in Chapters 2 (Assessment, Formulation and Beginning CBT) and 4 (Skills for Working with Negative Thoughts).

The word 'cognitive' refers to information processing and interpretation. I sometimes think that it might have been better to have named 'cognitive therapy' as 'appraisal therapy' because it is the cognitive processes of appraisal that are really the most important to successful CBT. Many automatic thoughts are about trivial matters. The negative thoughts of clients that most often turn out to be central to change in CBT are almost always linked to appraisals of meaning connected to who clients think they are, what they think they should be doing and with whom they think they should be doing it. Readers may care to bear this in mind as we shift through different layers of thinking, appraisal and meaning.

Suggestion

Think back over the last week or so and search for an incident where you felt a strong emotional reaction. For the purpose of this exercise, it is usually best to think of a negative emotion that you half know is a little problematic (for example, where you reflect that something got to you more than perhaps it should have done). If you are working with another person, you may need to think if what you plan to talk about is appropriate to the particular situation you are working in. See if you can trace out your reaction in terms of the pattern of thinking (appraisal) – emotion – behaviour. If possible, draw out as shown above.

Is there any 'vicious cycle' element in the reaction chain you have identified? Should such a situation arise again, how else might you care to react? What did/does this situation MEAN to you?

CBT base camp: the collaborative therapeutic relationship

I seem to have spent a good deal of the last 15–20 years of my professional life trying to convince therapists from other traditions that CBT therapists really do believe that building a therapeutic relationship is an essential part of what they do. My argument has been based on three main propositions:

- The therapeutic relationship in CBT has significant heritage and continuity from other therapeutic models (this point is further explained under the heading, 'Empathy, warmth and genuineness' below).
- CBT has, however, its own particular take on the therapeutic relationship (see 'A collaborative working alliance, empirical in nature and pragmatic in spirit' below).
- Although simplicity is one of the virtues of the therapeutic relationship in CBT, in informed and sensitive hands it is capable of responding to most of the subtle interpersonal processes that arise in psychotherapy, including transference and countertransference (see 'CBT as an interpersonal therapy' below and Chapter 3).

Empathy, warmth and genuineness

When Beck et al. (1979) wrote their seminal work on cognitive therapy, their description of the therapeutic relationship owes a clear debt to the ideas of Carl Rogers: 'As described by Rogers (1961), the therapeutic relationship in cognitive therapy is characterised by genuineness, respect and, within reason, warmth (Beck et al., 1979: 21). Equally, Albert Ellis (1973) describes REBT as a humanistic approach to therapy. Cognitive theory, however, suggests that the way in which the client perceives therapist empathy is filtered via the client's belief system: therapist behaviour experienced as empathic by one person may be patronising to another. Warmth in CBT is often accompanied by a degree of optimism, such as sometimes choosing to be a little 'upbeat' with the client, especially the depressed client. This can sometimes extend to the judicious use of humour. Humour has the capability of reframing certain ways of thinking and this is explored further in

Chapter 4. In addition, empathy can be extended by the reflection of meaning as well as by the reflection of feeling (Ivey et al., 1997). Van Deurzen-Smith (1988) has argued that exploring meaning is a central concern of existential therapy. A particular form of cognitive empathy (Burns & Auerbach, 1996) develops as the expression of feeling is accentuated by the expression of what that emotion means. The CBT practitioner can make this link explicit by saying something like: 'Anyone who is thinking "*I have lost everything*" would feel low, as you do now.' Empathy can also be extended by blending in reflections and Socratic questions, rather as is done in Motivational Interviewing (Miller & Rollnick, 2002), and by 'a rigorous search for solutions' (Wright et al., 2006: 19). An empathic client–therapist dialogue can also include challenge, although this may need a degree of diplomacy, but not to the point where it could interfere with genuineness – a quality as important to CB therapists as to others.

The CB therapist brings these qualities together to form the basic therapeutic relationship and also initiates 'collaborative empiricism' (see the next section). A study by Klein et al. (2003) showed that outcome in CBT is very much linked to the quality of the relationship. The presence or absence of this relationship is evident at a very early stage of CB therapy. Furthermore, Keijsers et al. (2000), in a major review of therapeutic qualities in CBT, show that CBT practitioners seem to be just as good at enacting these qualities as therapists in other traditions.

A collaborative working alliance, empirical in nature and pragmatic in spirit

CBT practitioners have gone out of their way to stress that the operation of the model does not depend on a clever expert being 'in charge'. Indeed, CBT is common sense (Beck, 1976), straight forward (Wright et al., 2006) and down to earth (Wills, 2006a). This is why such emphasis is placed on forging a collaborative working alliance between therapist and client. Collaboration, however, simply means working together: the client's work and the therapist's work are different but must dovetail with each other. The therapist works to identify and, often, challenge the client's thinking. The client works to honestly report examples of problem functioning and must commit to working on trying to change such patterns. Clients may experience being challenged on their thinking as an attack on the self. It can therefore be helpful to use the analogy that client and therapist form a 'team' against the problem. It can even be helpful to imagine that client and therapist are sitting on one side of the room and are working against the problem sitting on the other side of the room. Client and therapist share responsibility for work and progress. The collaborative structuring devices of agenda-setting and collecting feedback (see Chapter 2) can bolster this process. At first the therapist is likely to take more responsibility and will be more active, but responsibility and control can be gradually handed over to the client. The initial stance may be one of tutor-coach but, as time goes by, this will evolve more towards a consultative mode. The basic working alliance is an empirical (based on data collection) one because it relies on generating evidence about current functioning and about attempts to experiment with newer styles of functioning.

CBT as an interpersonal therapy

Therapy is an inherently interpersonal process and CBT is therefore subject to the same kind of interpersonal and transferential processes as have been identified more explicitly in other models of therapy. Becoming more aware of interpersonal processes allows CB therapists to make more flexible use of structure (Chapter 2). Without some such flexibility there is a danger that CB therapy can become stilted and lifeless. Learning what one might call the 'natural history' of therapy – how things turn out for the endlessly varied people we see – helps us to realise that CBT cannot be any kind of quick fix. Learning how to do CBT artfully must therefore be a life-long process. It has always seemed to me that being unwilling to learn from the experiences of other modalities is wilful ignorance. CB therapists have been showing more and more willingness to learn from other models. A good example is the way that we have opened our constructs to an understanding of interpersonal processes (Safran & Segal, 1990; Sanders & Wills, 2005; Bennett-Levy & Thwaites, 2007). The discussion of interpersonal processes is further developed in Chapter 3 but for the moment let us state its spirit in the words of Paul Gilbert: 'Cognitive therapists should take more time out of their technique-oriented approaches and consider what it is to be a human being' (in Dryden & Trower, 1988: 66).

CBT's strategic posture for helping

CBT has been established as one of those therapies more associated with shorter-term rather than long-term work. Important developments in CBT have made it necessary to add certain qualifications to this position. The context itself has been changing as various imperatives have raised the profile of shorter-term methods over the longer-term ones. The usual range of CBT – between 10 and 20 sessions – would once have seemed impossibly short to some, but now when I am training I am frequently told it seems luxuriously long and I am asked by some whether it could be done in 6–8 or even fewer sessions.[1] The 10–20 range emerged from research on CBT with depressed clients that suggested the most parsimonious results came from a mean of 17 sessions (Beck et al., 1979). This finding came at a time of increasing political and socio-economic pressure for more time and cost efficient therapies, trends which have, if anything, intensified in the succeeding years. A more theoretical justification, however, turns on the point that therapists rarely solve all the client's problems and should perhaps focus more on facilitating clients to solve their own problems by becoming their own therapists. This would help to prepare the client to resist future relapse, one of the major strengths of CBT (Hollon, 2003). Short-term work is, in my experience, popular with clients, especially if they are able to negotiate for extensions if they so wish.

The brief nature of CBT is very important because from it other aspects of working style develop. When therapy is brief, it is vital that it is educative and that it uses time well. It must therefore remain highly focused, and the most obvious focus is the problem and/or symptoms that the client brings to therapy.

A clear problem focus leads naturally to agreed goals. As Carkhuff (1987) has pointed out, goals are the flip side of problems.

As problems are assessed and a formulation of them is built up, it is often apparent that although there is a problem in current functioning, this problem has a 'history' and may be reflected in early development. Traditional CBT has been inclined to work with the current, present-time problem and has placed somewhat less emphasis on historical and developmental factors. This aspect of CBT developed because much of its theory and practice came from focusing on clear syndromes with relatively discrete symptoms, such as unipolar depression (Beck et al., 1979) and panic disorder (Clark, 1996). As CBT has expanded into wider areas, it has become noticeably more flexible in terms of length of therapy and in attitudes towards working with more historical and developmental issues (Sanders & Wills, 2005). Longer-term versions of CBT have emerged in the form of dialectical behaviour therapy (Linehan, 1993) and schema-focused therapy (Young et al., 2003).

Such flexibility of approach means that a CBT treatment may develop in a variety of different ways. It may opt for standard work with current symptoms within the traditional short-term framework. If this work is relatively successful, yet underlying issues are evident and the client wants to work with them, work can begin to refocus on those underlying issues, perhaps even within the range for short-term sessions. It is not always necessary to completely 'work through' all these issues: therapy may still be completed within the short-term frame. Alternatively, there is a set of criteria that allows a judgement that standard CBT would not be a suitable approach for this particular client (Young et al., 2003), and therefore the therapist may begin by using a longer-term, schema-focused model, perhaps going up to and beyond 40 sessions or the one-year duration. Carefully researched work by Cummings and Satyama (1995) suggests that most caseloads will carry around 10% of clients who will need longer-term help and 5% who may even need something like episodic help over many years. A paper by McGinn et al. (1995) nicely captures the current spirit of CBT by describing '[W]HEN and how to do longer-term therapy and not feel guilty'. It is interesting that a short-term version of psychodynamic therapy has produced good results for the treatment of panic (Milrod et al., 2007). However, this treatment is longer than the usual CBT treatments and it is claimed to be especially useful when panic is associated with interpersonal difficulties, a point also made in the CBT literature (Sanders & Wills, 2003).

Another factor that emerges from the short-term and problem-solving strategic posture of CBT is that the CBT therapist has traditionally taken a consciously educational role. This is sometimes referred to as 'psycho-educational'. This term, however, most usually refers to the relatively didactic aspect of the educational role and is exemplified when the therapist gives a depressed client 'normalising' information about the condition. A client, for example, may become very self-critical because of poor concentration and motivation, and it is often helpful for them to realise that these traits may well be 'the depression speaking', and are not the client's inherent personal qualities. This kind of normalisation also carries a meta-message of CB therapy: *This is something we can learn to manage.* There is, however, another and more subtle aspect to the educational role and one that is closer to the 'tutor-coach' role.

In this more tutorial dimension, the therapist's role is to help the client to 'learn to learn', which begins by trying to foster the quality of reflective curiosity in the client: *what is happening to me?* Gradually, reflection may become more active as the client learns to 'think about thinking' and then experiment with different styles of thinking and different types of behaviour via behavioural experiments.

CBT: the skills and techniques base

CBT skills and techniques will be described more fully later. Here the focus is on showing the relationship between skill use and the principles of CBT that influence how client problems are understood and how interventions are developed.

It sometimes seems that the CBT method would be more likely to be deductive – building up evidence from which to derive a theory – rather than inductive – testing a theory with facts. It is, however, inductive because it involves testing clients' current theories about their lives because we suspect that they are skewed by negative bias. This is the sequence used in the Socratic dialogues where the great philosopher asks his fellow debater to supply the first statement and then elicits evidence about that idea by asking Socratic questions.

We can see this process in dealing with rationale stories. Earlier, we discussed the role of these in building up the client's understanding of therapy. Another rationale story, one experienced by many, uses that common experience of trying to say hello to someone who apparently ignores the greeting. Most people, when asked their thoughts in this scenario, report thinking either 'He doesn't like me' (external appraisal) or 'I must have done something wrong' (internal appraisal).[2] If we encounter this situation when feeling very confident, we might stop the person and ask, 'Didn't you see me?' and might then get some information about what happened. More likely, though, we will review the situation and perhaps reflect, 'Have I done anything that might have offended him? I can't think of anything. Perhaps he was just distracted.' We are essentially 'reviewing the evidence': a normal everyday cognitive activity. If we were feeling low when we were 'blanked', however, we'd probably be more upset and would be much less likely to act assertively. Even later, we may find it much harder to review the evidence and come to a more positive view.

An isolated incident like this hardly adds up to a mental health problem. Once psychological problems start to develop, however, these incidents will tend to increase and begin to take their toll. Once a tipping point is reached, symptoms will occur in a syndromal way and then start to kick-start 'vicious cycles' of increased symptoms.

Breaking into these vicious cycles with therapeutic interventions may well begin with behavioural work. In depression, for example, the effects on concentration may make any kind of higher-order cognitive work too difficult, at least for a while. As we will see in Chapter 5, however, 'activation' – increasing levels of behavioural activity and encouraging more proactive behaviours – can result in early changes in mood that in turn make cognitive work and cognitive shifts more likely. Sometimes a behavioural shift alone can shift thinking. I might, for example, hold the negative and depressing belief, 'I can't make myself heard at work.' If I do somehow find a way of making myself heard and see for myself that I have done that, my belief systems, faced with this cognitively dissonant information, may start to shift to take in this new information.

Cognitive change takes place at different levels. Negative automatic thoughts (NATs) may be modified by techniques such as 'reviewing the evidence' and thought records (see also Chapter 4). These techniques essentially help the mind to process information as it does when it is functioning well. Sometimes the evidence is written down in a therapy notebook or on a white board, which helps the client to be more aware of their thinking processes. Having completed tasks in the therapy session, the client might be encouraged to practise them for homework. Homework completion is associated with greater gains in therapy (Kazantzis et al., 2005) and may be increasingly regarded as a common factor in therapy (Kazantzis & Ronan (2006). Using the time between sessions to practise also helps to compensate for having less time when working under time limits with some clients. All in all, time limits can have positive as well as negative effects.

Getting the client to write down things for himself also emphasises the client's responsibility for and control of change. It can be easy for a persuasive and practised therapist to think up good challenges to negative thoughts. The change that comes from therapist challenges, however, is usually short-lived and will not get the client into the habit of being his own therapist. The emphasis on getting the client to do work may be one of the reasons why CBT therapists report fewer problems with client dependency than other types of therapy.

As well as working on NATs, CB therapists are likely to work with deeper levels of cognition in the forms of assumptions, rules of living, core beliefs and schemas. These interventions are typically more complex, long-term and involve using more interpersonal, relationship-based factors (see also Chapters 3 and 7).

It can be seen, therefore, that CB uses a variety of techniques to change thinking, mood and behaviour.

Conclusion

CBT is a skill orientated form of therapy but its skills need to be firmly based on a set of principles governing how to understand client problems and to help in the planning and execution of interventions to ameliorate such problems. The principles serve as navigational devices to keep the CBT boat on course and to steer it clear of the shallow waters of banal therapy and the stormy waters of chaotic therapy.

Suggestion

Looking back down the list of principles in Figure 1.1, which of these principles do you find yourself in ready agreement with? Are there principles that you find more difficult to accept? If you had to 'sign up' or 'take the oath' for this set of principles and were allowed to amend one or two, which ones would they be and how would you amend them?

PRACTICE TIP: Fitting CBT to your client

Choose words carefully

Perhaps because of the historic link with psychiatry and mental health work, the language of CBT can sometimes carry meanings for people that are not necessarily intended by the therapist. Most therapy models have made attempts to de-stigmatise their languages. In the chapters on working with different levels of thinking I have preferred the word 'unhelpful' rather than 'dysfunctional', 'maladaptive' or 'irrational' to describe the ways that clients may be thinking. This is not just being mealy-mouthed or politically correct; there is a respectable intellectual case against all those terms. It is also likely to be why the client is coming to see the therapist: their current patterns – of which thinking is a part – are not helping them to get to where they want to be in life. Psychiatric language is helpful in guiding us to the right ballpark but is often a lot more categorical than the concepts it describes. The word 'obsession' is one that clients frequently find quite scary. In practice, I find that there are enormous overlaps between the concept of obsession and the concepts of intrusive thoughts and worries. Some clients will find it easier to think of themselves as working with worries rather than obsessions, and the rationale for ways of working with worries works in much the same way as the rationale for working with obsessions.

Titrating CBT structure

Learning to use therapy structure in a way that is comfortable to each individual client is very much one of the main skills of the art of CBT. We probably begin with the assumption that the therapy will be quite structured while at the same time retaining an exquisite sensitivity (Beck et al., 1979: 65) to individual client needs in this and other areas. Beck et al. (1979) refer to 'titrating' the degree of structure. Structure, for example, is often helpful to depressed clients because it helps them concentrate and remember. Many clients come from other therapists complaining of being subjected to over-long silences, during which they felt worse. Interestingly, they have often interpreted these silences as meaning that the therapist did not care about their problems. While I am sure that they were mostly wrong in this assertion, it does remind us of the cardinal cognitive principle that people will understand what is happening to them in terms of their current thoughts and feelings. As in the previous tip, words are very important here too. Many therapists working in other models seem to think that it is very bad for the therapist to be 'directive', but what about a therapy that 'lacks direction' or a therapist who is not able to communicate 'directly'? All these words and phrases are related to each other. Therapists should be aware of the client's language and meaning: they may frequently find that they are not derived from reading therapy books.

Further reading

Harvey, A. et al. (2004) *Cognitive behavioural processes across psychological disorders.* Oxford: Oxford University Press.

Rachman, S. (1997) The evolution of cognitive behaviour therapy. In D.M. Clark & C.G. Fairburn (eds), *Science and practice of cognitive behaviour therapy.* Oxford: Oxford Medical Publications, pp. 3–26.

Sanders, D. & Wills, F. (2005) *Cognitive therapy: an introduction.* London: Sage, especially Chapter 1.

Notes

1   A number of sessions now frequently specified in employee counselling and in the Health Service.
2   Trainee therapists tend to report the latter.

2

ASSESSMENT, FORMULATION AND BEGINNING CBT

*The devil is in the detail. The Irish grand
narrative is easy to understand but you
have to dig deep to really understand it.*

Mick Fealty, Guardian, 'Free to
Comment' Blog, 9 June 2006

Appraisal of meaning-giving events is a central concept in CBT. Several philoso-phers have suggested that appraisal is also a central aspect of human nature: people are naturally meaning-seeking animals (Kegan, 2006). Humans seem to assess and size each other up from the first few seconds of encounter. The appraisals are invariably interpersonal: Is this a person I can get on with? Might she be a threat to me? These factors mean that appraisal and assessment processes commence in the first moments of contact between therapist and client. They also mean that 'assessment' is a two-way process: the client is assessing the therapist from a very early stage – will this person like me, help me or exploit me? In a sense, therapeutic 'assessment' is only a formalisation of these natural appraisal processes, but it is vital because it will lead to our initial formulation and that in turn will act as a route map for our interventions.

This chapter will begin by describing some ways of using the initial appraisal exchanges to maximum advantage. It will then concentrate on the essential features of 'cross-sectional' assessment, especially gathering the detail of current functioning. This will be followed by some thoughts on client suitability for CBT. The chapter will then describe some of the skills needed to complete a satisfactory formulation of the client's problems, especially focusing on the client's developmental history. Finally, it will describe initial structuring steps to help therapist and client implement plans to facilitate change in the problems identified by the assessment and formulation.

First contacts with the client

First contacts with clients are influenced by the context of the work. Where the ther-apy service is located in large organisations, the initial session may be the first time that the client speaks to the therapist. In independent practice, the therapist may handle the initial inquiry via telephone or email and may also be involved in setting appointment times. These are important moments that often set the tone of therapy. It sometimes seems as if it gets harder and harder to get quality time from service providers in our modern economy. Technological advances such as websites can sometimes serve to insulate providers from service users: what clients want to know may not be covered by the frequently asked questions section of a website. People wishing to refer themselves are often nervous and on foreign ground, and usually value highly responses that are friendly, relaxed and open. Therapists should also note the questions people ask and the way they ask them: you are already getting glimpses into the client's way of seeing the world. Sometimes understanding emerges before contact. One client left a message for me to call but when I tried to do so, he always seemed to be at work, even later into the evening. This felt significant and indeed emerged as being so: he was going through a very stressful period at work and faced the possibility of redundancy. He was working all the hours God sent to keep on the right side of his bosses and was pushing himself inexorably towards stress-related illness. The initial contact call may be when a sense of hopefulness, sometimes referred to as 're-moralisation', is established. The client will often ask directly, 'Do you think you can help with my problem?' They are probably appraising whether the therapist is worth the expenditure of effort and resources that may be required. They have every right to ask about how long the process might take and the likely costs in time and money of seeking treatment. The therapist equally has a duty to ensure that CBT is a reasonable investment for them even at this stage. Shortly, we will discuss some criteria for suitability for CBT and these may even profitably come into play to rule out a 'poor bet' situation. The therapist can follow this discussion by sending information sheets and leaflets, using materials from professional associations such as the British Association for Behavioural and Cognitive Psychotherapies (see free downloadable material at www.babcp.org.uk). For a more customised version, see Horton (2006).

Client suitability for CBT

Decisions about client suitability can be difficult to make. This is because, although criteria for both inclusion and exclusion have been described, it may be hard to know how the person will react to the therapy until it is actually underway. Once meetings have taken place, however, it is then often difficult for a therapist to convey to a client that she is not suitable. Figure 2.1 contains a distillation of the main inclusion and exclusion criteria (see the further reading section at the end of the chapter for more detailed references).

When I look at the criteria for clients who do best in psychotherapy, I sometimes think that you have to be in good shape to do well in therapy. How helpful, for example, is it to know that the clients most suitable for CBT should have good access to their thoughts? Firstly, it would probably improve prospects for any type of therapy. Secondly, if we make the judgement that a client cannot access their thoughts, what then do we do? Suggest some other form of therapy or medication? Not necessarily, because it may be possible to help clients to recognise their automatic thoughts. Indeed, the ability to access thoughts is not an 'either/or' ability but is arranged on a continuum from very good to very poor current access. Perhaps the most we can draw from these criteria is that we should know when CBT might be a longer-term venture.

The reader will note some use of psychiatric terminology in Figure 2.1 and wonder how to understand psychiatric terminology in a way that is congruent

Inclusion:
1.   Can access thoughts and feelings.
2.   Accepts some responsibility for change.
3.   Understands a CBT rationale and basic formulation.
4.   Able to form a 'good enough' relationship with therapist.
5.   A degree of optimism about therapy.

Exclusion:
1.   Impaired cognitive functioning.
2.   Chronic or severe problems.
3.   Unwilling to let go of avoidance behaviours.
4.   Unwilling to do homework.
5.   A pronounced pessimism about therapy.

FIGURE 2.1   *Inclusion and exclusion criteria for 'standard' CBT*

with client-centred assessment of suitability. Because much of the developmental work for CBT was completed within the psychiatric sector, psychiatry has influenced its language use and conceptual thinking. CB therapists tend to make some use of the *Diagnostic and Statistical Manual (DSM)* of the American Psychiatric Association classification. They work slightly differently with panic disorder than they would with panic disorder with agoraphobia, for example (Hackmann, 1998). Some CB therapists are diagnosticians, though many are not. It is possible to regard the criteria in the *DSM* as useful general guidance to the sort of issues that are likely to cohere when working in that area. This need not tie therapists to any label or 'labelling' process. The use of these criteria is, in any case, rarely as clean-cut as is sometimes implied; clients often seem to meet the criteria for several different categories[1] and it can be hard to know which of them is the right starting point. The trickiest labels are linked to the controversial term 'personality disorder', a field muddied with misunderstanding. The word 'disorder' and its supposed link to anti-social behaviour put off some therapists from drawing on helpful aspects of the criteria. The criteria can help us to understand otherwise very puzzling symptoms. 'Personality' mainly refers to the fact that patterns of negative functioning are so wide and pervasive that they suggest a characterological dimension to them. The concept of pervasive patterns, perhaps dating back to childhood experience, is not foreign but rather a familiar concept to most therapists. The *DSM* criteria can offer route maps to understanding, though we should perhaps be travellers who are able to make critical observations of our own judgements. Any system is of course open to abuse, but readers may find it reassuring to read the introduction of *Diagnostic and Statistical Manual IV-R* (American Psychiatric Association, 2000), in which the careful and rigorous process of collaboration and consultation involved in defining the terms is described.

Thinking about client suitability criteria can also help us to anticipate certain avoidable glitches. We might ask ourselves and then test whether the client will be able to:

■   accept responsibility for change,
■   undertake out-of-session tasks ('homework'),
■   accept a structured approach,
■   settle into a CBT therapeutic relationship.

Hayes et al. (2004) suggest that CBT practitioners have tended to take an overly rational approach to client motivation, believing at times that because clients feel bad, they will necessarily want to work at feeling better. This ignores a tradition in therapy which recognises that some clients may need to go through twists and turns to get to this point. As Hayes (1998) has put it: 'The client comes in and says: This is my problem. Please help me to solve it by doing what has not worked in the past.' Psychodynamic therapists may think of Freud's observations about the 'compulsion to repeat' negative patterns. The motivational interviewing literature shows that motivation and commitment for change normally rise and fall through several cycles over time. The careful combination of empathy, probing and Socratic questioning has been shown to be an effective way of enhancing motivation and taking responsibility. Questions to facilitate 'I statements' are helpful, especially when clients tend to shift attention and blame to others. A client who keeps describing the impossible behaviour of an errant partner can be asked, 'So when he/she does that, what do *you* do?', a question to bring the focus back to the client.

Client's motivation for CBT can also be assessed by suggesting that they will be asked to do homework on a regular basis – a useful marker of future expectations. The therapist might, however, be wary of a client's undue optimism. Hard-won completion of homework tasks may prove to be most valuable in the end. The degree of preparation to engage in CBT may also be ascertained by observing how a client reacts to rationale-giving and to CBT structure. Some clients are resistant to structuring because it carries some meaning of being controlled: the therapist should show the ability to vary structure and the therapeutic relationship accordingly. Therapists may, however, react differently to these different client reactions. Some may back themselves to be able to win clients round and will enjoy the challenge of doing so.

---

1. Does the client seem more or less hopeful now?
2. Is there collaboration?
3. Are clear and realistic goals emerging?
4. What is the balance of work and responsibility between client and therapist?

FIGURE 2.2   *Questions to assess how therapy is going after three or four sessions*

Figure 2.2 contains a series of questions for the therapist to ask him/herself three or four sessions into CBT to assess how suitability factors are showing themselves in practice. Negative answers would suggest the need to review and perhaps amend the style of therapy.

Suggestion

Think of a current or recent client you have had and apply the questions in Figure 2.2 to your work with him or her so far. Do any of your answers point towards any technical or relationship problems in the therapy? If so, how can the work and/or relationship be amended in order to try to ameliorate them?

Some clients may present in a way that suggests that they are too disturbed to really settle into any kind of therapy. It is sometimes hard for therapists to make that kind of judgement because it can feel like negative labelling. It may be helpful to use 'mental state examination' criteria. These criteria focus on any obvious signs that may indicate anything about the client's current state of mind that might impact adversely or otherwise on therapy. For example, does the client exhibit any delusions? There are a number of detailed criteria on the web, but in practice therapists may find the simplified version offered in MacMahon (1996) particularly helpful. MacMahon acknowledges the danger of stereotyping coming into such assessment, but rightly suggests that items can be judiciously adapted to the needs of the therapeutic situation. If the client is demonstrating delusions, it is only right and proper to consider how that may influence therapy.

Getting the detail: cross-sectional assessment

Getting detail about the client's current functioning is extremely important because there are likely to be several ways for therapy to proceed and we need to know what will enable us to intervene in the most fruitful areas. Detailed information on the client's functioning is important because initial improvement might be very slight and we might not even notice if we do not have a good idea of pre-therapy functioning. To some extent, this part of assessment involves having the right kind of information-gathering format and then going straight ahead and gathering it. The format presented in Figure 2.3 is one devised by Diana Sanders and I from various sources. It has been tried and tested over a number of years.

Such a list can look rather daunting and may also raise the spectre of the CB therapist appearing with a clipboard and then doggedly ticking boxes on the list, regardless of the time and pain endured by the client! We have all known assessments conducted in this way. One of my clients described such an experience as 'death by clipboard'. It seems a world way from what Hobson (1985) called the 'conversational' mode of therapy. If we drew a continuum between the conversational mode and the clipboard mode, we would probably wish to take up a position near the middle for assessment purposes, but would wish to move towards the conversational as therapy proceeds. It can be useful for clients to fill out forms in between meetings to save session time. Therapists may also keep a list such as Figure 2.3 in front of them and make selective reference to it, or *after* assessment, to see what ground has already been covered and what else needs to be discussed next time.

Assessments should always have an element of provisionality, especially in the CBT model, whose very theoretical approach requires us to keep adjusting constructs as new data come in. One of the reasons why we do sometimes cling to ticking boxes is that we do not trust ourselves to remember what to cover and it helps to keep us heading in an appropriate direction. A major function of assessment at any stage, however, is to remind us of what we *don't yet* know as well as to formulate what we do know. It is only rarely that omissions cannot be retrieved at a subsequent meeting.

1. **Current problem:**
    What is the problem? Give a recent, detailed example, collecting information on:

    - Triggers to problem (external or internal)
    - Thoughts
    - Feelings

    - Physical factors
    - Behaviour
    - Environment

2. **What keeps the problem going now?**
    What makes things better? What makes it better?
    Safety behaviours and unhelpful coping strategies:

    - Avoidance
    - Checking of symptoms or danger
    - Seeking reassurance from others
    - Rituals
    - Suppressing thoughts or feelings
    - Worrying away at the problem continuously

    - Hopelessness and lack of belief in change
    - Other people's negative behaviour
    - Lack of social support or too much support and dependency
    - Continuing life events and stresses

3. **How did the problem develop?**
    History of the problem
    What started it in the first place?
    What was going on in the person's life at the time?
    Is it life-long or recurring?
    Main life events and stresses
    Key themes in the individual's or family's life
    Ideas about underlying assumptions and rules

4. **Developmental history:**
    Early life history, occupational and educational background
    Family and relationships
    Significant life events
    Themes within the family
    Medical and psychiatric history
    Previous experience of therapy

5. **General health issues:**
    Medication
    Prescribed or non-prescription drugs
    Alcohol, smoking
    History of dependency

6. **Expectations of therapy and goals:**
    Hopes for and fears about therapy
    Problem list
    Identify main goals for therapy

FIGURE 2.3   *Assessment information (to be adapted to client need) (adapted from Sanders & Wills, 2005)*

Suggestion

Think of a current difficulty you have and, without rehearsing it at all, talk about it for 5–10 minutes. If you are working with another person, she should note down what you have said. If working by yourself, you can speak into a tape recorder and then make brief notes. As you go over these notes, try to slot them into the various categories in Figure 2.3. Check where there are no entries. You can then repeat the exercise over several cycles. You may find that you automatically turn to areas neglected before. If so, what might be happening is a developing and iterative (repetition and deepening) process as the unstructured 'conversation' interacts with the structured format.

It may be a good idea to start with assessment items that make the least demand on memory – usually the most recent events. We have stressed the ubiquity of the 'vicious cycle' concept in CBT and it can be good to start by working back from today, sifting through recent experience and searching for occasions when negative functioning was triggered:

Therapist: Okay, so what sort of day are you having today so far?

Client: Oh today – not too bad. But I'm on leave at present so I've been feeling a bit more relaxed. I had a mooch round the shops this morning actually.

Therapist: Right, so although this stuff is not directly about work, being at work seems to make it more likely that you will feel down.

Client: Yeah, I quite like my job actually but it is stressful and then that can come on top of all my other worries about other stuff.

Therapist: How was the weekend?

Client: Funnily enough – good: I suppose because I knew I'd be on leave this week.

Therapist: Funnily enough?

Client: Yeah, because weekends are usually the worst times because I am by myself. I can't seem to work out what to do and I get this real dread about being on my own.

Therapist: Right. So how was the weekend before?

Client: That was a bad one. I had a crap email from Louise on the Saturday morning and then I somehow got left out of the five-a-side in the afternoon. I was a wreck by the evening and then I didn't sleep.

Therapist: Okay, that sounds like a good set of examples to put under the microscope. Let's go over what you were thinking and feeling first about Louise and then about the five-a-side. (**Client:** Okay.) These types of thing come up regularly in all our lives so it would be good to do some work on helping you handle them better.

Making a current example really work

It can sometimes be helpful to use the analogy of a computer program when trying to trace out client reactions to troublesome triggers. Computer programs work by one manoeuvre touching off several more and these in turn creating yet more, and it appears as though our reactions work in this way. It can be very hard for us to get hold of these reactions because they are so fast and so complex, which can make us feel as though we are not really in control of events and can add yet further negative elements to the reaction. The first thing that the therapist does is, in a sense, to help the client view the reaction in slow motion. Slowing down and reflecting helps the client to establish a better relationship with his pattern of reactions. Working on these vicious cycles may, however, misfire if the work does not raise enough relevant emotion. If CBT work does not engage the client emotionally, the results of the cognitive work will be akin to 'logic chopping' and will not usually be enough to inspire change. Both elements – emotional feeling *and* cognitive change – are necessary but alone neither will fully work to help to 'process the fear network' (Foa & Kozak, 1986). Using present-tense and personalised language to describe the traumatic situation as if it were happening now can enhance emotional engagement:

Therapist:	So let's go over what happened when Louise emailed you. I'd like you to try to speak in the present tense, sort of like, 'So I'm in my front room and I notice that an email has come in.' Can you do that?
Client:	Yeah, will it help?[2]
Therapist:	It seems to but let's see. So what time is it?
Client:	It's late, you know. Louise is in America so her emails come when I'm just going to bed. I told her to pick better times …
Therapist:	Just try to stay with what is happening in the present tense. How are you feeling?
Client:	Oh, right … Hot, you know, queasy. Oh … I'm feeling churned up, you know, things between us are fraught. I sometimes feel that she has gone off deliberately to get away from me. And now an email has arrived.
Therapist:	What is going through your mind?
Client:	This is it, the email will say it's all over.
Therapist:	And what would that mean?
Client:	She's been driven away by me and my crap ways of behaving. I'll never find another one like her.
Therapist:	So now you're reading the email, what does it actually say?
Client:	It's not what I feared but it is ambiguous …

Clients often report that when the story is told in this way, they do start to feel some of the actual emotion that they felt at the time. This usually gives a greater sense of 'felt meaning' to the account and thus gets us closer to the real cognitive-emotional-behavioural experience that was triggered in the real situation. Foa & Kozak (1986) add the rider that the feeling should not be so strong as to overwhelm the client's capacity to process the event. This stipulation is similar to guidance for dealing with emotions in post-traumatic stress disorder (PTSD) and requires the client to possess a certain degree of ability to modulate emotions. Clients can be helped to learn to modulate emotion with a 'safe place' procedure (further described in Chapter 6). Another method used to intensify emotions to the optimal level for processing meaning is described in Gendlin's (1981, 1998) 'focusing' intervention, again described further in Chapter 6.

Discussion of the intensity of feelings reminds us that intensity is part of the 'baseline' report of symptoms that the therapist is aiming to help ameliorate. The report should also include frequency and duration of symptom episodes so that changes for better or worse can be measured. CBT practitioners tend also to use validated symptom measures such as the Beck Anxiety and Depression Inventories (BAI & BDI) and others (a list of measure sources is included in Appendix 2) to measure change in symptoms. CB therapists have slightly different ways of using these measures but tend towards regular weekly use which allows monitoring and graphing of inventory scores. The sight of a downward curve on the symptoms graph, showing a decrease in symptoms, can reinforce a feeling of forward movement in the therapy. I often remark to clients that as long as symptoms show an overall tendency to fall, even with some ups and downs, the prognosis remains good. However, certain cautions need to be observed around measures. They are somewhat prone to the problems of all self-report accounts with demand characteristics. For example, some clients so want to 'reward' the therapist by seeming to be cured that they may fool themselves into under-reporting their symptoms. For this and other reasons, inventory scores should not be taken completely at face value and should always be discussed with the client (Sanders & Wills, 2005). The discussion can be opened with remarks such as 'Well, that's what the scores say, what do you say?'

Formulation:[3] putting the mud through fire to make crystal

As information starts to build up, there is a concomitant need to order it into meaningful and useful forms. One of the drivers of formulation is the need to link up the various aspects of client data and give them shape and meaning and begin to give the client a psychological explanation of the problems. There has often been a tension between psychological approaches that emphasise general patterns and those that put more stress on highly individual explanations. Formulation in the CBT tradition offers to bridge these two tendencies by developing an individualised explanation based on general principles: the general style comes 'off the peg' but the suit is highly tailored to the contours of the individual.

In essence, formulation consists of a synthesis of data that provides explanations of the origins, development and maintenance of the client's problems. It answers the client's questions, 'Why me? Why now? Why doesn't the problem just go away? How can I get better?' The contributing factors are shown in Figure 2.4.

Formulation helps the therapist on all sorts of levels: to understand the client; to make treatment decisions; and to understand why some clients press our buttons (Persons, 1989; Beck et al., 2003). It helps the therapist to feel more empathy for the client and the client to feel more empathy for himself. What helps the therapist can usually also help the client.

The following example shows how general factors and individual factors interact with each other. Dan was a young man who had quite severe social anxiety. There has been brilliant research into social anxiety and this

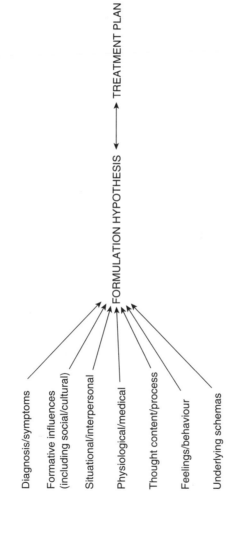

FIGURE 2.4   *CBT formulation: parts and whole (adapted from Wright et al. 2006)*

research has sketched out a detailed picture of how people think, feel and behave when they are socially anxious (Wells, 1997). The general cognitive theme shown by the research is a self-conscious fear of negative evaluation by other people. Dan suffered from this in the extreme, especially when other people were in authority. He was so in awe of his boss that he had to ask a colleague to lurk around when he got instructions from his boss – to hear the instructions that he himself was too over-awed to take in. A few weeks later I took on a new socially anxious client called David. He was suffering severe social anxiety after taking on a new job. I hazarded that he felt this with his boss. 'Oh no,' he replied, 'With my boss, I know exactly what to say and do. It is in informal situations with my peers that I feel anxious. I literally have no idea what to say. The Christmas party is next week – I am terrified. I'll have to be off sick that day.' The theory gets you so far, but in order to get the real fit, you have to dig deep to ask the client about his individual thoughts and feelings. Dan had highly critical and voluble parents, while David's parents were quiet people, 'laissez-faire' to the point of not ever giving him even a little help and advice about how to live his life. The experience of this hands-off parenting style may have influenced some of David's core beliefs, such as 'No one is going help me' and 'I have to work things out for myself.' Although CB therapists do not pursue clients' history in quite the same detailed way as psychodynamic therapists, they are becoming much more interested in historical factors. One technique that I have found helpful in striking a balance between exploring early experience and not becoming too entangled in it is to ask the client to give me examples and stories that seem to him to capture the flavour of his childhood experience. Dan told me, for example, about how his father had a school report day ritual. It was assumed that his report would be bad and his father had a slipper ready for ritual corporal punishment before he had even read the report. As a result, Dan believed himself to be a 'bad person'. David told me of several occasions when he had difficult choices to make at school and had asked his parents for advice only to be, as he described it, 'fobbed off with very dusty answers'. Further discussion of these and other methods to elicit core beliefs will follow in Chapter 7.

Later on, Dan revealed another more obsessional side to his anxiety. I began to grasp this when he started to turn up later and later for appointments, finally not attending at all. I was trying to work out whether to accept this as voting-with-his-feet or whether to pursue him by writing a letter. I looked at his formulation and was struck by the core belief that 'No one really cares about me.' In light of this core belief, actively writing to him seemed more likely to counter such thinking because it implied that I cared enough to write. Letting him go may have conveyed that I didn't really care if he came to therapy or not. Had his core belief been 'People do not trust me to decide for myself', I would have taken the opposite decision. Writing turned out to be the right strategy. He came back and completed therapy and was able to tell me that his lateness was caused, paradoxically, by being early. The sessions were at my home so that when he came in an obsessional fashion 30 minutes early, he couldn't come in. He then would go to look at some shops, forget the time and suddenly come charging over for his therapy late. That strikes me as a highly idiosyncratic causative factor and I do not think many therapists would have guessed it just on the basis of

Early Experience
Information about the client's early and other significant experiences which may have shaped core beliefs and assumptions.

↓

Development of Beliefs about the Self, Others and the World
Unconditional, core beliefs developing from early experience, such as 'I am bad', 'I am weak and vulnerable', 'Others will always look after me' or 'The world is a dangerous place'.

↓

Assumptions or Rules for Living
Conditional statements, often phrased as 'if … then' rules, to enable the individual to function despite core beliefs: e.g. 'If I am vigilant about my health at all times, then I'll be safe, despite being vulnerable'; 'If I work hard all the time. I'll be OK, despite being a bad person.'

↓

Critical Incidents which Trigger Problems
Situations or events in which the rules are broken or assumptions are activated.

↓

Problems and Factors Maintaining the Problem
Physical symptoms, thoughts, emotions, behaviours interacting in a 'vicious cycle'.

FIGURE 2.5   *The longitudinal formulation map (adapted from Sanders & Wills, 2005)*

what had happened thus far. Theory can take us so far but the devil *was* also in the detail in this instance.

The most comprehensive formulations are longitudinal and a common shortened format is shown in Figure 2.5, followed by a shortened version of Dan's formulation in Figure 2.6. Other fully written formulations are included in the website materials accompanying this book (see www.sagepub.co.uk/wills).

Empirically based theory gives us hints on where to look for relevant information for the formulation. As we will see in more detail in Chapter 4, recent research for problems such as worry and intrusive thoughts has pointed towards the thinking processes (especially attention), rather than thought content, as being the most relevant foci (Wells & Mathews, 1994; Wells, 2000). Social and cultural factors are now seen as having been neglected in previous theory and new work is proceeding on how they can most meaningfully be included (Tarrier & Calam, 2002). There is perhaps a tension between having fully inclusive formulation models that may become rather bloated and Beck's exhortation to 'simplify, simplify, simplify' our formulations and interventions (Beck et al., 1985).

CBT practitioners have a tradition of sharing formulations with clients and working collaboratively on them and are keen to review and question assumptions about the formulation process. There has been a useful debate in recent years on the validity and reliability of formulations (Kuyken, 2006). The debate

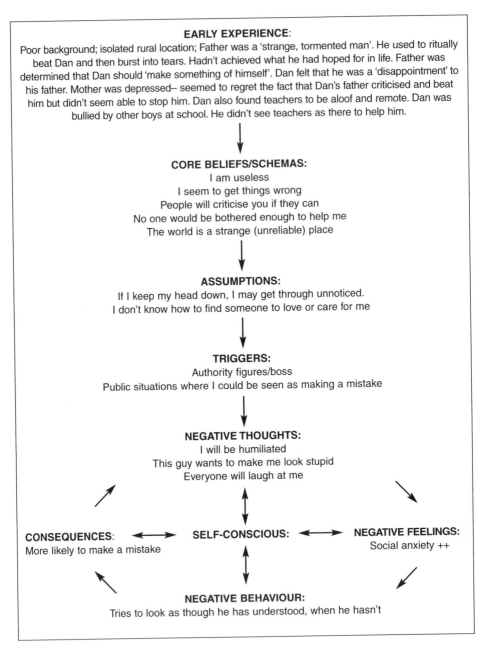

EARLY EXPERIENCE:
Poor background; isolated rural location; Father was a 'strange, tormented man'. He used to ritually beat Dan and then burst into tears. Hadn't achieved what he had hoped for in life. Father was determined that Dan should 'make something of himself'. Dan felt that he was a 'disappointment' to his father. Mother was depressed– seemed to regret the fact that Dan's father criticised and beat him but didn't seem able to stop him. Dan also found teachers to be aloof and remote. Dan was bullied by other boys at school. He didn't see teachers as there to help him.

CORE BELIEFS/SCHEMAS:
I am useless
I seem to get things wrong
People will criticise you if they can
No one would be bothered enough to help me
The world is a strange (unreliable) place

ASSUMPTIONS:
If I keep my head down, I may get through unnoticed.
I don't know how to find someone to love or care for me

TRIGGERS:
Authority figures/boss
Public situations where I could be seen as making a mistake

NEGATIVE THOUGHTS:
I will be humiliated
This guy wants to make me look stupid
Everyone will laugh at me

CONSEQUENCES: **SELF-CONSCIOUS:**   **NEGATIVE FEELINGS:**
More likely to make a mistake   Social anxiety ++

NEGATIVE BEHAVIOUR:
Tries to look as though he has understood, when he hasn't

FIGURE 2.6   *Longitudinal formulation: Dan*

is not yet fully resolved but one important factor that has emerged is that therapists should retain a degree of scepticism about their own formulations. The healthiest way to do this is to remember that even the best formulations are always provisional and that, wherever possible, they should be tested or at least testable. Figure 2.7 suggests some questions that attempt to pinpoint testable areas of formulations and ways of testing them.

1. To what extent would the client agree with this formulation?
2. Is this formulation more convincing than another rival explanation?
3. What significant issues in the situation does it not explain?
4. Does it fit with other available information: measures, clinical reports, etc.?

FIGURE 2.7   *Questions to test a formulation (adapted from Kuyken, 2006)*

Suggestion: Group discussion exercise

Download one of the fully written formulations from the SAGE website for this book. Test the formulation with the questions suggested in Figure 2.7. It may be more time-efficient to give certain questions and/or certain areas of the formulation to different pairs of group members and then for each pair to feed back to a plenary group session.

How did the formulation face up to scrutiny? What areas could be improved? Can you devise further questions and/or tests that might test the formulation?

Beginning CBT: from assessment and formulation to structuring the therapy

My research (Wills, 2006b) has identified that therapists' attitudes towards structure in therapy is one of the key determinants of how well therapists from other modalities adapt to learning CBT. I identified that there are several different layers of meaning linked to concepts of therapy structure. One of them may be termed 'surface structure', that is, the kind of structure an observer may see by watching what steps the therapist takes. For example, she may begin by asking a client to fill out a Beck Depression Inventory (BDI), ask for a brief account of his week and then set an agenda. Certain therapeutic traditions are quite hostile to such structuring, making it hard for people trained in these traditions to achieve clarity and efficiency in the way they practise CBT. This can delay the achievement of assessed competence in CBT. There is, however, another type of 'deep structure' that is not so easily evident in practice but is arguably more relevant to skilled practice. It is not so visible because it is in the therapist's mind and is guiding his moves rather than dictating them. Padesky (Padesky & Mooney, 1998) tells the story of the first time she saw Beck doing CBT. She found that his work seemed to lack structure and seemed to wander somewhat aimlessly. It was only later when she studied a recording of the interview in more depth that she realised the deep structure that Beck had been following. His laid-back manner had distracted her from seeing this.

We will start with the overt structure. A session structure for a post-assessment CBT session is shown in Figure 2.8. The assessment session itself has the additional items of identifying problems and setting goals, socialising the client into the CBT model, discussing the client's expectations of therapy and supplying any helpful and normalising information about the client's condition.

> 1. Brief update and mood check (including use of measures).
> 2. Bridge from previous session.
> 3. Collaborative setting of the agenda.
> 4. Review of homework.
> 5. Main agenda items and periodic summaries.
> 6. Setting new homework.
> 7. Summary and feedback.

FIGURE 2.8   *CBT session structure (adapted from J. Beck, 1995): Post-assessment*

Update and mood check

It is helpful to check how the client is at the start of each session, although keep it brief. Clients may have been thinking about what they are going to say for some time before they arrive, so the therapist may be greeted by a long account of recent stresses or sometimes a painfully obsessional and detailed story. At the other end of the continuum, especially when they are starting to improve, people sometimes say 'I don't really know what I am going to talk about today.' Some clients may have experienced other types of therapy based on getting things off your chest, so they may even think that they are required to do just that. If clients keep 'offloading' in this way, it can disrupt the more structured CBT activities. The therapist may use immediate statements such as 'I feel like we may be wandering off track here, what do you think?' to help to re-establish structure. This is not about preventing clients from expressing themselves but about helping them to use therapy well and keep on the track of problem-solving. The therapist must be sensitive and able to negotiate this collaboratively with clients. I have often been thanked by clients for doing so: they had a shrewd suspicion that they 'went on a bit at times' but were not really sure what was required of them in the therapy context.

Bridge

The therapist creates a bridge to the previous session by simply asking if the client has anything left over from the previous meeting. Although this is usually brief, occasionally clients will have been brooding on some point and until that is cleared, it may bubble away below the surface.

Agenda-setting

The therapist should try to get to agenda-setting in the first 10 minutes of the session. Trainees who have been trained in less structured methods often fail to keep these early items on track and so are then left setting an agenda when half the session has already gone. Unless caused by an exceptional item, it clearly doesn't make a lot of sense to take so long. Agenda-setting itself is not just about identifying any items to cover. Ideally, items should relate to the goals of therapy, a point which it is helpful for therapists to underline: 'Yes, it would be good to talk about that incident with Sam because it seems to relate to how fed up you get when you feel that people haven't respected you and we have identified helping you to manage that better as one of our goals.' The skill of agenda-setting also implies an ability to keep to the agenda (within reason). It can help to set time boundaries and a running order for various items.

Main agenda items: focusing on issues

The overt structuring principle is very evident in this section of therapy. As I write, I can't help but feel that it will sound either slightly controlling or even anally retentive to some readers. It is good to acknowledge that structure can indeed be used in either of these ways. I believe that all therapy models have their characteristic problems: being over-structured is one of the main problems of CBT. What stops CB therapy from becoming irredeemably problematic in this respect is the drive towards collaboration with the client. For example, if you felt a client was straying from an important focus, you can say, 'Mary, before, we were talking about how you find it difficult to work with certain people and how that gets you down. I wonder if we may now have strayed a bit into details of the work itself and how you got into it. It may be important to discuss that but it may also be important to try to get back to the previous topic. What do you think?' Padesky & Mooney (1998) note that therapists can sometimes feel nervous about this kind of intervention because they hold 'therapist beliefs' such as 'If I structure clients, they will resent it.' This may be true of some clients, especially those who are ambivalent about being structured, but my experience is that most clients react well to it, provided they understand and respect the therapist's motives for doing it. Finally, I do think that it is possible to 'wear the structure lightly', as I believe Aaron Beck, for example, and hopefully myself do. Some trainees have said to me that they have become aware that they adopted non-directive values in therapy to counterbalance a tendency to be a bit over-directive in their work. I think that this may work the other way: if you have an ambivalent attitude about structure, then that may be the very way for you to go.

Homework and feedback

Other principles of CBT's structure are the importance of feedback in maintaining good collaboration, and using homework. It is extremely valuable to ask the client what she has found helpful in the session and if anything was awkward or unhelpful. Therapists are probably just as prone to the problem of seeking approval as anyone, but getting feedback should not be about that. We can, of course, enjoy positive client reports but we also need to know about what is not working for them if we are to keep therapy collaborative and on track. The task of setting homework will be covered again in Chapters 4 and 5, but the structural principle to get hold of is that if clients go to the trouble of doing homework, it must be discussed, otherwise they may become demotivated. Given how busy most of us are in modern society, I confess that I always feel mildly surprised when clients do homework and I therefore pay a lot of attention to trying to work out realistic and do-able tasks. It is obviously important that clients understand why homework can help and are able to negotiate a task that means something to them and is likely to be completed. Like all aspects of CBT structure, most clients adjust to it well and have often reported to me that they enjoy the sense of knowing how their sessions will run. It can, of course, all become too predictable sometimes and some variations will be considered in Chapter 7.

Suggestion

How do you feel about implementing the CB therapy structure? If you have reservations, you wouldn't be the first to do so. This may be a bullet you will have to bite though – and there's no time like the present. (Most trainees find that with a little persistence, what at first seems 'strange' becomes second nature eventually.) Look down the structure items and pick out one to practise right now. On this occasion, you should also include a 'rationale' in your own words, for example 'Charlie, I suggest that we now set an agenda for our session today. I suggest that we do this every time we meet. I'll ask what you would like to cover today and sometimes I will make suggestions too. The reason for an agenda is because this is short-term therapy and we want to try to make sure that we use the time well and cover all the concerns you might have. Does that make sense? Do you have any questions about it?'

Earlier I mentioned that overt structure is only one aspect of structure in therapy. The other is the more strategic one of having a structure in your head that constantly directs your radar towards three questions:

- Why did this problem start?
- What keeps it going?
- What will bring it to an end?

As CBT practitioners listen to clients, they may well find themselves thinking about these questions and about alternative frames of reference for responding to them. For example, a client may be berating herself as being 'useless' and the therapist may be looking for signs of usefulness. CBT theory, and all its levels of thoughts, beliefs and schemas, is wonderfully helpful in suggesting possible areas for alternative ways of seeing things. The concept of 'self-focused attention' and its role in social anxiety helps us to realise that the signals of anxiety noticed by the client are likely to result from paying too much attention to internal feelings and not enough attention to external reality (Wells, 1997). Knowledge of the growing CBT research literature also helps by giving excellent estimates of characteristic thoughts and thinking processes for people with various types of problem (see the chapter on anxiety disorders in Wells, 2006). A therapist can use all these ways to understand client experience and build up a CBT radar that informs the CB therapist's clinical judgement and intuition. There is, frankly, an element that is creative and slightly 'left field' about the ability to sense alternative, more positive ways of thinking that may help the client. It can be difficult to describe this skill in words and within an entirely logical framework. The desirability of mixing theory and intuition will emerge again as an issue in Chapters 4 and 5, where we will see how this combination can guide and direct cognitive and behavioural interventions.

Conclusion

This chapter has covered much terrain as we have moved from collecting glimpses of clients' mindsets in the first interactions with them through to more detailed information to establish their current problems. This kind of detail, together with more historical material, is built into a formulation, driven by identifiable and testable psychological mechanisms. A collaborative therapeutic relationship is established and maintained during these exchanges. This relationship is then used to establish goals for therapy and structured methods to attain progress in achieving those goals. CBT principles inform each step of the journey, though there is much to be said for using the principles and the structure with a light hand. The following chapters will provide a more detailed description of the CBT skills needed for implementing techniques on the subsequent steps of the journey.

PRACTICE TIP: Helping the client to see that things can get better

Initial contract and re-moralisation

Psychologists have generally suggested that first impressions from initial contacts are powerful and long-lasting. Clients who come for therapy are often feeling demoralised and the extent to which initial contact 're-moralises' the client is often thought to be vital in maintaining clients' motivation during the normal ups and downs of therapy – especially in the early stages.

At a seminar, a trainer asked 'What would you feel most fed up about not getting from this session?' I think that this is a good question for therapists to consider in relation to clients. When I have discussed this with clients, they have invariably said that they would like to leave the first session with some kind of idea of how the therapy might go and how it might work for them. Given that they could be about to invest a lot of money and/or time in this process, this question seems entirely fair to me. There has sometimes been a tendency for therapists to regard such requests as rather neurotic attempts to establish certainty where it cannot exist. Therapists should certainly be wary about giving promises of a 'cure', but can, in my view, be helpful to clients by suggesting some lines along which therapy could proceed and how it could be helpful to a client. If I were a client, I would be fed up if I left an initial session without some such understanding.

I therefore try to finish initial sessions by:

- summarising what has been said,
- summarising the sorts of things that might help, for example doing thought records to tackle negative thoughts,
- suggesting that 'there may be bad days', and, finally,
- asking the client what they think of my summary.

The point about bad days reinforces the fact that expectations for therapy may need to be positive but they also need to be realistic.

Further reading

Grant, A. et al. (2004) *Cognitive behaviour therapy in mental health care*. London: SAGE.

Kirk, J. (1989) Cognitive behavioural assessment. In K. Hawton, et al. (eds), *Cognitive behaviour therapy for psychiatric problems*. Oxford: Oxford Medical Publications, pp. 13–51.

Westbrook, D. et al. (2007) *Introduction to cognitive behaviour therapy: skills and applications*. London: SAGE

Notes

1   The technical term for this is 'commordity'.

2   The reader may observe that clients give their consent quite easily in these examples. Readers will find more material on 'consent' and 'resistance' in Chapters 7 and 8.

3   In earlier joint publications, Diana Sanders and I used the term 'conceptualisation'. The term 'formulation' has exactly the same meaning but has become the dominant term used through all modalities (Eells, 1997). I have therefore decided to switch to this term in the interest of therapy integration and 'common coinage' throughout our profession.

3

USING INTERPERSONAL SKILLS IN CBT

There are certain politicians who cannot stand to be in the same room as one another, even if mutual interest dictates that they should try to get along. ... This is what the Stoics fail to grasp when they assert that reason rather than emotion should play the dominant part in human affairs...

Robert Harris (2006: 83–4)

Interpersonal processes saturate therapeutic work. They emerge as significant in the assessment of the client's past and present functioning and in the interaction in the therapy room. The interpersonal dimension is now firmly established in CBT theory and practice (Gilbert & Leahy, 2007). This chapter will describe the skills that CB therapists can use to conduct therapy in an interpersonally sensitive way. It has been particularly informed by the approach of Kahn (1991), who describes the convergence of humanistic and psychodynamic therapies around the theme of interpersonal exchange, and the approaches of Safran & Segal (1990) and Gilbert & Leahy (2007), who have covered similar ground from the CBT perspective.

The chapter will begin by showing how CB therapists can recognise moments when interpersonal factors particularly impact on continuing therapeutic work. These moments often have a slightly unexpected feel to them and will be illustrated by clinical examples. CB therapists are able, however, to recognise these moments more easily when they have identified significant interpersonal elements in the client's formulation, as introduced in Chapter 2.

The chapter then moves on to suggest that the recognition of interpersonal factors is aided by understanding their role in the development of psychological problems. Therapists can use relationship skills better when they understand the processes described in attachment theory and the way such processes exercise interpersonal influence in the client's life and the way they interact in therapy. I focus especially on using immediacy in interpersonal work, which allows the therapist to acknowledge what is going on between her and the client in the here and now, during assessment and ongoing therapy. Further links to interpersonal skills in working with emotions and schemas are made in Chapters 6 and 7 respectively.

Recognising the influence of interpersonal processes in everyday therapy

BRON: It was a cold day in January and I wanted to greet my morning clients with a roaring log fire as they came in from the cold. On this morning, however, the wood was slightly damp and the fire spluttered rather than roared. I tried to keep my attention on my client, Bron, but I also wanted to revive my fire and eventually, I asked her if I could pause the session for a few minutes to do this. As I bent down to remake the fire, she said, 'I am sorry.' A few minutes later, with the fire now ablaze, I said I'd noticed she had apologised and asked her why. 'For causing you trouble. If I had not needed therapy, you would not have been on your hands and knees.' This led to an interesting discussion about both her apology and *my* discomfort at taking my attention from her. Bron said, 'I seem to have to apologise for being alive sometimes.' The week before we had sketched out a preliminary formulation and we now consulted it:

Her mother had died when Bron was 12. Bron had gone to live with Aunt Gwen, who was a Welsh Congregationalist and a complex character: both dutifully giving and subtly withholding. Bron was deeply grateful to Gwen but wondered just how 'kindly' her aunt really was. One day she had overheard two neighbours talking about the situation; one had said, in a world-weary way, how sad the situation was but that 'Gwen had been a true Christian' and 'taken Bron in'. Bron had understood from this that she was a 'burden', a 'charity case' and that she must evermore be grateful that she had been 'taken in'.

These facts exercised some interpersonal influence on me: I had known Aunt Gwen types in my youth on the Anglo-Welsh borders. In addition, the fact that the fire needed boosting was at least partly connected with one of my patterns: trying to do too many other things had not left me enough time to set the fire properly. This little incident said much about us both. Highlighting the interpersonal content came from noticing a small discordant phrase, one that could have easily been overlooked. Reflecting back to the client and listening carefully to what she said about it enhanced the quality of therapy. The material gleaned was extremely helpful in understanding Bron's situation more deeply and in building up knowledge of the belief changes most likely to help her move on.

Recognising interpersonal content in CBT formulation

The process of developing a client formulation within a sound therapeutic relationship was described in Chapter 2. During this process, the therapist is looking for significant client material that seems likely to be linked to core problem areas. The therapist will find much of this type of material in the client's current and historical interpersonal functioning:

DON was raised in a tough part of Newcastle. Both his parents had severe drinking problems and were highly inconsistent in their parenting. Don had joined the Army, learnt a good trade and had prospered after coming back to civilian life. Now years later, he was struggling to establish a good relationship with his partner. She, fed up with his behaviour, suggested a trial separation, during which he should sort himself out. He was depressed. While discussing his history I asked Don for a typical story from his childhood (see Chapters 2 and 7) and he told me the following:

Often when I came home from school, I would find my parents lying drunk on the floor. There'd be no food for tea. Often there'd be no heat or light: the gas and electric had been turned off due to debts. The final disillusion came when I returned from a school holiday in the Lakes. The coach got back to school at four on Friday. All the parents were there to meet the kids: all except mine obviously. The awful thing was I had to walk past all these 'happy families' to get my bag from the back of the coach. That was the walk of shame. But it was a historic moment for me: as I did it, I said to myself, 'I'll never be humiliated again. I'll never rely on anyone again. From now on, I will look after myself.'

We can see that Don's recent experiences connect with his more distant past. The strategy of 'looking after me first' probably worked well in the Army but was less useful when trying to make an intimate relationship now. How can one fit a drive for independence into a situation usually characterised by a degree of mutual dependence? Don also showed a particularly strong need for love yet struggled to trust enough to allow it to happen, which was hardly surprising given his earlier experience. He had antagonistic schemas: one driving a need to attach, the other driving a need to detach. We built a short formulation and used it to understand his negative reaction to an incident when a friend failed to call (see Figure 3.1).

Looking at the formulation in Figure 3.1, interpersonal material seems to come at us from every angle. Distant and current trigger events are interpersonal in nature, hinting at a long, interpersonal learning history. The key cognitions are all interpersonal, even the thoughts that Don has about himself are in relation to other people: what trust and love can there be between the self and others? Even the planet is anthropomorphised into a person who has intentions or, in this case, lack of intentions towards others. The behaviour is a measure of how the client might move towards or away from other people, and the negative feeling is, as we will see shortly, a wired-in propensity to react to aversive interpersonal events.

It turned out that Don's partner, who had manoeuvred him into therapy, had in fact been having an affair with another man, potentially confirming all his most negative interpersonal schemas. We weathered this period by helping him to apply his already established problem-management and problem-solving

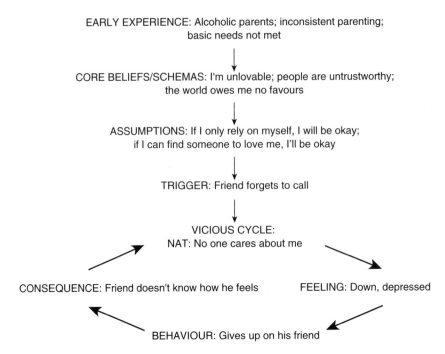

FIGURE 3.1   *Don's CB formulation*

skills to deal with the impact of feeling so hurt and lost. Towards the end of the therapy, Don emigrated and made a new relationship. He wrote to me two years later, reporting friendship with his previous partner, a happy new marriage and a new sense of peace with his family of origin. Reflecting on my work with Don, I used standard CBT skills of identifying his various strands of belief, relating them together and conveying the patterns back to Don verbally and in written formats. I can also identify 'soft hand'[1] skills of a more interpersonal nature. These skills resemble those described by Young et al. (2003) in implementing 'limited re-parenting' (see also Chapter 7) and acting as a reference point and transitional figure with whom various forms of pain and change could be worked through and resolved. Finally, although I am sure that the therapy played an important role, I believe that these changes were finally secured by the success of his new relationship.

Suggestion

Think of a client you have seen recently. What sort of client material might fit into a formulation such as the one shown for Don? What did he/she tell you about current and past relationships? How was/is your therapeutic relationship? What elements in all these factors seem to fit into common themes and what discrepancies are there?

Understanding the relationship between interpersonal and psychological problems

Some early critics of CBT maintained that the cognitive model of depression did not give sufficient emphasis to relationship difficulties as causes of psychological problems. This critique and Beck's responses are described in Weishaar (1993). There was some truth in this criticism and Beck, in particular, characteristically responded by widening some aspects of the theory and clarifying others (Beck, 1988, 1991). It has been long known, for example, that early loss of a mother and the lack of a confiding partner are major vulnerability factors leading to depression in young mothers.

As well as acting as historical triggers of psychological problems, relationship factors play a major role in the maintenance of depression. The depressed client can become unrewarding company. Most partners of depressed people begin by feeling sympathetic but the self-preoccupation of the depressed person can quickly overcome this good will (Papageorgiou & Wells, 2003). One study found that 40% of partners of depressed clients themselves present sufficiently strong symptoms to meet the diagnostic criteria for depression (Safran & Segal, 1990). It has also been argued that relatively simple behavioural and interpersonal interventions with such clients can be just as effective as more complex psychotherapeutic ones (see Chapter 5 on 'behavioural activation'). Dealing with interpersonal material can involve sophisticated psychological work based on deep self-knowledge, but this should not lead us to neglect simple and straightforward interventions. These new developments in CBT clarify the fact that the model needs to take the social environment seriously and should not be over-reliant on explanations based on psychological deficits. The famous dictum of Epictetus[2] can be misunderstood. Disturbance usually results from the views people take of *actual* events: without such events, the negative views would not have been taken in the first place.

Some depressed clients may be unrewarding to therapists and may test our acceptance and empathy to the full. It still surprises me that quite a number of therapy trainees express a fear of depression, almost as if it can be catching – perhaps because in an interpersonal sense it can strongly affect other people. I think that it can be helpful to acknowledge these problems with clients: quite often they are more than half aware of how people see them anyway. A kind of grimness and over-seriousness can settle in with depression and this can estrange some clients from their former selves and thereby their partners. The therapeutic session can be a safe environment where newer ways of behaving (and/or recovering older ways) can be played with and tried out experimentally. The idea of lightening up can sound a little trite, but I have put this to a number of clients who *have* been able to identify with this point and *have* benefited from thinking about how they might do it. Lightening up may perhaps sound less worrying than having to 'overcome depressogenic tendencies'. Interpersonal experimentation ties in with the principles of activation and reframing discussed in Chapter 1. Crucially, it can help the client feel that it is possible to reclaim a former self that was not depressed. It goes without saying that this idea should emerge from within the client's frame of reference and that launching it from outside that frame could be hazardous.

Using an understanding of attachment

Attachment has proved to be a powerful idea in therapy. It can help clients and therapists understand how intimate relationships work. Bowlby's (1980) working model of attachment has similarities with Beck's concept of mode (Beck, 1996). Human infants have particularly long periods of dependence so that secure attachment bonds have survival value and appear to be wired-in responses for mother and baby, evident from the very first moments of life. Beck (1996) has described some of the evolutionary underpinnings of CBT theory. Anxiety, for example, can be seen as a wired-in response to the possibility of danger, without which proper life precautions may be neglected (Beck et al., 1985). Depression may also be an evolutionary response, in this case to defeat, when it makes sense to withdraw resources or conserve energy from a failed project (Gilbert, 1992). From a more interpersonal perspective, there is potential danger in being excluded from the group. Perception of such a possibility is likely to trigger anxiety as a motivator to the 'two Fs': fight or flight. Some clients with social anxiety have, for example, described how they see certain work colleagues as 'predators', circling the flock waiting to pick off the weaker animals that get pushed to the edge of the herd (Sanders & Wills, 2003). While moderate anxiety about such possibilities might be adaptive, severe anxiety seems to block adaptive behaviour and results in freezing so that the possibility of escape may be inhibited. If an infant has a secure base, it appears more confident to explore. Anxiety, however, seems to inhibit exploratory behaviour. Bowlby (1988) shows how a developmentally secure base facilitates exploration and an expansion of the child's safety zone, whereas an insecure base may lead to negative modes of attachment. Liotti (2007) suggests that if rational collaboration breaks down in a therapy relationship, then clients may revert to previous modes of negative attachment in the way they relate to their therapist. Therapists should therefore strive to develop containing relationships to promote sufficient security for the client during therapy.

Therapists are certainly asking clients to explore the way they function. Hence clients need to feel that they will not be negatively judged as they do so. Winnicott (1965) describes a situation of 'being alone in the presence of the mother', in which the child oscillates between exploring and returning to base. Exploration raises understandable anxiety which can be tolerated if the therapist can facilitate a secure base so that the client experiences security as being close at hand. Detachment, however, is also an important stage of attachment (Guidano & Liotti, 1983). Secure attachment makes secure detachment possible. Similarly, therapists have to help clients to detach at the appropriate time. Anxiety can, however, reach problematic levels and may result in exploration becoming blocked and appropriate detachment delayed. Behavioural experiments (described in Chapter 5) can be seen as forms of client exploration from the secure base of the therapy relationship. The attachment concept also gives us a language to talk about developing and ending patterns in relationships, including the therapeutic relationship. It is important to be aware of and to respond to different client needs in this respect. Attachment may also be understood in a wider sense that can be seen as the desire to have a reasonable, secure relationship with one's surrounding social group. Mythology contains widespread representation of the fear of being turned on by the group in (Girard, 1977) which be present in the underlying fears of socially anxious clients.

Suggestion

Draw a continuum line with 'attachment' on one end and 'detachment' (or 'autonomy') on the other) and place various people on it. For example, some people have strong needs to be attached, whereas others seem happier with autonomy. Start with yourself and then add clients on to it. What are the implications of the various places assumed by these people and the relationships between them? For example, what happens when people with strong drives towards attachment have to link up with people who have strong needs for autonomy? Are there productive ways in which families and organisations can balance everyone's needs in this respect?

Skills for promoting change in negative interaction patterns – first catch it

Negative interpersonal behaviour often seems to exert a pull that draws others into a 'complementary response' that in turn merely confirms the first person's worst fears (Safran & Segal, 1990). During early training, I felt disengaged in an experiential group and became preoccupied with negative feelings about another group member. The group facilitator suddenly asked me what I was thinking. I might have held my tongue but instead I blurted out, 'I'm so pissed off with R___ . He sits there with a superior smile on his face and never says anything.' My eyes met those of R___ in a sudden, pure 'meeting'. I saw that he was very *scared* in the group and he saw that I saw that. I saw that he saw that I saw that! We both giggled at the absurdity of the situation. It was the start of a nice friendship between us. I have found this same pattern among many clients suffering from social anxiety.[3] When people are scared, usually of being judged in social situations, they can take on a defensively detached state that others may see as 'superior'. This pattern draws both unwanted attention and hostility from others, the very things the person most fears. They want to deflect unwanted attention but frequently only attract more of it (Sanders & Wills, 2003), a pattern which can result in a self-fulfilling prophecy: 'people do not like me and will criticise me'. This is the classic 'vicious cycle', first described by Karen Horney (1951) and later by Paul Wachtel (1982), and now very much part of CBT formulation (Sanders & Wills, 2005).

Self-fulfilling patterns are so well established that they often seem like the natural order of things. They may repeat themselves in sessions without the therapist really noticing. One day, however, especially if therapists are sensitised to such things, the pattern will suddenly grab our attention and we will think back and begin to identify them as part of a pattern seen in previous interactions. The therapist has caught hold of the pattern. Supervision is a place where these insights can be tested and thought through. Even where there is an obvious pattern, how, or even whether, to respond may not be so obvious. One source of data that may help us decide these questions is the formulation, that is, what we have already learnt about the client's interpersonal functioning in current and historical contexts. Interpersonal strategies will often be evident in schemas, core beliefs and assumptions.

Interpersonal CBT: assessment skills

Many of the questions asked during the assessment process will build a picture of the client's interpersonal functioning. Some repetitive themes may cause the therapist to wonder about the possibility of certain blind spots:

> **RACHEL**: Her work as a nurse was clearly a very important issue for Rachel. She defined herself by how 'important' she thought her work was. She went through frequent periods of considering that her work was not important enough and that she should seek a job in another field. As well as that, she was a harsh critic of her productivity during every day of her current job, even though she undervalued it. As we tried to assess the extent of the problem, she described her recent work history by exploring her last five jobs. Rachel assessed each one as a failure and laid the blame at the feet of her nurse manager in each instance and always because the manager had failed to appreciate Rachel's individual talents. The therapist was quite open to the possibility that some of her nurse managers matched a preconception that the standard of management in the NHS is frequently criticised, but when it came to five managers in a row, he did begin to wonder if Rachel had a bit of a blind spot with managers.

Besides themes emerging naturally from the therapy material, there are two other sources of interpersonally potentially significant information: **relationship signals** and **relationship breakdowns**.

Relationship signals ('interpersonal markers') are incidents that reveal underlying interpersonal patterns. They are samples of behaviour that are 'windows into understanding the whole cognitive-interpersonal style' of the client (Safran & Segal, 1990: 82). They often have a slightly off-key feel to them and may become evident to the therapist when she finds herself reacting to a client behaviour by musing, 'What on earth was that all about?'

> **MARY** sat down for the first session and immediately bombarded me with questions about myself. With a rather fixed smile, she asked me about my training, how I had got interested in the work, how I organised my practice, and other questions. before saying anything about her own problems. Therapists would perhaps tend to think that such behaviour might signal anxiety or an issue of trust. Later on in the session, however, Mary gave me an entirely different and more

idiosyncratic motivation for her questions. She was basically an ill-favoured eldest child, who had been used as a 'skivvy' to look after the more indulged younger children. She came to believe, that 'I just don't measure up: I am not as good as other people.' No matter what she achieved or how hard she tried, she expected to be judged negatively by people, who would never be interested in her. Years later, on a sales course, a tutor had unwittingly given her a strategy to overcome this problem. 'Ask about your customer, be interested in him and he will be interested in you', she was instructed. By asking me lots of questions, she was saying to me, 'I am interested in you, please be interested in me.'

By asking further questions, it emerged that this very specific strategy was part of a more general 'people-pleasing' strategy that Mary followed zealously. Going back to our earlier point about the ironic consequences that often result from such strategies, this behaviour really got up the noses of Mary's work colleagues, who took her for granted and treated her like a skivvy. In supervision, I role-played Mary's people-pleasing style and my supervisor commented 'Wouldn't it be great if she could lighten up and be a bit more playful.' I fed this back to Mary and she got it right away. I sensed a great relief at identifying a potential solution and she moved forward rapidly from then on.[4] It is often helpful, having got a breakthrough in this way, to capitalise on it by facilitating the client to brainstorm a range of situations in which she might try out the new strategy – in this case, playfulness. Egan (2002) suggests a series of steps for giving forethought to how various options that emerge from brainstorming may be tested in the imagination for viability and effectiveness. One such step, for example, is to try to work out who might be the first person with whom to practise 'playfulness'. Perhaps the person most likely to respond positively? This kind of anticipation can help to gear the client up for action. The action has the additional benefit in Mary getting some positive feedback – something she has been striving for but had been striving in all the wrong ways. It strikes me that it must have been much nicer for Mary to have a problem in needing to 'be more playful' than to have a nasty sounding 'disorder' called 'social phobia'.

For Mary, the effect of her interpersonal 'marker' behaviour was relatively benign and was in any case identified and worked through at a relatively early stage. Other interpersonal markers – for example, ones betraying a lack of trust in the therapist – are more likely to cause problems in the therapy relationship if left unheeded. We will explore these more difficult disruptions or alliance ruptures, and ways of handling them, shortly and in Chapter 7.

Suggestion

Think of any incidents that may have happened between you and your clients over the years. One trainee told me about a client who regularly brought a bag of chips into the session with her. Thinking back, do of any these incidents seem like they may have been 'interpersonal markers' for the client's underlying interpersonal patterns and/or the way they may have interacted with your underlying interpersonal patterns?

Skills for working on clients' interpersonal patterns outside therapy

When clients report interpersonal experiences that have gone badly, they often express intense emotions and negative thoughts:

> **ALAN** described how a work meeting had triggered a depressed reaction. He had a personal history where people had not 'really been there for him'. His parents were not 'bad' parents, but had somehow never been really active in helping him deal with things. He grew up to believe that 'people will not really help me'. His work situation was pressured and redundancies were rumoured to be imminent. Alan saw some colleagues as competitors and 'predators'. At the meeting he had to present a report. He described the experience as 'horrendous ... everyone seemed to want to have a go at me. My report was rubbished. ... I felt so bad when I came out that I went straight home and went on the sick.'[5]

As he was describing the meeting in this way, Alan had no doubt that this is exactly what had happened. Safran & Segal (1990) describe this state of mind as being 'fully immersed' in his negative thoughts. The therapist is less enmeshed in the client's version of reality and is therefore freer to wonder what had actually occurred. A good starting point is a thorough knowledge of 'cognitive distortions' (see Chapter 4). CB therapists should be highly versed in distortions so that they can spot them quickly:

> **ALAN:** The therapist helped Alan to think about the possible effects of 'overgeneralisation': would an entire meeting of nine people, it turned out, have viewed Alan and his report with total unanimity? A more common experience of meetings is that, in free discussion, it is often very hard to reach even a degree of unanimity. The therapist went over the whole experience, asking Alan to recall as much detail as possible. As is often the case, the devil *was* in the detail. Alan wrote down all the comments he could remember and found to his surprise that, of the comments he could recall, only 10% were critical. He also recovered memories of some positive comments: actually as many were positive as negative and the overwhelming majority of comments fell into the 'neutral' category. Reality turned out to be more benign than he had thought at the time, when feeling so anxious. The good relationship between Alan and his therapist meant that an attempted reframing was seen as a challenge of his perceptions rather than a challenge of him as a person.

From a skills perspective, where you have a client with whom you have a good relationship and the client is convinced by his negative cognitions, challenging those cognitions is likely to be therapeutic because it will probably reveal new ground. The previous perception, influenced by the fact that the client was anxious and depressed, is now being rethought from a newer perspective derived from higher order reasoning. The appeal to reason does not, however, mean emotions play no role. Change in CBT is more likely when adaptive thinking is experienced alongside the negative emotion (Foa & Kozak, 1986): without emotions, reframing is mere 'intellectualisation'. The client is more likely to be able to accept his contribution to the negative pattern. This is an internal process such as saying to oneself 'Yes, that's it; I *am* seeing this as more personal than it was probably intended.' The discomfort of the initial dissonance is a part of the necessary motivation for change. The empowering and liberating notion that nestles in the new position is 'If I talk myself into this, I can talk myself out of it.'

Another possibility, however, is that the client is not fully convinced by his negative thoughts and conducts a running argument with them (Safran & Segal, 1990). The client has already felt some cognitive dissonance and is actually now in two minds. Two minds can be seen in Bron, whom we encountered in the opening pages of this chapter. Contemplating her 'apology', Bron commented, 'I know it's crazy, isn't it? I don't know why I have to apologise all the time. I seem to have to apologise for being alive sometimes.' It might be thought that this was an even better position from which to launch a challenge: since Bron is half-way there – perhaps we could encourage her to go the last few yards by allying with her rational side. It may go that way on occasions, but may not. One possible extension of the dialogue may show us why:

Therapist: So you apologise for situations that you have no active part in bringing about.
Client: I know. Why do I have to do that?
Therapist: How do you answer that question?
Client: Because I'm bloody stupid.
Therapist: What evidence can you give me that you are bloody stupid?
Client: Because I do bloody stupid things like apologising for silly things all the time!
Therapist: Is there any other way of seeing what you do there?
Client: (looking very distressed) Oh I don't know… I just feel so lame.

This scenario represents an example of how challenging negative thinking can be ineffective. If such challenges are over-zealously pursued, they can even alienate the client. The problem is that the client is probably arguing with herself about her negative thoughts so that the therapist is pushing at an open door: nothing new is happening. Therapeutic gain is more likely to come from the dynamic interplay between the force of the intervention and the unquestioning clients' resistance when their minds are in the fully 'convinced' state. It is important for the CB therapist to bear in mind, therefore, that the client not only has negative thoughts but also has relationships with those thoughts. Many clients are debating with their thoughts all the time. The problem, however, is often maintained by the way they pay attention to and conduct this debate (Williams et al., 2007), a paradox which can seem puzzling to the therapist because sometimes one side of the debate will command the client's voice and at other times another will do so. Therapists need not only to monitor thoughts but to be aware of the client's relationship with those thoughts. Furthermore, the interventions shown in the last dialogue, though well meant and 'technically correct', are not interpersonally well informed. Bron is a highly intelligent, capable person and yet one who is capable of feeling stupid a lot of the time. The client can easily experience the therapist's intervention as patronising and as implying that the therapist does in fact see the client as stupid. This can be a powerfully negatively confirming experience, fitting quite snugly into the negative self-schemas that the client is trying to get away from. We are not helping the client to experience her role in maintaining the negative thinking in an open way. According to Safran & Segal (1990), the correct therapeutic manoeuvre here is the counter-intuitive and homeopathic one of directing the client back into the negativity by facilitating emotionally felt experience by 'focusing' (Gendlin, 1981):

Therapist: You apologise for situations that you have no active part in bringing about and you feel stupid about that. Let's go into that. Let's stay with that feeling.

Client: How do you mean?

Therapist: Well, now you try to push it away, let's do the opposite. Let's welcome it in and feel what it is like to be with it.

Client: (intrigued) Okay then... if you think that would help.

Therapist: Is there any body feeling that goes with it?

Client: There's a headache, a pressure in my brow, like a bursting. It's like I feel sometimes on a thundery day. You know, the atmosphere is brooding.

Therapist: So let's keep that thundery, pressured feeling for a moment. Just hold it and see what happens. ...

Client: There's a kind of cloud that has been following me. It has been following me all my life. It's not very nice... but it is mine... my weather, part of my climate... It is something I can live with... it is just a quirky part of me.

There is the start of a therapeutic shift in the way Bron attributes cognitive-interpersonal and cognitive-emotional meanings as she processes her own functioning: She realises that there is a difference between 'stupidity' and 'quirk-iness'. Quirkiness is easier to live with and may even give a sense of attractive-ness to the person. The incident that led to the above exploration was something that happened in the session but the therapist shifted the focus to a more general pattern that Bron experiences in her life outside therapy. We will now turn our attention to therapeutic incidents that occur in the here and now of the session. The therapist's aim is now to stay with what is going on between her and the client to try to work the incident through in the session.

Relationship breakdowns (alliance ruptures) occur when the relationship between client and therapist begins to falter. They are not necessarily always very dramatic events and may even seem to be about some apparently rather minor detail of the therapy, but what marks them out is an intensity of feeling on one or other or both sides.

Skills for working on interpersonal patterns in the therapy session

Focusing on the here-and-now interpersonal process between therapist and client becomes appropriate when a relationship signal occurs within a therapy session, especially when it results in the breakdown of therapy – 'an alliance rupture' (Safran & Segal, 1990).

Safran & Segal (1990) name seven types of common alliance rupture in CBT:

1. The client is sceptical.
2. The client is sarcastic or otherwise negative.
3. The client alludes to problems in the therapy indirectly by reference to another relationship.
4. Client and therapist disagree on goals or tasks.
5. The client is over-compliant.
6. The client does not respond to an intervention.
7. The client activates 'therapy safety behaviours'.

Breakdowns may first become apparent as uncomfortable bodily sensations: for me, a prickly feeling in the neck. They can, however, present great opportunities for therapy to move forward. Therapists should try not to feel too wrong-footed by them and may also need to step back from reacting too quickly. Such responses tend towards retaliation and may result in putting down the client or too hasty reassurance or apology (though it is always good to bear in mind that the therapist may have made a mistake). Using empathy is usually an integral part of healing a breakdown and may offer a chance to compensate for an earlier lack of empathy. Sometimes breakdowns occur because a client has experienced a sense of shame in a session (Gilbert, 2006). Going over old wounds can easily trigger shame. Sometimes a therapist can unwittingly imply that a client is 'stupid' by artlessly challenging one of their negative automatic thoughts.

It is important that the first move of the therapist is to become 'unhooked' from the client's interpersonal pattern. This demands the ability to use what Casement (1985) has called the 'internal supervisor'. As described in other therapeutic models, the therapist must be quite comfortable with his own feelings, especially negative feelings that arise in therapy. Such feelings are sometimes blocked by what Padesky & Mooney (1998) have called 'therapist beliefs', such as 'I shouldn't feel angry about clients', or 'It is bad to feel bored by clients.' It is important to realise the pressure we sometimes put ourselves under by adhering, even unconsciously, to such beliefs. They may make us over-concerned to 'achieve something', 'be something' or 'do something' – perhaps especially the latter in CBT. Therapist can work on developing a different type of attention: a kind of non-attached awareness, close to what I shall discuss as 'mindfulness' elsewhere in this book. Joyce & Sills (2001: 38) describe such an attitude in Gestalt therapy as 'the fertile void' or 'creative indifference':

> It does not mean ... an attitude of not caring. ... It involves the counsellor truly embracing the practice of genuine interest combined with an equally genuine lack of investment in any particular result.

Sometimes the interpersonal breakdown has indeed started with the therapist and we should be ready to own appropriate responsibility. For this reason, and because of the danger of coming over to the client as a 'clever clogs', we should record the discomfort of possible breakdown as 'information about something' and try to be as honest as possible in our subsequent review – perhaps in supervision – of what that something is. A supervisor can frequently help us to formulate the situation and our role in it, and then form testable hypotheses about its mechanism. The formulation needs to be testable because our hypothesis might be wrong and because client–therapist collaboration might be able to find a more accurate one.

JO was a final-year undergraduate who had been dreadfully depressed and was close to giving up on her degree. Therapy coincided with a remarkable recovery (and eventually a good degree). The recovery was assured from February onwards and the therapist noted that Jo kept adding extra sessions as they approached the end of each contracted period of therapy. This was slightly puzzling, as Jo had shown strong tendencies towards an autonomous streak throughout therapy. Discussion in supervision revealed that the therapist himself felt pressure to close as much work as he could because of ongoing pressure of other referrals. It was decided to put the whole situation to Jo in as open a way as possible, asking her to help the therapist resolve it in a way that met both of their needs and interests. Interestingly, Jo was quite amused at the thought that she might be seen as 'dependent', but revealed that she wasn't really sure how therapy ended. The theme of 'not quite knowing how to end things' was also evident in her formulation: she spent a long period of alternating between her mother and father after they divorced and found each and every transition difficult, partly because of the actions of one or both parents. Once this issue was surfaced, however, she and the therapist were able to devise an appropriate 'fade out' period of therapy and follow-up.

The message conveyed in this instance may be regarded as the type of communication that aims to identify problematic interpersonal patterns in the client and in the therapist and then initiate joint exploration. The starting point is often about helping the client appreciate the impact that they may have on others.

When I act as a supervisor, I frequently find that supervisees have difficulty dealing with clients who overwhelm them with material – trainees often describe the feeling of 'being dumped on'. When I am faced with this situation, I have generally felt comfortable saying something like, 'Can we just hang on a moment: I am finding it a bit hard to keep up with you. It would help me if we could slow things down and focus a bit more?' Clients invariably give such permission and often add, 'I'm glad you said that. A lot of people reckon I go on a bit. I'm never quite sure about what detail might be required so it would help me if you did focus me.' Trainees often fear that saying something like this would be seen as rude or 'cutting across' the client, but that fear makes an assumption about what clients feel. Rather than make assumptions, it is often easier to ask them straight out. Getting a better handle on how we really come over to other people can give us a terrifically empowering capacity for insight. The ways that we use to make impressions on people are behaviours that can usually be modified. New behaviours that are generated and rehearsed in therapy can help clients have more rewarding relationships with their environment and the people in it.

The best way to share impressions about how people come across is by using 'immediacy' (Inskipp, 1996), also termed 'you/me talk' (Egan 1975). Egan (2002) distinguishes between 'relationship immediacy' – the ability to reflect on the history of your relationship with the other person and how it might have developed in the way it has – and 'here and now immediacy' – the ability to use the reflections from the relationship immediacy and use them in the here and now with the client. It is helpful to think of this as a two-stage process. It is usually helpful to reflect first, in supervision, for example, and even wait until an incident has occurred several times before moving into using immediacy. Egan (2002) offers useful steps in delivering the immediate statement:

- Say how you are affected by the client.
- Explore your contribution to what is going on.
- Describe the client's behaviour and offer 'reasonable hunches' about what is happening.
- Invite the client to consider what is happening.

One factor that makes such 'immediacy' work well is when we are able to offer feedback that the other person can swallow, that is user-friendly feedback that often stresses the deliverer's behaviour and emotions rather than the receiver's. My earlier response to feeling overwhelmed and needing to 'slow down' uses the first two of Egan's steps. The starting point is *my* frailty – *I* can't keep up – and the proposed action is a joint one – that *we* slow down and focus a little more.

A more difficult situation occurs when the client is sarcastic, angry or dissatisfied with the therapy. Firstly, it is natural for the therapist to feel disappointed about this and it can be okay, even helpful, to own this, provided it is not retaliatory and acting *out of* the disappointment. It is hard to be criticised by clients and it is natural to want to defend oneself. If we defend ourselves too readily, however, we would often miss a golden opportunity of finding out about something therapeutic: the client's interpersonal patterns, one's own interpersonal patterns or the way both patterns interact with each other. Therapy often proceeds much more quickly when clients are able to take responsibility for their own functioning. If we therapists are able to acknowledge our role in proceedings, then it should help the client to do the same. Sometimes neither party may be very clear about what is going on, however, and it may then be useful to do what Joyce & Sills (2001) describe as 'micro process investigation' and a 'frame by frame' exploration of a passage of therapy, with both parties noticing what is going on for them.

Developing interpersonal responsiveness over time

Therapists will develop their own styles of interpersonal responding. As well as learning about different client patterns, they can also learn much about their own patterns and how *they* respond to different client challenges. It is often helpful to review this development in supervision and it may even help to keep a reflective journal for a time. Once a therapist has made a few successful interpersonal interventions, such work can seem intoxicating. Therapists should, however, be wary of analysing interpersonal breakdowns as if they all emanate solely from the client's 'stuff'. Kahn (1991) eloquently makes the case for considering how the therapist's own issues and behaviour, including errors, should also be examined as possible factors in therapeutic breakdown. In this way, we can do intoxicating work and yet stay grounded.

Suggestion

Work in groups of three. Each group member should present a client with whom he/she had protracted difficulties. (Hint: it may be helpful to present a 'critical incident' in which the difficulties were encapsulated.) The other group members (one as 'client advocate' and one as observer) should try to help the presenter to map the underlying interpersonal patterns, including any contribution from the therapist. They may also try to formulate and deliver an alternative response.

Conclusion

Other models of therapy have been explicitly based on the interpersonal dimensions of the client's life and the encounter in the therapy session. Theorists and practitioners from these perspectives have added much to our understanding of the therapy process. Such a perspective was not initially very explicit in CBT theory and practice but has become more so as practitioners engage with the necessarily messy processes of trying to help people. CBT has developed an enriched understanding of interpersonal dimensions in the lives of clients and how these may play themselves out in therapy sessions. It has also developed more ideas to help its practitioners respond to clients' interpersonal needs in a more informed way.

Suggestion: Kagan's Interpersonal Process Recall (IPR)

Format: Small group (two, three or four participants)

Audio and video recordings of therapy sessions are often excellent sources for detecting interpersonal processes in therapy and are often therefore used in supervision. IPR, first devised by Kagan (1975), is an excellent procedure for tracking interpersonal processes in a learning or supervisory context. The basic method is for the person who is reflecting on their therapy to be able to stop the tape at moments that strike them as containing learning and for the other party to use 'inquirer leads' to help them reflect on what was going on for them. Participants can begin to explore the session by trying to pick up new awareness of how their own body and mind reacts as they listen. They can think about whether there seem to be any unspoken feelings evident in the session and what else might have been said.

(For a detailed description and exercise, see Inskipp, 1996: 96–100.)

PRACTICE TIP: Right here, right now...

Immediacy

It has been said that 'immediacy' can be 'strong medicine'. It can indeed, and big doses are therefore not recommended. The interpersonal dimension is an intriguing one. As a therapist first learns about and then attempts to operationalise interventions based on interpersonal material, it can become quite heady stuff. It is important, however, for the therapist to remember that she enters these exchanges with many advantages. They are usually launched at her initiative. She has a theoretical and practical approach that informs and shapes how she will react. The client can be quite thrown by this departure from the usual script. The intervention works by the client becoming a little more self-conscious, but it is easy for the client to become a lot more self-conscious and thereby very uncomfortable. This can result in the therapist seeming to be a 'clever clogs'. The signs of this developing are usually quite clear and early: puzzled, uncomfortable facial expressions, body shuffling, and verbalisations like 'Are you saying that...?' and 'I'm not sure what you are getting at here.' In a way, one is in a new alliance rupture. Usually it is best to back off at this point. The rupture must be repaired at some point but moments of extreme self-consciousness may not be the right time to do so. It can often be picked up during the feedback section of the final part of the session structure or even at a subsequent meeting. Egan (2002) presents some good training exercises on the various aspect of immediacy.

Role-plays

Role-plays are often a good way of evoking emotions and immediacy when exploring both client patterns and new ways of responding. They are especially good for eliciting interpersonal appraisals and negative automatic thoughts. There are quite a few options available to therapist and client and with creativity even more can be added. For example, if the client has just suffered some kind of interpersonal rebuff or humiliation, the client can role-play the person handing out the rebuff and the therapist can play the client, or vice versa, or both. Creativity can add different aspects. We can, for example, really ham things up: bring on the man with the most humiliating tone in the world or the woman with the coolest riposte. I usually find it is helpful to try 'every which way'. Not all clients respond to role-plays: some just seem to be left cold by the process. Do not be over-persistent here as they may just not have this one in their repertoires. It may be necessary to de-role therapist and client to avoid the therapist getting contaminated by role-playing a baddie. For people who can do them, they can feel very empowering and can inject a feeling of 'doing something right now about the problem'. It is also possible for clients to get over-enthusiastic about the process and they may need to be reminded that what happens in the role-play in the session may not be the way it pans out in the world outside the session. With situations that are likely to be tricky, it can be helpful to think about how the client could cope with a possible further rebuff. The message to go for is not 'This will help you win out in the situation' but 'Most people feel better if they have at least tried something.' Some clients may also benefit from 'de-role' – that is, consciously putting away the role – after a role-play, much as one would do in experiential group work.

Further reading

Gilbert, P. & Leahy, R.L. (2007) *The therapeutic relationship in the cognitive behavioural psychotherapies*. London: Routledge.

Safran, J.D. & Segal, Z.V. (1990) *Interpersonal process and cognitive therapy*. New York: Guilford Press.

Notes

1 There may be a good analogy here with the game of cricket where it is said that 'soft hands' on the bat allow one to hit the ball harder.
2 'People are disturbed not by events *alone* but by the view they take of events.'
3 For a royal example, see Juliet Nicholson's description of the supposedly 'haughty' Queen Mary in *The perfect summer: dancing into the shadow in 1911* (Nicholson, 2006).
4 For further description, see Sanders & Wills (2005: 13–20).
5 See also Sanders & Wills (2005: 82–3).

4

SKILLS FOR WORKING WITH NEGATIVE THOUGHTS

Cleanse the thoughts of our hearts...

Prayer of Preparation (Church of England, 2005)

Identifying and challenging negative thinking are keystone activities of cognitive behaviour therapy. The changes brought about by such interventions lie at the heart of the CBT enterprise. This chapter will begin by considering why such work is therapeutic and will emphasise the importance of 'emotionally felt' cognitive change.

The chapter will identify three distinct stages in cognitive interventions directed at changing the content of negative thoughts: identifying, evaluating and, finally, responding to and challenging them (J. Beck, 1995). Each stage has two phases: verbal and written (Sanders & Wills, 2005). The stages and phases can be used separately at different times but essentially build up into the quintessential CBT method: using a thought record. Contrary to some glib representations of the process, difficulties are frequently encountered during this work. These difficulties and possible remedies will be described. The cognitive interventions directed at cognitive content are essentially phenomenological in that they involve describing and evaluating experiences. Evaluation is typically concerned with confirming or falsifying thoughts and beliefs, using insights from the principles of science derived from Karl Popper (1959). The work involved in challenging negative thoughts has particularly benefited from some of the vigorous techniques associated with Albert Ellis and rational emotive behaviour therapy (REBT) (Dryden, 2006).

In recent years, it has become clear that the relevant experiences of psychopathology are not just concerned with the content of negative thinking, but are also linked to cognitive and meta-cognitive processes involved in functions such as memory and attention (Harvey et al., 2004). Furthermore, these processes seem to cut across traditional diagnostic categories, suggesting that *DSM* labels are less useful to therapists than a 'trans-diagnostic' approach to symptoms across various disorders. Worry, for example, is a prominent feature of many disorders. It has many normal and functional aspects: we all need to be somewhat vigilant for future dangers. The psychological problems of worry, however, begin to arise when we are not able to 'switch off' these processes once they have had their beneficial effect. Worrying may then begin to dominate our attention in highly destructive ways, leading to experiences that are like continuously streaming 'videos' of negativity. The chapter will therefore finish with some of the newer cognitive interventions that focus on processes of worry and attention.

Although behavioural and cognitive interventions have been divided into different chapters in this book, readers should note that in practice they are very often 'joined up'. The cognitive intent of 'behavioural experiments' is described in the next chapter. Equally, the methods for working with thoughts described below also involve the identification of feelings. Identifying feelings will be dealt with in this chapter in so far that it connects with cognitive work but will also be given fuller consideration in Chapter 6. It is perhaps a tribute to the increasingly joined-up nature of CBT thinking that it is often difficult to know the best location for various concepts and methods.

Why do cognitive interventions work?

CB therapists essentially use scientific and rational methods to invite clients to explore thoughts, assumptions and beliefs about their lives. These methods focus on certain ways of functioning that have been found to play both a causative and a maintenance role in psychological problems. Though the methods are mainly rational, we also know that they are unlikely to be very effective unless they evoke and modify key emotions (Foa & Kozak, 1986). The idea of interplay between 'heart and head' in psychological functioning is an ancient and familiar one. The relationship between cognition and emotion is complex and subject to different theoretical explanations: most of these, however, stress the fact that problem-free functioning seems linked to establishing a degree of balance between the two factors. This balance can, however, show considerable variation. People who over-rely on emotions may show 'emotional reasoning' and not think things through as thoroughly as may be desirable. On the other end of the spectrum are the 'intellectualisers': who may suffer from being out of touch with their feelings and being unable to trust gut feelings. One client, a scientist, told me recently that the only way he could tell whether he loved his partner was to ask himself, 'If I were dying, would I want her by my side?' This turned out to be not a sign of 'intellectualising', as I first thought, but a desperate attempt to rein in ultra strong but fluctuating feelings.

Teasdale (2004) has identified different ways of processing information: a 'propositional' mode that deals with essentially factual and specific quantitative knowledge and an 'implicational' mode more concerned with more evaluative and qualitative knowledge. The former establishes the 'facts of the case' and the latter establishes what those facts mean. Epstein (1998) also has developed a twin-track theory, suggesting that there is a rational information processing system and an 'experiential' or intuitive one. Epstein has argued that optimal functioning is linked to the degree of harmony in the way these systems are able to work together. Clients who are suffering from the intense emotions of anxiety and depression may not be able to use rational processing functions well because their

Mainly good for people

psychological functioning has been 'flooded' by material from the experiential, *good people and emotional* emotional system. Cognitive techniques may help such clients by reinstituting the basic steps of rational processing and re-teaching clients to use them in 'battle conditions' (that is, when the whole system is flooded by negative emotions).

From our own experience, we know how the feeling of being upset can be followed by quieter moments when we re-examine and re-process our experience: 'Hang on a minute, was it really the case that Katie ignored me? Or was she just under pressure from other sources?' The more upset we are, the longer it may take us to be able to undertake the natural steps of reality-testing. Clients who are very emotionally disturbed, however, may have lost touch with these rational processes in a more consistent way. They may need the conscious and deliberative steps of CBT, especially reinforced by writing them down. Some readers may at this point begin to fear that I am advocating a triumphalist rationalism. The case is rather that rational and emotional functioning need to work together harmoniously. This is why 'intellectualisation' in therapy can be just as much of a problem and why healing requires 'emotionally felt change', a *metanoia*, a change of heart, as much as a change of mind. Metanoia may be elusive because language itself may hinder us in finding it. Pierson & Hayes (2007) contrast the process of the ACT (Acceptance and Commitment Therapy) model with more traditional CBT by saying that whereas CBT aims to deconstruct negative language, ACT aims to deconstruct all language. They express the spirit of the 'third wave' in CBT well by saying 'a person who says "I am bad" and then changes it to "I am good" is not now a person who thinks "I am good" but a person who thinks, "I am bad, no, I am good" (Pierson and Hayes, 2007: 207).

As we will explore later, cognitive change may come less from change in the content of negative thought but more from changes in the thinking *processes* associated with negative thought.

Some clients may also need to be encouraged to be more aware of and in touch with their feelings. Classically a humanistic activity, working with feeling will be presented from a CBT perspective in Chapter 6.

Suggestion: Thought experiment

Try the following thought experiment on your own or in a group. You are driving to the station to catch a train to London to receive a prized professional award. You run into heavy traffic delays and arrive 20 minutes late at the station. In scenario 1, the train left on time 20 minutes ago and you must wait another 1 hour and 40 minutes for the next train – it is not clear if you will get to the award ceremony on time. In scenario 2, the train was delayed and only left 2 minutes ago. You still have to wait for 100 minutes. Would you feel differently in these different scenarios? Why?[1]

Identifying negative thoughts

In the assessment phase of CBT, the therapist will naturally find his attention focuses on the content and processes of negative automatic thoughts (NATs) that arise in the client's account of his situation. The therapist is aided by having a good knowledge of current generic formulations for various areas of psychological functioning. Westbrook et al. (2007) and Sanders & Wills (2003) have, for example, provided a number of short readable chapters describing up-to-date formulations for the anxiety disorders, and Wells (2006) has developed a short-hand pro-forma version of their main points in a way that can be kept on hand for immediate use in sessions. While recognising the utility of generic formulations, therapists also need to listen very carefully for the actual individual and idiosyncratic thoughts that each client will report as variations on generic themes. It is also essential for CB therapists to be sensitive to feelings, and in order to do this they need to be excellent listeners. Counselling education has led the way in training people in careful and skilful listening. The listening skills tradition has been strengthened by well-established skills training methods (Inskipp, 1986, 1996). Listening skills are essential for effective CBT practice and should not be left outside the CBT consulting room.

The excellent formulations of the cognitive content and processes of various problem areas are, however, some of the greatest strengths of CBT. Following Beck's (1976) early lead that specific modes of thinking could be linked to specific problem areas ('the cognitive specificity hypothesis'), an ever-increasing number of areas have been provisionally mapped (Salkovskis, 1996a). The word 'provisional' here acknowledges that our formulation maps are probably closer to those of explorers in the eighteenth century than the Google Earth satellite maps of today. Even so, these maps are very helpful to therapists and often suggest where to begin looking for key cognitions and the questions that can lead us there. In social anxiety, for example, we know that people become very self-conscious and preoccupied with negative evaluation in social situations (Wells, 1997) and this can guide our questioning. Here is a brief edited extract where the therapist is exploring the experience of a client who becomes anxious while giving a pharmaceutical sales talk in a hospital. The therapist's framework of understanding is guided by extensive findings about the how socially anxious clients think and pay selective attention to negative signals in difficult situations:

Therapist: What do you see in the room?
Client: ... Just tiers of people in front of me and they haven't dimmed the lights so I can see them all and they're in their white coats and they're wearing their stethoscopes so I can tell they're doctors...
Therapist: What is going through your mind?
Client: (Looking distressed) They are not listening to me. They're bored... I am not making any sense here... they are cleverer than me. [...]
Therapist: How many people don't seem to be listening?
Client: About four or five.
Therapist: About how many people are in the room?
Client: About 50, I'd say.
Therapist: So about four or five people out of 50 don't seem to be listening to you?[2]

We can see in this extract the start of a sequence of questions that lead further into the client's frame of reference and we can see that, as the process unfolds, the client's feelings also come to the surface. The series of questions

helps to identify therapeutic targets in the form of modifying negative cognitions. Sometimes merely identifying negative thinking in itself, without conscious modification, sets off a process of change. Reflective discussion itself can
be change-producing because it can help the client to really 'hear' his internal
processes of thinking and feeling for the first time (Nelson-Jones, 2005). Clients
often make comments like 'I know it sounds crazy when I say it' and 'that sounds
daft, I know, but that is how it feels when I am low'. One can almost feel the tides
of change flowing here but it may also be useful to underline the point by reflecting, 'So there can be a type of thinking that goes with feeling low that isn't there
when you are feeling better?' The therapeutic manoeuvre here is that of 'staying
with' the negative feeling, and thinking and letting them unfold, rather than
pressing on to more deliberate attempts to change. Later we will consider
whether this process can be accelerated by getting a handle on the emotion
(Gendlin, 1981) or by other interventions.

The client is prepared by presenting the rationale for CBT and by training
clients to understand the link between thinking and feeling (Wright et al., 2006).
Good opportunities to begin this process can come from spotting when a client's
mood intensifies during a session. A client may suddenly become tearful during
discussion of a current difficulty or a piece of history:

Therapist: It seems like you became upset when we mentioned your dad just now?
Client: Yeah (pause and sobs). Yes, it is just so bloody sad... I didn't get to say
goodbye to him and it was all out of so-called loyalty to my mum. I really
regret it now.
Therapist: So just now you thought 'I should have said goodbye' and then you feel...?
Client: Yeah, really guilty. I feel angry too, actually.
Therapist: And the angry thought is?
Client: My mum shouldn't have interfered... she should have seen that was a
special moment anyway.

If it proves helpful, in session, to identify thoughts which lead the client to feel
upset, then the same work can be generalised into helping the client herself spot
such moments outside sessions. The client can be encouraged to record thoughts
and feelings in a simple diary, which can then be built up to fuller thought
records, described below.

Suggestion: Fieldwork assignment

Many clients have told me that once they become aware of the concept of negative thoughts, they often experience hearing other people say them, especially people close to them in their families and workplaces. It may at first be
easier to hear such thoughts in others than in oneself. Hearing one's own
thoughts is a new insight that may come a little later. For some people, this
extremely valuable extra insight is hastened by writing down overheard NATs
and then periodically asking oneself 'Do *I* ever have a thought like that?' You
may wish to try this as a fieldwork assignment.

Identifying cognitions by intensifying emotions

One of the significant aspects of negative thoughts is the degree to which they generate significant, usually intense, emotions. Sometimes the degree of emotional intensity is muted because of either certain beliefs about emotions (for example, that they are 'dangerous') (see also Chapter 6) or for some other contextual factor. Clients suffering from post-traumatic stress disorder, for example, have often been instructed to tell their stories in highly factual ways for police and legal personnel. They may simply have developed a standard way of telling the story without becoming overwhelmed. Sometimes a therapist can get a more emotionally live account by simply asking for or giving permission for it to happen. At other times the therapist may need to be more active to achieve this result. In the earlier extract on helping a client to review an anxious experience in a lecture theatre (p. 56), the reader may note that the therapist encouraged the client to respond in the first person and in the present tense, that is as if the event were happening now. This seems to intensify the degree to which the client is able to experience some of the feelings they experienced in the actual situation. Intensifying feeling can help clients to identify their thoughts in the situation more accurately and it can also help them to move towards more felt change.

Emotion and belief ratings

CB therapists frequently ask clients to rate both the intensity of the emotions they feel in trigger situations and, once they have established the NATs, the extent that they believe those negative thoughts. Therapists ask for these ratings in ways similar to those illustrated in the following extract. Frequently, they might also write down these ratings in a simple two-column record that is likely to be mirrored in sections of a fuller thought record, constructed now or later (see Figure 4.1):

Therapist and client are discussing the client's reaction to a dysphoric telephone call.

Therapist: So you felt upset after your dad's phone call. What was said?

Client: Basically, he called to remind me not to forget to get a birthday card for mum.

Therapist: So how did you feel about that?

Client: I felt pretty angry, you know, like that he thought I might forget. I never forget! Why did he seem to think that I might forget this time?

Therapist: What is your theory on that? Why did he seem to think that?

Client: He just doesn't trust me. He has never seemed to recognise me as a competent adult. (Looks very upset)

Therapist: What's the feeling now?

Client: Sad, sad... a bit forlorn, you know, it will never change.
(A little later)

Therapist: So there seemed to be two feelings just now: anger and sadness. Can we take them one by one and look at them and see what's behind them? The angry bit first. If 100% were the angriest you have ever been, how would you rate how you felt then?

Client: Not too bad; 40% maybe. I am used to it with him, you know.

Therapist: And the thought there seemed to be 'He thinks I will forget mum's birthday', is that right?

Client: Yes, but I don't really believe that. It is just his interfering ways really.

Therapist: So how much out of 100 do you believe that thought?

Client: Not so much; about 30% I suppose.

*They go on to identify that the sadness rating is much higher at 80%, twinned with a
belief rating of 90% for the thought 'He has never recognised me as a competent
adult'.*

This establishes that the sad thought and feeling are more 'salient' to the client
and probably should be tackled first.

Thought	Emotion
He thinks I'll forget mum's birthday (30%)	ANGRY (40%)
He's never recognised me as a competent adult (90%)	SAD (80%)

FIGURE 4.1   *Thoughts feelings ratings*

Often the client will reveal many negative beliefs but not all of them are relevant. As shown above, the process of rating beliefs and thoughts often helps to
target the therapy on to the most significant negative beliefs. Additionally, belief
ratings carry two crucial meta-messages: beliefs can vary over time and not usually in either/or (100%/0%) form. These messages prepare the client for the
possibility that thoughts and beliefs have differing degrees of validity and
usefulness.

Evaluating thoughts: Socratic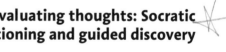
questioning and guided discovery

It can be tempting for CB therapists to become overly persuasive. As you practice CBT regularly, certain patterns of discussion of NATs will start to become
familiar to you. It is unlikely that clients will be as familiar with the form of
these discussions as you are. CB therapists must therefore put a brake on the
tendency to use this knowledge to overpower clients. Firstly, only the client
can really know what will prove most persuasive to him, and, secondly, there
is evidence that when clients begin to see their therapists as being too persuasive, they become much more resistant to what the therapist is saying
(Heesacker & Meija-Millan, 1996). It is preferable to use guided discovery
rather than persuasion when trying to help a client to open out her thinking.
Guided discovery involves asking questions that invite the client to explore
what she is saying and then to look at things from different angles and look
'outside the box' for additional information. These questions are Socratic
because they are similar in intent to Socratic Dialogue. Socrates was an
Athenian philosopher who displayed a seemingly endless delight in getting

- What do you mean when you say x?
- What is the evidence that x is true? What is the evidence against x being true?
- What might be the worst that could happen?
- What leads you to think that might happen?
- And if that happened, what then?
- If it did happen, what would you do? How would you cope?
- Have you been in similar situations in the past? How did you cope then?
- How does thinking that make you feel?
- Are you thinking in a biased way? (See Figure 1.2) e.g. are you predicting the future or mind reading?
- Are you paying attention only to one aspect? What if you looked at it from a different angle?
- What would you say to a friend who kept on saying x to herself (e.g. 'I'm stupid'; 'I'm terrible')?
- How would that work in your body?
- Is there an alternative explanation?
- Is there any other way of seeing the situation?
- What are the advantages and disadvantages of thinking that?
- Is it helpful, or unhelpful?
- What would it mean to you to see things differently?
- Are you making decisions based on your feelings, or is reality telling you something different?
- What might you tell a friend to do in this situation?
- What would your friend say to you?
- Is there something else you could say to yourself that might be more helpful?
- What do you think you could change to make things better for you?
- How would you like things to be different?
- What would you like to do instead?
- What would have to happen to make that possible?

FIGURE 4.2   *Socratic questions*

people to examine the assumptions of their arguments. He hardly ever expressed his own opinions but asked questions that made his debating partners think more deeply. These debates often ended in what has been called *aporia*[3] – a kind of confusion resulting from the abandonment of an old idea without entirely being sure of what to replace it with. This state of mind has some similarity with the modern psychological concept of cognitive dissonance, when ideas or facts seem incompatible and irresolvable. Cognitive dissonance theorists have considered that such dissonance produces the necessary discomfort that often precedes change, that is, the discomfort motivates us to think out the resolution. Therapists should learn not to be too alarmed when initial cognitive interventions lead to apparent confusion. Over time confusion may result in higher-level resolution. This 'harder won' change may prove more meaningful and therapeutic to clients.

It is worth having a list of Socratic questions on hand for both therapist and client (see Figure 4.2). It is important that Socratic questions are used in an unfolding way in order to help the client expand her horizons. Padesky (1993, 2004a, 2004b) has identified a four-stage process for building such questions into a guided discovery sequence:

1. Ask questions to uncover information outside the client's current awareness.
2. Accurate listening and empathic reflection.

3. Frequent summaries.
4. Ask synthesising questions that help to apply the new information to the client's original thought.

In the example that follows, client and therapist are discussing the client's statement that he feels that his boss has become critical of his work and that the boss is 'dangerous':

Therapist: So, how is that dangerous, do you reckon?
Client: Well, it means that I'm out of favour; he won't give me any plums, any of the good work. I'm used to being one of the players. I might get left on the shelf now.
Therapist: You'd be left out. What is the worst that could happen with that?
Client: I could lose my job...nah but that's not very likely, I don't think. More likely I could just become one of the old lags.
Therapist: The 'old lags'?
Client: Yeah, you know the guys who are just hanging round for their pension.
Therapist: That isn't how you see yourself there. How would you cope if you became an old lag?
Client: Well, I'd be fed up but I could hack it I suppose. There are worse fates. I'd probably start applying for other jobs.
Therapist: And would you find something, do you reckon?
Client: Eventually, I guess.
Therapist: Okay, so let's gather that up. It seems like you have been in favour with your boss but now, for some reason we haven't yet established, you're a bit out of favour. You might now get left out of certain things and if that went on long enough, you might leave. So how does that tie up with him being 'dangerous'?
Client: No, no: not dangerous. It's just that he is a bit cold. To be honest, I was always quite glad to be on his right side and now I'm not on his right side and I'm not sure where that could go.
Therapist: Okay but saying he is dangerous ... how did that affect you?
Client: I have been a bit paralysed, I think.
Therapist: Yeah, using a strong word like 'dangerous' may act as an 'amplifier' that inhibits your problem-solving. In a way, the problem is relatively straightforward: things have slipped with your boss and you're not sure how to put them right. Those are problems we can work on.
Client: Yeah, I think I have built up the fear and that's just got in the way really.

Therapists should not expect the identification of negative thoughts to go smoothly at all times. In practice a variety of problems occur and these require therapist patience and creativity. If the client finds it difficult to make the link between thoughts and feelings, the therapist may need to proceed more slowly and adopt a more educational style of work. This problem, other problems and frequently used solutions are shown in Table 4.1.

In order to use CBT methods well, the client should be able to distinguish between thoughts and feelings and be able to make links between the two. In everyday language, however, people regularly say things like 'I feel like I will fail the exam' when this statement masks the fact that 'I will fail the exam' is a cognition and a negative prediction. CB therapists need to gently point this out to clients without sounding pedantic. The best way to achieve this clarity is to work through examples with

Table 4.1   Problems and solutions for difficulties in identifying negative thoughts and feelings

Problems working with negative thoughts	Possible solutions
The client confuses feeling with thinking: E.g. 'I just feel like I'm going to fail the exam.'	*Reflect back to the client with the correct terms: 'So you think you'll fail the exam, I guess then you feel anxious?' Refer back to the terminological difficulty when the client has put it the right way round.*
The client cannot identify a clear thought associated with distress: E.g. 'I was on my own, I just started feeling anxious. I didn't seem to have a thought.'	*Work back to a set of theoretical explanations and ask the client which one seems closest to his experience. 'When people are anxious they often fear something bad will happen. Does that ring any bells for you?'*
The client's negative thought is a 'megaphone statement': E.g. 'When my car failed, I thought "typical".'	*Reflect back and add a probe: 'So you thought typical... of your luck? Like fate is against you?'*
The client's negative thought is in the form of a question: E.g. 'Why was it me who was left out?'	*Point out that the question could mask a negative thought and ask, 'If so, what would the "negative answer" to the question be?'*
The client's negative thought is hidden in other material: E.g. 'I was thinking about how my work had been going' (in relation to feeling low).	*Make the thought/feeling link by asking 'Does the fact that you were feeling low imply that you fear that your work hasn't been going well?'*
The client cannot identify the negative feeling associated with the negative thought: E.g. 'I just felt yewk.'	*Go with the client's vocabulary in the belief that a more precise feeling is likely to emerge as therapy progresses.*
The client cannot rate the emotion experienced.	*Use an analogue scale (draw a line with the two extremes of emotion on either end and a mid-point), and ask clients to indicate where their emotions would fall on the line.*

clients in sessions, clarifying that it is the 'appraisal' (what the thoughts mean) element in cognitions and the link to feelings that makes them significant. Other problems listed in Table 4.1 include the way certain other figures of speech also mask cognitions: 'typical' in the third statement, for example, seems to mask the thought 'This is typical of my bad luck.' CB therapists may take educated guesses at what the underlying thought is, though they should be wary of engineering or gaining shallow consent. Certain clients seem to have difficulty identifying any kind of thinking. Therapists can then go back to the rationale-giving stage and build up understanding in simple steps or even put the main emphasis on behavioural work.

It should also be remembered that negative emotions and thoughts are only part of the client's way of functioning. CB therapists probably have had a tendency to be over-concerned with the problematic in both its general formulations (Kuyken, 2006) and its general ways of working (Seligman, 2002; Duckworth et al., 2005). The 'positive psychology' and 'solution-focused therapy' movements may help us to balance this tendency by, for example, asking clients about exceptions[4] to periods of feeling bad:

Client:	I just get these periods of just feeling so stressed. I do a fair amount of work at home and sometimes after a difficult customer has called and asked me to do something that pisses me off, I get so morose. ... The other day my wife said to me, 'You're having an Eeyore morning.' And I thought 'Yes, you're right, I'm turning into a misery guts.'
Therapist:	Okay then, some mornings you feel like Eeyore and that seems to be morose and depressed, I guess. But some mornings are you more like Pooh? (**Client:** Yeah.) So what happens then when a difficult customer calls?
Client:	Oh, I don't know, I just shrug it off, I suppose. I can be pleased to hear from them, pleased to give them a service or I just roll up my sleeves and get on with it.
Therapist:	Okay, so it could be good to work out the thinking that goes with Pooh and 'sleeves-up' days and the thinking that goes with Eeyore days and to see if we could get more Pooh and less Eeyore?
Client:	(animated) Yeah, that would be good!
Therapist:	It may also be worth thinking about whether Eeyore has any good points too. Many people do find him quite endearing.

It is helpful to ask questions about 'exceptions' early in therapy: they set a good tone but also point to goals in user-friendly terms, for example 'less Eeyore, more Pooh'.

Suggestion: Good day/bad day

Writers from Marcus Aurelius (*c.* 100 CE) to Carlson (1997) have noted our proclivity to 'sweat the small stuff' (that is, over-react to the minor frustrations of life) so I assume that the reader is no exception! Taking one such frustration, work out your negative thinking, feeling and behavioural reaction to such frustrations on a 'bad day'. Then trace out your reaction on a 'good day'. What is different between the 'bad day' and the 'good day' reactions? How would you have to change your reactions to get more good days and/or less bad ones? Would it be worth the effort?

Evaluating negative thoughts: testing cognitive distortions

Everyone is familiar with the scenario in which one attempts to cheer up a friend who is thoroughly fed up. All the things that used to be a joy to him seem now beyond imagination. If you try to remind him about a good thing about his life, he will tend to 'disqualify the positive' by saying something like 'Oh anyone could do that!' Beck (1976) identified these as 'cognitive errors' and distortions that affect or exacerbate psychological problems. A certain degree of negative thinking is normal and non-problematic, but, as negative feeling states become more permanently established, distorted ways of thinking may play a maintenance role in problems such as feeling low and fearful. Early stages of working with negative thoughts involve helping clients to identify them, a process aided by learning to spot cognitive distortions as they arise. We will now discuss how therapists can facilitate this process.

Most books on CBT contain lists of cognitive distortions with definitions and examples in the belief that such a list can aid the process of recognising negative

Table 4.2   Distortion types and domains of negative thinking

Distortions	About the self	About the self in relation to others	About other people	About life and/or the world
APPLYING A NEGATIVE LABEL: Attaching a highly negative and over-generalised label to oneself or others	*I am boring. I am worthless. I am a real Eeyore. Everything in my life is only ever half done. I am 'Billy No Mates'.*	*I just don't fit in. I don't measure up to the people around me. I have to placate people. Without a partner, I'm useless.*	*My boss is an idiot. He's a wee man in a big job. My wife is self-indulgent about her illness. My 4-year-old tries to wind me up.*	*The world is a cold, cold place. Life now is just a jungle. My workplace is full of sharks.*
MAKING NEGATIVE PREDICTIONS: Making predictions about the future based more on how you feel than on what is knowable	*If I take the exam, I will just go to pieces. I will never find another partner. I will never get back to how I used to feel. I won't enjoy that now.*	*People will think that I am pathetic. No one will be attracted to me now. If I tell people how I really feel, they will just use it against me.*	*Girlfriends will always dump me. My colleagues will criticise anything I say in the meeting. If I ask people to help, they will let me down.*	*It will be downhill all the way from here. People won't be prepared to give me a chance. I'll end up an outcast if I screw this up.*
OVER-STATEMENTS: Over-emphasising the bad aspects of a situation and/or understating or ignoring the good aspects	*The fact that I lost that account means I'm incompetent. All my good work goes up in smoke in light of that failure.*	*Life without Sam is unbearable. I just don't know what to say in social situations. It's horrible if people criticise my work.*	*They never think about other people. People always put their own advantage first.*	*Life is pointless. There is so much violence and hatred in the world. Society is very unforgiving of mistakes.*

thinking. The number of terms in these lists has increased over time and I have found that sometimes trainees and clients may find them hard to use. They are perhaps too complex and contain too many overlapping concepts that are rather technical for easy take-up. In a recent paper (Wills, 2007), I analysed the negative thoughts and cognitive distortions from my therapy notes for a full year. I was able to discern four main subject areas: thoughts about the self, the self in relation to others, other people and life/the world. I was also able to discern three main types of distortion: applying a negative label, making negative predictions and making over-statements. I have put these two dimensions together in Table 4.2.

A simplified list can help both the trainee and the client to get hold of the important idea of distortions. This is not to say that a fuller list of distortions cannot be used later in therapy, as the ability of therapists and clients to spot them develops. Some helpful categories of distortion can be profitably linked to certain problems. 'Catastrophisation' (subsumed under 'over-statement' in my short list), for example, is a very frequently found factor in anxiety problems of all types. A fuller list of distortions is therefore given in Table 4.3. In this list, however, the examples do

Table 4.3   Cognitive distortions (adapted from Sanders & Wills, 2005: 7)

NB: *The distortion types below are not listed opposite appropriate examples. This is an exercise to train readers in being able to identify different types of distortion. The answers are given on page 82.*

Cognitive distortion types	Examples
1. EITHER/OR THINKING (about oneself). This style of thinking makes extreme demands on you to be one way and, if not, condemns yourself totally to the other extreme.	a. *Work was hell today. Ron didn't like my report and then no one seemed to have a good word for me.*
2. MIND READING. Assuming that people are thinking in a certain way.	b. *I forgot my wallet this morning: that's proof that I have really lost it.*
3. PREDICTING THE FUTURE. Assuming that you know what the future will bring – aka 'crystal ball gazing'.	c. *A few of my customers seem to trust my judgements but they are just the minor customers.*
4. DWELLING ON THE NEGATIVE. Over-emphasising a negative feature of living and ruminating on it.	d. *Unless pretty well everyone likes me a lot, that means I'm a failure.*
5. DISQUALIFYING THE POSITIVE. You reject good personal qualities you have by putting them down.	e. *My boss is just a total idiot. He deserves no respect at all.*
6. BLOWING UP THE NEGATIVE. Exaggerating things that go wrong.	f. *There's no way that I'd be offered a job like that.*
7. LABELLING. Attaching a highly negative label to something.	g. *I just have this real dread that everything will fall apart.*
8. CATASTROPHISING. Thinking that the very worst possibility will happen.	h. *Everyone will think that I am really stupid.*
9. EMOTIONAL REASONING. Assuming that something you feel strongly must be true.	i. *I'll lose my job and then my family – I'll have nothing left to live for.*

Answers

1	
2	
3	
4	
5	
6	
7	
8	
9	

not match up with the definitions because it is doubling as an exercise in helping the reader to become thoroughly conversant with helping clients to recognise them. This exercise aims to help the reader to learn for herself, and thereby become an even better tutor for the client. This type of exercise has also been included in the client self-help books by writers such as David Burns (1999a, 1999b).

There are other helpful traditions in psychology that identify biases and distortions in thinking (Harvey et al., 2004). Cognitive theorists have pointed out that there are various homeostatic tendencies in thinking styles that keep distortions in place. Self-serving biases, for example, may stop people from identifying their own role in relationship breakdowns. Cognitive mechanisms such as 'limited search routines' may prevent people from searching widely enough to find appropriate evaluative evidence regarding their thoughts. In these circumstances, therapists must be prepared to be persistent and devise creative Socratic questions to overcome these limitations.

Evaluating evidence on thoughts: validity and utility

If there is one sentence that captures the spirit of CBT, or perhaps more accurately cognitive therapy, it would be 'What is your evidence for that thought/belief?' followed shortly by 'What is the evidence against that thought/belief?' Because the client's negative thoughts often make highly malevolent charges against himself, some aspects of cognitive therapy have an uncanny resemblance to a 'defence attorney' (Leahy, 2003). I often ask my clients questions like: 'Is that (usually a minor discretion) really a *hanging offence?*' and 'Would that (self) charge (of being 'totally incompetent') *stand up in court?*' Ironically, I have had experienced lawyers as clients who have surprised me by finding it remarkably difficult to acquit themselves – testimony perhaps to the compelling plausibility of negative thoughts. Albert Ellis advances a telling argument against any form of judgement on the self: 'the results are not yet all in'. Usefulness is established over a lifetime. Late goals can change football matches. Churchill was considered a political failure in 1939. Furthermore, the accusation 'I am useless' implies a basic, core personality judgement, whereas usefulness and uselessness, in as much as the terms can offer any utility at all, emerge from many separate behaviours. This does not preclude the validity of judgements on some aspects of a person's behaviour.

These facts confront us with an aspect of evidence review in CBT: all the relevant information is hardly ever completely available. This is true, for example, by definition of the kind of negative predictions that so often accompany anxiety: we can never know how a future event will turn out. The best we can hope for is a range of probabilities concerning particular outcomes. Life and the universe remain frustratingly short of certainties. Clients who worry and obsess usually require more certainty than is available in life as we know it. They never look entirely convinced when I suggest that life might be boring if we could be as certain of key outcomes as they would like to be.

Also there are often issues concerning the relative strength of the quantity and quality of evidence. For instance, one big example of incompetence is usually remembered more fully and counts for more than many small examples of competence.[5] The therapist, however, has no other choice than to look for the devil in the detail: collect the small evidence along with the big. The overall evidence thus gathered is usually mixed and often allows therapist and client to come down against gross generalisations and may well promote more benign views of life than are usually held by people in the grip of painful emotions.

Modifying and challenging negative thinking using thought records

The nature and purpose of thought records

The thought record sums up many of the manoeuvres we have already described in the identification and evaluation of negative thoughts:

- It specifies trigger events that lead to negative thoughts.
- It describes the thinking, feeling and behavioural responses to those triggers.
- It evaluates evidence in relation to the negative thoughts.

The thought record also helps reframe negative thoughts:

- It develops alternative, more adaptive thoughts or ways of thinking about specific trigger events should they arise in the future.
- It summarises key elements of a new cognitive, emotional and behavioural response in light of the review of the original responses.

An example of a thought record is presented below so that the reader can match up the manoeuvres listed above with their appearance in the actual columns of the thought record. The client who completed the thought record was a well-qualified health professional who suffered from obsessional and intrusive thoughts with a theme of contamination. Some of her main obsessions were about fears of contamination coming from touching blood and other materials that result from medical work. She met the criteria for both obsessive compulsive disorder (OCD) and Simple phobia: Blood (*DSM-IV-TR*). The thought record shown in Table 4.4 is an exact copy of the original thought record filled out by a client and then amended by the therapist and client working together. The upper part of the form (written in italics) shows the client's first attempt to fill out a thought record for homework. The bottom half of the form shows how the client and therapist reworked the form in the next session. There are skilled and unskilled ways of completing thought records and these skills have to be learnt and developed by both client and therapists. The way the client filled out the form for homework shows some misdirection and this meant that the thought record was not effective in helping her to manage her negative feelings better. The client reported that the reworked form made more sense and helped her to understand and feel better about her situation. This was the first thought record that she had completed and it is therefore perhaps not surprising that it went a little off target. I had gone over one example in the previous session with her. In retrospect, I was a little over-hasty in encouraging her to use a full record so soon. I normally give clients a guide to using thought records[6] but on this occasion did not have a copy to hand. Each section of the thought record will now be described, opening with a statement of the basic aim of each section and

Table 4.4   Seven-column thought record (worked example)

Trigger	Emotion	NAT	Evidence for NAT	Evidence against NAT	Alternative adaptive thought	Outcome
Blood on money from cash point	*Anxious 80%*	*I have to wash my hands. I have to change my clothes.*	*Not hygienic*	*No infections transmitted this easily. Probably very common.*	*I should rationalise that the risk is negligible.*	*Anxiety 60%*
Blood on money from cash point	Anxious 80%	I have got dangerous germs on my hands. I could kill my son and husband.	Germs are everywhere.	Germs are only very rarely dangerous. Blood infections aren't that hardy.	I may have germs on my hands but they are almost certainly harmless.	Anxiety 30% Resist washing hands/ changing clothes.

followed by comments for each section of the original and reworked thought record entries shown in Table 4.4.

Trigger/Emotion

The aim of these columns is to establish a specific trigger that leads to the specific problematic reaction. The trigger situation may be very obvious but is not always so. The problematic reaction might be part of the syndrome that constitutes the main aspect of the problem for which the client has been referred. In this case, anxiety is very much part of the criteria for OCD.

In the top part of Table 4.4, the client makes an effective entry for these two columns. She has found a specific trigger that constitutes a moment when the thought and emotion, in her words, 'kicked in'. Sometimes thought records do not work because the client refers to a more general trigger in this section, such as 'my girlfriend finished with me'. Such an experience usually takes place over a number of days, weeks or months during which the client has many different thoughts and feelings. The therapist can encourage the client to make this type of trigger more specific by asking 'Which was the worst moment?' This may produce an answer that can be translated into a specific trigger: 'When she rang and told me that her ex had been in touch and she was having doubts about us now.' Getting the specific moment usually evokes a much stronger emotional reaction and is more likely to get to the most telling and significant negative thoughts. The negative emotion in Table 4.4 is clearly defined with a simple word for a primary emotion, but again we have to be prepared to deal with clients who are not always so clear in the way they identify feelings (see Tables 4.1 and 4.5).

Negative automatic thought (NAT) or image

The case has already been made for the importance of negative thoughts and images in the maintenance of emotional and psychological difficulties. As testing a specific thought is a key part of the thought record and CBT generally, it is important that the thought or image is clearly defined in a way that can be tested. It may be helpful if the client's reported thought is probably not exactly as it was in the moment. There is already some reconstruction in the memory of it so that a therapist can feel legitimacy in working to define the thought further – in ways that clarify its underlying meaning and make it more testable in the thought record.

In Table 4.4, the reported thought probably was something like what went through the client's mind but really amounts to a behavioural disposition rather than an appraising negative thought. It is sometimes difficult to define salient thoughts but, if in doubt, the therapist should ask herself 'Does this thought explain the negative feeling?' In this case, the answer must be 'no' because washing her hands would relieve the anxiety: it is a response to the anxiety, not the thought that evokes the anxiety. As they reviewed the thought record, the therapist asked the client 'Why did you think you should wash your hands and change your clothes?' The client answered 'Because I felt I had germs on my hands.' The therapist then asked a 'downwards arrow' question: 'And what was bad about that?' She answered 'They could be dangerous. I could infect other people. I could kill my son and husband.' These thoughts do explain the anxiety. Notice also that the client did not rate the strength of her belief in the NAT. The therapist did not ask her to do so as they reviewed the form because her rating of the thought now in the relative calm of the therapy session would not have reflected how she would have rated it at the time. This is a frequent problem with thought records that are not filled out in the heat of the moment – in 'battle conditions'.

In a therapy session, unless a NAT comes up in the session itself, retrospective reports of negative thoughts are simply the best that can be achieved. The therapist can always encourage clients to fill out their thought records as close in time to the actual moment as possible. This may not, however, always be practically possible. Clients are often concerned that other people may discover their thought records and thus only ever fill them out when complete privacy is assured. When I kept thought records myself for three months, I devised a version that could be fitted into a pocket book and was surprised how often I could use it there and then. Practical issues should be discussed with clients when setting homework. For example, there may be various fears, including feeling more disturbed by a clearer recognition of thoughts that once were vague. Some people find it hard to access their thoughts and some, even when they can, find it hard to report them. Sometimes people find it easier to access what was in their minds by describing images that they experience. One client, for example, reported feeling depressed on deciding not to apply for a job. When we went further into her experience, it turned out that, as she was thinking about whether to apply, she had a vivid and detailed image of being rejected by the interviewing panel. I asked her to describe this image in great detail, which struck rich veins of negative meaning. I then explored these meanings with her. She imagined, for example, the interviewers shaking their heads as they read her application form. When I asked what this meant to her, she said 'They thought that I had a cheek to apply and that I was wasting their time.'

Evidence for and against the NAT and images

The aim of reviewing the evidence for and against the negative thoughts and images is to help the client to step back from them and consider them in a new light. This is because we know that when people are emotionally disturbed, they are likely to take negative thoughts as facts rather than interpretations or hypotheses. The negative thoughts play a major role in maintaining negative mood and thus their hold on the client's mind needs to be loosened.

In Table 4.4, the client has produced good pieces of evidence in the 'for' and 'against' sections, but they are responses to the behavioural disposition and so do not get at and evaluate the negative thoughts and underlying beliefs. The evidence presented in the reworked version is similar to the client's original entries but *does* get closer to the underlying thinking. It is also more realistic. It accepts that there may be germs in public places but that the risk of harm is remote. Interestingly, we later realised that the chances of any possible infection were greatly increased by skin cuts, and skin cuts were made more likely by her excessive hand washing which can damage the skin. Images can be reviewed in very much the same way. For example, with the woman who had the negative image about applying for a job, we could examine the evidence on how likely it was that the image was a reasonable estimate of what might happen if she did decide to apply.

Alternative thought/outcome

The aim of establishing an alternative thought from the evidence columns is to make the point that it is possible to learn to think in another way when confronted by triggering situations. In Table 4.4, the non-avoidant tone of the second version is more realistic and produces a decrease in negative emotion. The therapist strengthens the outcome column by initiating a conversation about 'dropping the safety behaviour' of hand washing. In this case, the client agreed that this could be undertaken but 'at a time to be negotiated and agreed'.[7]

Looking back over this thought record, I notice that it is not wordy but comparatively parsimonious, that is it has only a single situation and thought and does not amass a great deal of evidence. In many cases, the thought records may contain multiple entries for all the columns which can make it harder to use them effectively. Simple thought records showing simple and understandable links between thoughts and feelings seem to work best. Sometimes a client's difficulty with obsessional thoughts and making lists interferes with simplicity, since every nuance of every thought and feeling is recorded. Obsessional thoughts may also be harder to evaluate because they often concern 'risk assessment': just how 'safe' do you have to be to be 'safe'? It is true, however, that thought records do vary enormously in the amount of material they throw up. I considered this example to be a good one for my purposes because it was parsimonious and therefore allowed parsimonious discussion. Thought records, however, can sometimes be counter-productive for clients with obsessional and intrusive worries. There is now more interest about working with intrusive and obsessional thoughts by working with cognitive processes, the subject of the final section of this chapter.

Using thought records in practice

Sanders & Wills (2005) show that it is possible to use thought records more slowly and cumulatively by breaking up their various elements into smaller separate records, for example with just a few columns at a time. This chapter has shown that the various elements of a thought record can be used separately and it is now time to consider how they can be used in a wholly assembled format. It is usually suggested that the whole form (as in Table 4.4) is actually given in two phases. The first phase consists of giving just the columns for identifying triggers, feelings and negative thoughts, while the other columns are either left off or blocked out. The therapist should produce the form and explain it to the client, fielding questions as appropriate. Client and therapist should then fill out the form in the session, taking a recent incident in the client's life as the subject for a worked example. It is usually helpful to stress the collaborative element by encouraging the client to fill in the actual entries, perhaps running them past the therapist for comments first. Working with thought records rarely runs as smoothly as it is often portrayed in some textbooks. Most clients can make some connection with the logic of the thought record but are quite likely to report difficulties with getting it to work for them. It is likely that therapist and client will hit at least some of the problems described in Table 4.1 and 4.5.

Table 4.5   Problems and solutions in evaluating and responding to negative thoughts (seven-column thought record)

Problems	Solutions
Problems with evidence (columns 4 & 5)	
Strongly adverse life events.	*Focus on empathic listening. Identify ways of thinking that may be making the problem even worse. Suggest that it may be useful to review how helpful these thoughts are.*
The quantity of the evidence favours the negative. The quality of the evidence favours the negative.	*Discuss the balance of the evidence. Where either the quantity or the quality of the evidence balances towards the negative, suggest an 'open verdict'.*
The client finds it difficult to evaluate a negative thought as anything but true (negative evidence is more compelling or credible).	*Use belief ratings: anything less than 100% indicates a degree of doubt that can be built on.*
Problems with the alternative thought (column 6)	
The client describes the alternative thought as having intellectual but not emotional conviction (head but not heart).	*Go back over the whole sequence. Check the exact wording of the NAT and the alternative. Recheck the quality of the evidence. Also suggest that emotional conviction does take longer and may take some time to 'bed in'.*
Clients say things like 'Yes (I know I'm not really a failure) but...'.	*Draw out the 'but'– often it is underlain by some unspoken fears or even by a meta-cognitive rule such as 'If don't worry about this, I'll get complacent.'*
Problems with the end result (column 7)	
Client reports no change in negative feeling.	*Discuss the need to use the method over time. Write in a comment on how it could be different next time. If persistent, review focus and consider shifting focus to cognitive processes rather than content.*

Client difficulties in responding to thought records are sometimes the result of a pessimistic belief about therapy: a lurking suspicion that it might work for some people but will not work for them. This belief can seem as though as it has been confirmed when they first hit a snag such as a thought record that leaves them both baffled and not feeling any better. The problems of the first three columns – identifying and rating thoughts and feelings – have already been shown in Table 4.1. Table 4.5 focuses more on difficulties that arise in relation to generating evidence and alternative thoughts (covered in columns 4 to 7). The process generated by these columns strives for credible evidence and credible cognitive change.

Problems with evidence

A major impetus to the growth of CBT was the recognition that depressed clients in particular tend to be ruled by cognitive distortions. Obviously, though, at times clients report severe adverse life experiences which are not at all exaggerated – life-threatening illnesses, for example (Moorey & Greer, 2002). The evidence about such events may well confirm the negative thoughts. Apart from expressing empathy and being supportive, additional cognitive work would involve looking at ways in which the client's thinking is unhelpful to them as opposed to ways it may be 'distorting' reality. For example, when working with a person with cancer, cognitive therapy can help the client think about how ruminating about how little time may be left to them, may get in the way of making use of the time that is left. This kind of dialogue must not be led in a superior, knowing fashion; the therapist must herself become vulnerable to the hard truth of this moment and to the sheer difficulty of what the client may be facing.

Problems of evidence may also arise in other cases where the client's approach to evidence may seem to give disproportionate weight to some factors rather than others. It can be helpful to weigh the balance of the amount and quality of evidence, sometimes settling for an 'open verdict'. The credibility of evidence to the client can be assessed by the belief ratings they apply to the beliefs relating to them.

Problems with the credibility of cognitive change

Clients may quite often report that they believe the positive alternative thought with their heads but not in their hearts. It is actually in the nature of things that intellectual conviction often does precede emotional conviction and often this is just a sign that the client needs, in Albert Ellis' words, to 'work and practice' (Dryden, 1991). It is often helpful to recognise that the credibility of alternative thoughts and beliefs and change may take time to develop. One's view of self and life have developed over years and it may take constant repetition of alternatives to produce change. Sometimes, however, these problems are a sign that the therapy is not on track and the therapist may use them to consider alternatives, especially working on cognitive processes rather than on content and especially if the client has difficulty with intrusive thoughts, obsession, ruminations or worries (see later section in this chapter).

We must always try to empathise with any client difficulties with these processes. Thinking about our own attempts to change virtually any aspect of our lives tells us that such change is most frequently gradual and incremental. We may listen to some music several times before we really hear it, for example. Therapists and clients can sometimes be too eager for immediate change. Sometimes it takes time for new evidence and ideas to sink in and come to conscious realisation. Therapists should also be wary of arguing with clients when they seem to be blocking out new information. It can be very valid to simply acknowledge the client's doubts about the new information: 'So, the idea that you may actually be an okay person is simply not credible to you right now.'

It is important for CB therapists to take the time to deal with client reservations and difficulties as thoroughly as possible in therapy time, as the next move will be to ask the client if he can use thought records regularly at home. There is a good deal of evidence that clients who do homework regularly get significantly better results with CBT than those who do not (Kazantzis et al., 2005). If the client is able to bring one or more thought records, completed as homework tasks, with him to the next session, these should be put on the agenda as an item and given attention and time. If the client has taken the trouble to do the task, it can be very disheartening if the therapist gives them only cursory attention or even fails to review them at all. Thought records require time and effort and clients can feel afraid that their efforts will be judged negatively. They may find it helpful if the therapist clarifies in advance that spelling and grammar, for example, are not an issue.

As we move into filling out the response and challenge columns of the thought record it becomes helpful to have more discussion about the therapeutic aims of the thought record and how it may best be used. The prime aim of the thought record is to help the client to develop a more reflective relationship with their thoughts. This new perspective can raise the hope that the client can feel better and think more clearly in both the shorter and longer terms. Sometimes a client will be able to progress to being able to reach a new alternative thought during a testing negative event. Alternatively, they may be able to use it in retrospect and thus prevent themselves from going into prolonged negative rumination. When I kept thought records for three months, I found it a highly instructive experience. Firstly, I was amazed by the amount of rubbish that came out of my head. Secondly, I found that writing down my thoughts and evaluating them often made me feel better and clearer, helping me to get on with my day. Thirdly, I noticed that records were sometimes ineffective in the short term but that I would find, later in the day, that my mood had lightened. The experience emphasised for me the importance of persistence in keeping thought records. I would recommend the experience to all CB therapists. Having kept a record for oneself, the therapist can ask the client to follow suit with more authority and understanding. Leahy (2003) emphasises the need for over-practice and over-learning. This is because the sheer weight and persistence of negative thoughts[8] means that 'one swallow' most definitely does not 'make a summer'. The best prescription for problems with thought records is usually to troubleshoot in sessions but then to suggest *increasing* practice rather than any kind of backing away from using them. Hollon (2003) reinforces the view that CBT techniques often do need to be persisted with to achieve enduring effects for CBT.

Developing a creative use of thought records

The real aim of cognitive work is to generate alternative ways of thinking. Such shifts in consciousness and thinking can be elusive and may occur in unusual ways at times. I recently dreamt that my father used a thought record as a client. The final alternative way of thinking, however, was presented to him as a logo written on the side of a mug. My Dad loved his mug of tea and I reflected afterwards that it might have been a highly evocative and effective way for him to complete his experience of using a thought record! I sometimes feel that we could be a lot more creative in our working ways. Once, after participating in a particularly effective assertiveness training workshop, the presenter gave me an individualised badge that said 'I may not be perfect but parts of me are really nice.' I felt that this badge particularly spoke to my condition at that time and I treasured it for many years. I once made a customised T-shirt with a picture of Tim Beck and the slogan 'Put Your Beck into it!' for a CBT conference. As it happened, Tim and his daughter Judith were at the conference and Judith asked me if he could have the T-shirt. I duly posted it to him in Philadelphia. As CB therapists use coping cards with slogan-like adaptive thoughts, I have occasionally used the badge and T-shirt concept with clients (although it is helpful to discuss how other significant people in their lives are likely to react to them using such things).

I have identified over 20 different forms of thought record used by different CB therapists. They all include most of the steps indicated above, though they sometimes use different vocabularies and running orders. I usually use a version based on the 'Seven-column Thought Record' shown in Greenberger and Padesky (1995), though I sometimes find it helpful to use some other types of thought records with different clients. I find, for example, that some clients particularly benefit from using David Burns' self-help books as an accompaniment of therapy and therefore find it most congruent to use his version of a thought record that he calls a 'Mood Log'. I generally favour customising CBT materials for the idiosyncratic needs of both therapists and clients. Some thought record materials that can be used to customise exercises for the client are presented in Table 4.6 and are followed up in the next 'Suggestion' box.

Suggestion: Make your own thought record

Using the various elements and language of the thought record shown in Table 4.5, construct your own version in a way that will best suit you and your estimate of your clients' needs.

In the spirit of using different types of material, I follow the situation presented in the worked example of the seven-column record in Table 4.4 with the same example presented in the ABC format used in REBT in Table 4.7 (Dryden, 2006).

Table 4.6   Elements of a thought record

Language	Conceptual
THOUGHT RECORD: Mood Log;[1] Daily Thought Record; Dysfunctional Thought Record.	
TRIGGER: Situation; event; antecedent (A)[2]	Might include questions on time, place, who with, what doing, etc.
EMOTION: Mood; feeling; emotional consequences (Ce = emotional consequences)[2] (Also includes Cb = behavioural consequences)[2]	Might include intensity rating out of 5, 10 or 100.
NEGATIVE AUTOMATIC THOUGHT: Thoughts; cognitions; beliefs (B)[2]	Might include type of cognitive distortion.[1,3] Might include negative images.
EVIDENCE SUPPORTING NAT:	Evidence columns only included in seven-column record.[4]
EVIDENCE NOT SUPPORTING NAT:	
ALTERNATIVE BALANCED THOUGHT: Rational thought/alternative. Dispute (D)[2]	
OUTCOME (Change in emotion rating as result of holding alternative balanced thought) Effect (E)[2]	Might also include behavioural outcome or future plan based on alternative thought.

Notes:
1 See David Burns (1999b)
2 See Albert Ellis & Windy Dryden (1987)
3 See Gary Emery (1999)
4 Greenberger & Padesky (1995)

Table 4.7   ABCDE analysis (worked example)

A (Antecedent)	B (irrational Belief)	C (Consequences) emotional and behavioural	D (Dispute for each iB)	E (Effective rational beliefs)	F (Feelings and behaviours arrived at after considering effective rational belief)
Blood on money from cash point.	This is dangerous.	Anxiety. Urge to wash hands & change clothes.	Am I exaggerating the danger here? Do I really need to take these precautions? What is reacting this way doing to me in the long run?	There is a small possibility of harm but I am greatly exaggerating the danger. I can live with this possibility of harm without reacting like this.	Less anxiety. More resistance to washing hands, changing clothes.

Working with cognitive processes

At various points throughout this book, I have referred to a new understanding in CBT: therapists must focus on cognitive processes as well as on cognitive content. Many of us have the thought 'I am so useless' at times when we fail to do something we'd like to do. What happens next depends a lot on what type of attention we pay to that thought. For many of us, fortunately, the thought kind of slides away and does not give us any further trouble. A person vulnerable to depression, however, might start to ruminate endless on this thought and remember incidents in her past that seem to bear it out. The question is: how can the CB therapist help clients to give more appropriate attention to such thoughts?

Many of the newer CB approaches are suggesting that we need to help both ourselves and our clients to develop more mindful, non-judgemental and accepting ways of relating to these thoughts. Such a way of thinking stresses acceptance of the idea that thoughts and beliefs are mental events and processes rather than reflections of objective truths. These ideas have been operationalised by the development of mindfulness-based cognitive therapy group programmes, designed to work against relapse in depressed clients. There is now an impetus, however, for CB therapists to find ways of operationalising these ideas in their everyday practice – because they can be helpful to many of our clients.

Fennell (2004) describes how they can help with depression and low self-esteem for clients in individual therapy. She is clear, however, that bringing mindful techniques into everyday practice is not a question of learning new techniques but of importing the ideas, spirit and therapeutic style from mindfulness-based cognitive therapy practice. I would guess that there are CB therapists throughout the country trying to integrate mindfulness in their own individual ways and that, in future, these ways will develop into models of practice. At present, however, such models do not exist, so I must describe my own efforts to bring a mindful dimension into my practice.

The worked example for the thought record in Table 4.4 showed the responses of a client suffering from intrusive, obsessional thoughts, worries and phobias. A consensus is now building among CB therapists that working with the content of such thoughts is often only partially effective. This is because the problems they cause are crucially influenced by the amount and type of attention that clients pay to those thoughts. It has been shown, for example, that almost 90% of people have thoughts similar to those that afflict sufferers of OCD (Rachman, 2003). The difference between these 'normal' and 'abnormal' obsessions lies in the way that people react to them. Most people dismiss the thoughts in rather a light and easy way, whereas for OCD sufferers such thoughts are so personally objectionable, carrying such profoundly negative meaning, that they attempt to suppress them. Unfortunately, this suppression works in a way that only succeeds in producing a 'rebound effect', making the thought ever harder to suppress. Similarly, with the problem of worry, the content of worry does not differ much between sufferers and non-sufferers. Worry is functional – up to a point. Most people need to be concerned about things that could go wrong in their lives and would be 'unprepared' to meet crises if they weren't. Leahy (2005) distinguishes between 'productive worry' and 'unproductive worry'. Butler & Hope (1995) describe how worry is productive when it leads us to take reasonable action about our problems, but is unproductive when 'ruminative worry' blocks such action or prevents us from, as Carnegie (1993) puts it, *cooperating with the inevitable.*

I am suggesting here that it can be helpful to develop a different type of relationship between your mind and its worries, intrusions and obsessions. The way we think about our cognitive processes ('meta-cognition') may determine how we can relate to these problems. Rethinking our meta-cognitive beliefs can be a helpful first step in making such new relationships. Wells (1997, 2000) has suggested a number of helpful ways of changing the way we pay attention to negative thoughts: rethinking meta-cognitive beliefs and being more 'mindful' about them.

The theoretical understanding of these helpful processes is still some way ahead of more practical versions of how they can be implemented by therapists. Some strands of the new thinking have focused on devising mindfulness programmes designed to prevent relapse in depression, such as mindfulness-based cognitive therapy (Segal et al., 2002) and attention training (Wells, 2000). Others have focused more on how therapists can use some of the methods in one-to-one therapy (Wells, 1997; Fennell, 2004; Leahy, 2005). It is sometimes difficult to put these ideas into words. We have all known that wonderfully relaxed feeling that can steal over us lying in the sun on a summer's day, but would we be able to instruct someone to repeat our experience? Leahy's approach to worry does, however, contain a really useful set of 'think steps' that, in my experience, have been very helpful to clients trying to evolve a less enmeshed relationship with their own tendency to worry. I will therefore conclude this chapter with a description of this version of mindful therapy.

Leahy (2005) has developed a seven-step approach to overcoming worry. Worry is an acute and persistent negative state linked to anxiety, especially to Generalised Anxiety Disorder (APA, 2000). Like Segal et al.'s (2002) mindfulness programme, Leahy's mindfulness steps are woven in with more active cognitive steps that are focused on restructuring. The seven steps are shown in Figure 4.3.

In the steps, which attempt to help clients to learn how to use mindfulness, the client is encouraged to develop 'mindful detachment', a state that strongly

1. Distinguish between productive and unproductive worry.
2. Accept reality and commit to change.
3. Challenge worried thinking.
4. Focus on the deeper threat.
5. Turn failure into opportunity.
6. Use emotions rather than worry about them.
7. Take control of time.

FIGURE 4.3   *Seven-step worry cure (Leahy, 2005)*

emphasises non-possessive awareness and radical acceptance. Step 2 is called 'Accepting reality and committing to change' and clearly mirrors aspects of Steve Hayes' ACT model (Hayes et al., 2004). Hayes is another therapist strongly associated with the 'third wave' in CBT (Beck, 2004). Acceptance involves mindfulness and accepting one's limitations. To accept reality in this sense means that we have to move towards a way of accepting life as it is and not as we may demand that it should be. It is interesting that the mindful strategies associated with Leahy's acceptance step come *before* the more traditional cognitive intervention steps, such as the suggestion to challenge worried thinking. This order of precedence implies that it is important for the client to develop a different type of relationship to their worry processes before starting to challenge the content of their worrying thoughts. One of the important functions of worry may be to protect the client from feeling certain other negative emotions (Leahy, 2005: 293). Disowning emotion in this way would mean that cognitive work could fail to evoke the appropriate emotions and would therefore fail to meet the criteria that would be needed for *metanoia*, that is emotionally felt cognitive change.

Therapists can help worried clients to become more mindfully engaged in present time because worry is a problem orientated towards the future, such as the fear that some catastrophe will unfold. Worry can also lead to depression, and depressed thinking is typically global and non-specific. The therapist therefore helps the client to come to and stay in the present moment by describing concrete experience and 'noticing' what is happening around him. In the following example – a heavily abbreviated client dialogue – I have followed some of the suggestions proposed by Leahy (2005) for promoting the acceptance of worry (see also the final Suggestion box on p. 80). The therapist can introduce these concepts – gaining distance, describing what is in front of you, suspending judgement and, in imagination, fading out of the scene – and then work them through with the client. The client, Bella, had perpetual worries about her interactions with people who mattered most to her. She had visited her brother in the morning before our afternoon session and had come away feeling preoccupied that she had upset him:

Therapist: Okay, Bella, let's see if we can try to contemplate this worry about your brother more calmly. You have read this part of the Worry book, so we'll begin by trying to view the worry more distantly. The author begins by suggesting 'I am having the thought that…'

Client: Oh, it feels a bit silly.

Therapist: Yes, I know, but how about we give it a go anyway?

Client: Okay then, here goes (long pause). I'm simply having the thought that I may have said something about dad that upset my brother yesterday and that now he will be fretting all night about it… Because I know him and how upset he can get… (Silence)… It is funny I can see him in my mind's eye, sitting there… That was so vivid… it is fading now.

Therapist: Okay, you're doing well. Let us take your mind away from that thought now and just tell me what do you see in front of you now?

Client: (Looking out of window) I can see the garden and there is a bird hopping across the lawn… I think it might have a worm in its beak … and now it is flying up and away… and on to the roof of the house opposite … It is

Therapist:	sitting on the ridge, kind of puffing its chest out... and now it has taken off again up into the sky and way across Bristol and out of sight...

Therapist: Great, now let us look back at the worry about your brother but this time try to think about it without saying that the situation is good or bad... it is just a thought, neither good nor bad.

Client: I can see my brother again and I can see me saying what I said about dad... My brother looks quiet, perhaps a bit sad.

Therapist: If this worry were a thing, what would it feel like?

Client: Like a lump... but one that is now softening, melting perhaps... I can see my brother again. He *is* sad and a bit, you know, wistful maybe. I am remembering leaving his house. He did smile as I left. I think that he probably will think a lot about what I said about dad, but he will be sad, not hurt. I mean it is sad about dad – I feel sad about it too but it is just life, isn't it?

Therapist: Life can be sad... Your brother is now feeling sad, can you fade yourself out of the scene and just leave him to it?

Client: (Longish pause) I am stepping away from it now, from him. I am walking out of thinking about it like I walked out of the house. I am thinking about my brother living his life and I can leave him to do it. I care for him but I am not responsible for him. I can accept him being sad a bit more. I can accept myself feeling low as well.

As I mentioned earlier, it is hard to reproduce the *quality* of mindful functioning. Written down, these responses can appear trite and clichéd. It is important to understand that this was a reflective discussion and did not unfold as quickly as it is shown in the dialogue. It took some encouragement for Bella to find these words. Indeed, I suspect that the slowing down of speech and the reflective quality of it is an important aspect of these mindful interventions. To some extent, a dialogue like this is trying to promote contact with the present moment in which people even experience something of a transcendent sense of self. Leahy (2005) comments that worriers have often put themselves at the centre of the universe – not in an eccentric way but in a way that shoulders all the burdens of the universe. Bella found the part particularly helpful and commented similarly to Leahy that 'There's a sense of peace, you know, in stepping back sometimes and letting life go on by itself.'

As I wrote this section, I noticed some worries of my own and used the first 'think step' on myself. My response to the 'gaining distance' step is shown as Figure 4.4.

---

1. I am simply having the thought that I am going to be even later with this book than I said I would be.
2. I am simply noticing that I am feeling uncomfortably anxious and frustrated.
3. I am simply having the thought that I should make a massive effort to speed up.
4. I am simply having the thought that my CB colleagues will think this book is rubbish anyway.
   (Pause)
5. I am simply noticing that I am laughing!
   (Frank Wills, 3 May 2007)

FIGURE 4.4   *Simply having the thought...*

To gain distance, firstly we need to remember that a thought is just a thought. A thought is not reality. We can do this by using the formula 'I am simply having the thought that...' and 'I am simply noticing that I am feeling...'. We can bring our minds into the present moment by looking at what is around us and describing it in simple and concrete terms. I was sitting in my garden, the same garden that Bella looked out on, as I did this and became aware of the flowers and the insects. The moment stood still and, for some reason, I was reminded of the scene with the swirling paper in the film *American Beauty*. At this stage, we can also suspend judgement over our experiences and our thoughts. Evaluation is only ever provisional, as Albert Ellis has reminded us (Dryden, 1991). Evaluation can tie up immense amounts of mental energy and yet the finding of real value can be elusive. The final moves in Leahy's sequence involve 'taking yourself out of the picture', by imagining the world and life proceeding without you. This may sound scary but it can also be very liberating. The effect of all these steps is to take the sting out of nagging worry. A key element is the slowing down and 'gentling' of thinking processes. Finally, for the last suggested exercise of this chapter I give a shortened version of Leahy's 'gaining distance' steps. He suggests trying it next time you are stuck in traffic.

Suggestion: Flowing through you like a river...

1. Gain distance from your worrying thoughts by saying out loud (or writing down) 'I am having the thought that...' and 'I am noticing that I am feeling...'. Let the chain of thoughts and feelings run on as long as it wants.
2. Get to the present by describing what is around you in concrete, non-evaluative language.
3. Try also to take any evaluation out of any thoughts that crop up.
4. Think again about the situations that have evoked worrying thoughts and imagine yourself out of those situations. Imagine the situation, indeed the universe, going on without you.
5. Finally, imagine yourself disappearing altogether. Imagine yourself to be a grain of sand on a beach blown into the distance by a gust of wind.

We have reached a different CBT from how some people imagine it – perhaps a more balanced therapy that is freer to converge or diverge. Some parts of Leahy's work read almost like Zen *koans*. It is perhaps fitting to finish this chapter with one of them:

Change and progress involves successful imperfection and constructive discomfort. (Leahy, 2005: 95)

PRACTICE TIP: The great CBT takeaway

A key element in CBT, and indeed in most therapy, is that the client somehow reaches a new view about what is happening to them and how they can deal with it. The new view can surface in a moment – and dissipate just as quickly. Although CBT is most well known for processes which continually present and re-present chances to achieve change by relatively rational steps, we all know that change can be capricious and sometimes can only come at the 'auspicious moment' – called *kairos* by the Greeks. I am slowly but surely collecting the idiosyncratic and often unexpected ways in which people have reported catching themselves thinking negatively and finding a way to respond. I offer a few examples below and sometimes these can be useful suggestions for others. My main point, however, is for therapists to be alert to what their clients' idiosyncratic ways are.

'Seeing' negative thoughts on a white board

'I find it really helpful that you write up my negative thoughts on the white board. It makes it much more clear to me that they *are* negative. Recently, when I have had some negative thoughts, I have been able to visualise them on the white board and I have been more able to deal with them successfully.'

Hearing the therapist's voice

'I felt really pressured to accept extra typing work at the office yesterday but then I remembered our discussion about assertive rights, especially what you said about everyone having the right to ask for time to consider. Then I thought "Right, I'm going to march right in and ask for extra time to think about it. And I did it! I amazed myself."'

The loo as behavioural escape

'I found that situation at Maud's house really hard to deal with. Then I was thinking of those tactics we devised for dealing with stress situations and I thought 'Escape! Where can I escape? I could only think of the loo in that house but that was enough. I went in washed my hands few times and calmed down. I came out of there knowing how I could get round the difficulties Mike was creating.'

Further reading

Leahy, R.L (2003) *Cognitive therapy techniques.* New York: Guilford Press.
Leahy, R.L. (2005) *The worry cure: stop worrying and start living.* London: Piatkus.
Wells, A. (2000) *Emotional disorders and metacognition.* Chichester: Wiley.

Notes

1   This is a variation of a thought experiment devised by Christine Padesky. People come up with different responses: some show the emotional response that the second situation would be much worse, while some rationally say that the end result is in the same in both scenarios.
2   This is an extract from a CBT demonstration DVD/video (Simmons & Wills, 2006).
3   Originally, in Greek, *aporia* implied 'no crossing point'. The term has come to be used to signify an impasse in debate.
4   I am grateful to my colleague, Rosa Johnson, for suggesting this point to me.

5   I am personally grateful for my own 'naffness' and have been pleased to find that my clients with strongly 'self-perfectionist' traits seem to quite like it too! One client gave this kind of feedback recently and I found myself saying 'Yes, I'm pretty good at not being perfect.'
6   Stored in the 'Materials' section of the SAGE website accompanying this book.
7   A graduated programme of delayed hand washing subsequently made rapid progress.
8   With the possible exception of obsessional difficulties mentioned earlier.

Answers for Table 4.3

1	a
2	h
3	f
4	a
5	c
6	b
7	e
8	i
9	g

5

SKILLS FOR WORKING ON CHANGING BEHAVIOUR

---

*Cato took the news of Lepida's marriage
quite as badly as one would have
predicted, striding round and swearing,
which reminds me of another of Cicero's
witticisms – that Cato was always the
perfect Stoic, as long as nothing went wrong.*

Robert Harris (2006: 122)

Behaviour therapy preceded cognitive therapy in the history of the development of modern psychotherapy. Beck and Ellis, however, were both keen to bring behavioural methods into their cognitive therapy models. Importing behavioural methods made sense for two good reasons. Firstly, they had been shown to be effective as interventions with pervasive problems such as phobias. Secondly, behavioural and cognitive change can act in mutually supportive ways. Behavioural problems, such as withdrawal in depression, may be strongly related to specific negative thoughts and beliefs, such as 'No one will want to see me anyway.' Problematic behaviour may also be related to more general negative beliefs about the self – 'I must be weak to have a problem like this.' Converting negative into more adaptive behaviour may therefore also impact on these beliefs. The therapist should choose behavioural interventions based on the individual formulation of the client. Sometimes belief change can occur as a by-product of behavioural change but there are also times when therapists should consciously design behavioural experiments to allow clients to test and change beliefs that are not working for them. Some rules for devising and running behavioural experiments are presented later in this chapter.

Therapists are often very attracted to pursuing change at the deepest levels. It can seem very persuasive to pursue schema change as the most fundamental type of change, but it may be that more benefit could come from simple behavioural change. If you have been brought up to believe, for example, that you cannot really have much effect on your life or the world, sometimes even a small example of acting positively can have a big impact. The idea of deep transformative change can seem so alluring that it results in therapists overlooking smaller and less glamorous steps to change, even when this is exactly what the client may be looking for.

This chapter is about such small but cumulative changes and the skills that are needed to take them forward into positive life changes. We will explore identifying and assessing behavioural problems, activating missing behaviours, building more rewarding, self-efficacious behaviours and facing up to fears. As we do this we will see that developing positive behaviours is usually beneficial in its own right but such behaviours will often also reinforce positive beliefs about the self and about life more generally. We will particularly examine examples of work with problems such as the avoidance associated with anxiety and the withdrawal associated with depression and unhappiness. The methods described have utility across the board but are well illustrated in the context of these problems. We begin the chapter by considering two clients who asked for help with a behaviour they wanted to change:

> **MICHAEL** had a long-term physical illness and was also depressed. He had a good job that kept him busy in the day but in the evening he just sat and watched TV with his flatmate, who was also depressed. As the months went by, he became more depressed and isolated, losing the confidence to make contact with his friends.
>
> **CLAUDIA** was anxious in social situations. She had started a new job and the stress of fitting in had pushed her over the edge and into therapy. At her office Christmas party, she had hidden in the loo for almost an hour before going into the party. She then walked across the room slowly (so that people would notice that she had come) and returned to the toilet for a while before grabbing her coat and going home.

The way people behave when they are suffering from emotional or physical pain can reinforce their problems. Michael had lost some of his active social behaviours and this loss was leading to a vicious cycle of loneliness and depression. Michael needed to behave in a more socially engaged way after work. Claudia's tactic of hiding away and avoiding things only made her more anxious. Ironically, it probably ensured that people noticed her all the more. She needed to behave in a more confident and proactive way.

Suggestion

Can you think of some clients who are like Michael and Claudia? Try to define their behaviour. If things were getting better for them, how might that behaviour start to change? If the clients did start to make these behavioural changes, how would that impact on their beliefs about themselves, other people and about the world?

Traditionally, behaviourists have stayed a little on the outside of the therapy community, perhaps holding reservations about the unscientific ideas of the other traditions. Therapists from other schools have responded with equal reservations about the supposed coldness of behaviour therapy. The behaviourists, however, have always had good things to offer and have got on with developing some neat and effective interventions, especially for anxiety problems. Yet their insistence that only observable behaviour was worthy of being a focus for therapy had put an artificial ceiling on what they might contribute to the wider therapeutic field. A big break-through came with the recognition that it was possible to identify 'internal behav-iours' such as thinking, and that this opened up a wider view of the possible factors that could be defined as behavioural triggers and responses. Claudia's thought, 'People find me boring', for example, seems to trigger an intensification of her anxi-ety. Behaviourists then developed new insights as they developed a richer under-standing of behavioural triggers and responses. They realised that people appraised and evaluated these triggers and responses. What one person regarded as a reward, for example, another might not. These breakthroughs fostered a powerful alliance between the behaviourists and the emerging 'cognitive revolution' (Rachman, 1997).

On the cognitive side of the alliance, Aaron Beck (1970) and Albert Ellis (Ellis & Dryden, 1997) both came to stress the importance of working with behaviour. They realised that proactive behaviours were bound to have a positive impact on self-efficacy beliefs such as 'I can take effective action on issues that matter to me' and 'I don't have to passively accept things.'

Behavioural assessment

Most people know behaviourism from the work of Pavlov, Watson and Skinner. It is now considered that phenomena such as conditioning are a lot more complex than the original formulations (Rescorla, 1988; Staddon, 2001). Their work, however, remains important as signposts to the key areas of behaviour change. Pavlov and Watson both worked on the 'antecedents' (the 'what went before') of behaviour. They showed that one could change the way a person behaved by manipulating environ-mental conditions to trigger actually very specific behavioural responses. Skinner, on the other hand, worked more on the 'consequences' of behaviour that either reinforced or did not reinforce it, so making it more or less likely to reoccur.

One reason why therapists are sometimes reluctant to consider the benefits of a behavioural angle is that so much of the behavioural research was carried out with animals and may not therefore transfer easily to a human context. A major thrust of more recent behavioural therapy with humans has been the recognition of the power of simple social reinforcement, such as smiling, attention and praise – some of the basic building blocks of relationships. As CBT practitioners are involved in intense human encounters, they can use an understanding of social reinforcement to help clients develop rewarding interpersonal behaviours, such as positive attention, posi-tive regard and seeking intrinsic personal satisfaction to enhance therapeutic change.

Analysing the client's situation from a behavioural angle

The initially rather different concerns of both Pavlov and Skinner are now seen by behavioural therapists as playing key roles in most forms of learning. Concern with analysing the client's situation by identifying antecedent triggers and con-sequent reinforcement is shown in **behavioural assessment** or **behavioural functional analysis**.

The behavioural **ABC method** is a useful mnemonic for **functional analysis**. A stands for antecedents, **B** stands for 'behaviour', **C** stands for consequences.

The format used in the example below follows Sheldon's (1995) user-friendly language and is stored on the SAGE website for this book (see Appendix 1 for information on finding and using the website). We can apply the ABC concept to the situations of Michael and Claudia (Table 5.1).

We can see from Table 5.1 that all sorts of triggers, observable and unobservable, can act as 'antecedents': events such as meeting someone, thoughts such as 'It would be mean not to sit with him', and physical feelings such as tiredness and social events. Furthermore, laying things out like this helps us to look for things that might change and make a difference, and these things can be linked to any or all the A, B and C columns.

Table 5.1   ABC analysis

What happened before what happened	What happened	What happened after what happened
A: Antecedent	B: Behaviour	C: Consequences
Michael is tired when he comes home from work. He sees his flatmate and thinks 'It would be mean not to sit with him.'	Michael watches TV all night. He no longer makes plans to see friends. As he goes to bed, he thinks 'I do nothing with my life.'	Michael feels less energy. His routine becomes more and more rigid. He feels isolated and this intensifies his depression.
Claudia worries all the way to the office party. She thinks, 'People will think I'm weird.'	Claudia goes and hides in the loo. Later, she walks through, trying both to be unobtrusive and look as though she were enjoying herself.	Claudia feels anxious throughout the evening and bad about herself afterwards. Some fellow workers notice her behaviour and think it odd.

MICHAEL and his therapist decided that:

■ On returning home from work, he would first go to his room for a short rest.
■ Planning to meet friends occasionally did *not* mean he was 'abandoning' his flatmate.
■ Going out once or twice a week might increase his energy levels and decrease his isolation and depression.

CLAUDIA and her therapist decided that:

■ She should try to tolerate her anxiety more in social situations. She could work on tolerating five minutes and then build that up to six, seven and more minutes.
■ She might be less nervous if she believed she could engage with people to at least a minimal extent. She could practise conversational exchanges in safe situations, such as in therapy, and gradually extend this into other situations step by step. If confidence grew during these tasks, she could practise taking the initiative in social situations in the same way she practised responding socially.
■ One powerful and genuine way to break the ice socially can be to share one's sense of nervousness with someone likely to be sympathetic. Claudia could be encouraged to try sharing her feelings as a behavioural experiment. The experiment might allow her to test her belief that few other people were nervous in this way and that saying it would put people off.

Both clients did indeed try these strategies and were helped by doing so.

> ### Suggestion: Behavioural fieldwork exercise – Figuring out an ABC pattern
>
> **Form:** As an individual or in small groups.
>
> **Aim:** To become familiar with using the ABC pattern.
>
> Popularisation of the behavioural approach has come more recently in the form of 'behavioural analysis'. A simplified version of this can be found in TV programmes such as *Supernanny.* While some behavioural analysts frown at this populism, I find it quite useful in identifying the ABC pattern. The task, then, is to watch one of these types of programme and to make notes on some of the patterns that you observe, using an ABC form. This is essentially a solo activity but, if you can, compare notes with others afterwards.

It can be seen that developing ABCs is really a type of 'behavioural formulation' (Hersen, 2002) like the CB formulation we looked at in Chapter 2. As we noted earlier, formulation is something that can be used from very early on in therapy. Sometimes the behavioural factors in formulation may be overlooked. The therapist can strength the formulation by building up a comprehensive profile of the client's problematic behaviours – the examples above are likely to be reproduced tenfold for any one client. Such a wide approach is justified by the fact that once clients' problematic patterns take root they are likely to spread across more and more areas of their lives. The wide approach also gives the therapist a good working window on the client's current problems and thus increases the chances of identifying patterns and spotting areas more susceptible to change than others. If this is helpful to the therapist, then it is likely to be helpful to the client. It can therefore be beneficial to engage clients in recording their own ABC patterns as an ongoing part of the therapy, especially during early phases. We have already mentioned the importance of goal formation as the culmination of the assessment process. Goals are often the flipside of problems. This can be seen clearly in the strategies that seem to have evolved naturally from the ABC analysis of both Claudia and Michael.

Questions likely to be helpful in ABC analysis are shown in Table 5.2.

Table 5.2   Useful questions when formulating ABC analysis

A Questions	B Questions	C Questions
What happens just before you...?	How exactly do you react?	How do you end up feeling? Any relief?
Were there any body sensations...?	Any avoidance behaviours?	How do other people react to what you do?
Any thoughts?	Any safety behaviours?	Are there any longer-term consequences to you behaving that way?

Self-monitoring and diary keeping

At first, it is best for the therapist and client to do the ABC analysis together in session. As the client grasps the task, it can then become a useful homework assignment. As ABC analysis is carried out over a number of weeks, it becomes a form of self-monitoring. The suggestion that the client should take up self-monitoring carries several very powerful meta-messages:

- You are an active partner in this therapy.
- You can do things that can make a difference.
- You can develop a different relationship from the way you are living.
- You can become a reflective observer of yourself as a well as an active doer.
- Change is likely to involve 'work and practice' (Ellis & Dryden, 1997).

It is worth spending time and effort to introduce this important task, also preparing the client for any problems that might arise. A dialogue discussing such a task might run something like this:

Therapist: I'm going to ask you to keep a kind of diary about the things that trouble you for a while… I'd like you to use this ABC form here to capture some of the ways you get drawn into negative behaviours during each day. Try to record several instances for each day. When you realise that you have been upset, try to figure out what was happened just before you felt upset and write it here (pointing to A column), then how you felt or what you did here (B column) and then what happened after that in this column (C). This will help us find areas that we can work on. You may remember me doing this earlier when you told me about how fed up you are in the evenings. Now before we go any further, how do you feel about me asking you to do this for yourself at home?

Client: Well… okay I suppose. I mean I can see the point of it… but I wonder if I will do it, it is just that I feel so low, I may not be motivated… and since I've been feeling this way, I forget a lot of things.

Therapist: Yeah, I'm glad you are being realistic, it could be difficult. I'd like you to understand though that it is not a pass or fail thing – anything you are able to come up with is going to be helpful. Even if you do nothing, we can try to figure out why it was difficult. Quite a few of my clients only remember that they were supposed to do it just a few hours before therapy and they then scribble down some things for the whole week! What they do write is nearly always useful though.

Client: So is it best to write it down as soon as it happens then?

Therapist: Ideally, but that's not always possible, so whenever you can find the time really, and ideally that should get easier as the therapy rolls on.

Once the client has shown interest in taking up self-monitoring, it is worthwhile going over the rationale for the procedure. Everyone has his or her favourite way of giving and/or hearing a rationale. It can be helpful to match the explanation with the client's interests. It may be worth stressing the following points:

- It is often helpful to be able to step back from an upset and think 'What is this really all about? What is actually happening here?'
- It is good to be able to stop negative reactions at an early stage: 'Problems tend to be like boulders rolling down a slope. The further they roll, the more force and momentum they develop and the harder they are to stop.'

- It is good if you can spot the types of trigger that give you problems: 'being forewarned is forearmed'.
- It is good to develop several different ways of dealing with difficult situations: 'You don't want to be like a one-club golfer, trying to get round Gleneagles with just a putter!'

Diaries can be highly flexible devices for recording feelings, behaviours, thinking, physical reactions, substance use and social behaviour. They can be used:

- retrospectively – to reflect on what the client has been doing in recent days, or
- prospectively – to forward plan for the coming days and/or weeks.

Some of these activities have already been covered in the discussion of thought records in Chapter 4. The behavioural uses of diaries will now be examined against the backdrop of more general strategies commonly used in CBT.

Activating behaviour (increasing the scope of what you do) in depression

The body language and posture of a depressed person can be striking: the shoulders become hunched and the more depressed the person, the more the shoulders turn in on themselves, until the person seems to be shrinking before our very eyes. The self seems to be turning away from the world and the body slows down in unison. As the body dips below levels of optimal activity, performance drops below par as well: memory, concentration, appetite and sleep all suffer, movement and motivation seem to take more effort. It is as if the body's batteries are running down and the resulting dip only leads to less charge being received. One early nineteenth-century physician, Johan Reil, apparently made the unethical suggestion of infecting 'melancholic' patients with scabies to get them moving!

Extreme inactivity may take on the form of a desire to stay in bed. Some clients seem to believe that they will feel better if they do this. There may be some kind of 'sick role' satisfaction that rewards this behaviour. The belief is nearly always wrong and unhelpful. Aaron Beck has suggested that therapists can counter this tendency by encouraging clients literally to get up and get going. A realistic plan for gradually increasing behaviour levels is often the best way to go. Clients who are very depressed, especially those with impaired concentration, may find cognitive work just too difficult. A simple behavioural approach may be best at this stage (Fennell, 1989; Emery, 1999). The two best known strategies for such an approach are **activity scheduling** ('planning balanced levels of engagement with life') from the cognitive therapy tradition of Beck (Beck et al., 1979) and **reward planning** ('making sure that we are doing some things that give pleasure and meaning to our lives') from the behavioural tradition of Lewinsohn (Lewinsohn & Gotlib, 1995).

Activity Scheduling

We need to think about both the *quantitative* (how much) and the *qualitative* (what kind) dimensions of our clients' activities: both dimensions suffer when people become unhappy. As the person becomes more depressed and demotivated, he may well be withdrawing from everyday activities – often those very things that have made life worthwhile. Albert Ellis makes the excellent point that getting absorbed in 'a real vital ongoing interest can help many people to overcome their disturbance or at least live more happily in spite of it' (in Dryden, 1991: 40). If clients are just mechanically going through the days, life becomes humdrum – a low temperature existence lived without passion. One client was very embarrassed to tell me how he had once been really into stamp collecting: he feared that it meant he was 'un-cool' and 'an anorak', yet as he talked of the different colours, styles of stamps and their historical and geographical significance, I felt a real sense of passion in him. I encouraged him not to let himself be robbed of that by the tyranny of 'cool'. It may be that our modern society has lost the art of simple pleasures. Therapists could perhaps help clients to reclaim these lost simple pleasures.

The Activity Schedule has a simple format but one that is capable of being used in a variety of different and increasingly sophisticated ways. We can choose where to start on this spectrum but often begin with *quantitative aspects of behaviour* ('doing more things') and work up towards the *qualitative aspects* ('doing things that count'). Table 5.3 shows a worked example of the basic format of the schedule and is reproduced as Form 5.3 on the SAGE website. Table 5.3 shows an hour-by-hour monitoring of a client's mornings for the first three days of the week. It allows the therapist and client to reflect on the way the client was spending his time. Firstly, we notice that there is a pretty steady daily pattern for Monday and Tuesday. The client said he did not much like the sound of that boring phrase 'desk (aka 'computer') work'. Wednesday was like a liberation day for him. There are little personal clues about him too. He values a spiritual discipline in his week and he is fond of books. We are perhaps getting to know him from just these few jottings. Imagine what we might learn from a whole month of this type of material – provided he had been honest, of course.

The client did not feel depressed in those few days; if he had, the activity level might not be so high. If the activity level had been higher and we knew he had been depressed, we might guess that he had been working hard to keep going. We can see how we are getting to know the person and starting to be able to make reasonable inferences about how he is functioning. The therapist can also help the person to reflect on the balance of various factors such as work–life and self–others. This type of reflection naturally makes you think about 'What I'd like to do a bit differently' or 'How can I re-balance this?' Simple mood monitoring can also be added by asking clients to record how they feel for each segment of each day (see Wednesday in Table 5.3).

In reviewing a week, the therapist and client can look for periods of relatively high or low activity and/or periods of feeling low (1 out of 10) or good (9 out of 10). They can work collaboratively to see if there are patterns that it may be helpful to clarify and work on: typically, things like bad starts to the day or early evening dips in mood. Insights generated from this kind of review – for example, 'I generally feel better if I can start the day with some relatively undemanding tasks' – can be used to forward plan a new or better pattern for the upcoming week. These plans are usually in the spirit of 'try it and see' how they work and can be thought of as **behavioural experiments**.

Table 5.3   Activity Schedule with basic self-monitoring

	Monday	Tuesday	Wednesday
0600–0700	Sleep	Sleep	Breakfast 5
0700–0800	Breakfast	Breakfast	Getting ready and travelling to Cardiff 5
0800–0900	Getting ready for & travelling to work	Getting ready for & travelling to work	Finding venue in Cardiff 4
0900–1000	Morning prayer	Desk work	Setting up teaching room 6
1000–1100	Desk work	Library	Meeting students and teaching 7
1100–1200	Coffee, desk work	Desk work	Coffee 8
1200–1300	Library	Meeting and lunch	Teaching 7

Suggestion: What do our behavioural patterns look like and how could they change?

Form: Individual or counselling pairs (counsellor and client) or trio (counsellor, client and observer)

Aim: To experience skills of using the activity schedule.

Using the form for the Activity Schedule, trace out the daily patterns for the last few days. Look out for patterns and rhythms within and between the days. Go for as much detail as the client seems comfortable with. Be prepared to offer some personal feedback on how the patterns compare to your own and how you might feel about days structured like that. Ask the client if there is anything about their patterns that they might like to change. Devise a brief two- or three-point plan for making such a change. Finally, take brief feedback from all the participants in the exercise.

A behavioural review of the week can be linked with other aspects of the CBT work. The cognitive work with 'Don', described in Chapter 4, came from simply spotting that his mood had been particularly low early one evening but led on to an extended and significant cognitive-interpersonal intervention focused on the significance of relationships in his life. Sometimes more general, 'across the week/s' or across situation patterns show themselves. From reviewing schedules with clients over the years, I have come to see that the way a client starts a day is often a crucial influence over the way the rest of the day develops. Frequently, clients report that they wake and quickly have negative thoughts. One frequently encountered pattern has been that clients quickly ask themselves 'How do I feel today?' They then go on to predict that they will feel lousy all day. They then scan their bodies and minds and are usually able to find some minor negative feeling which they then latch on to and amplify. A good strategy to counter this tendency is to suggest that the client postpones evaluation of how they are feeling. It is relatively normal for people to feel quite disorientated immediately after waking. The best thing is to get up, move around, do some things and see how you feel later. The majority of clients who have been able to do this report that they find that they are okay later, presumably because they have avoided negative rumination by making a shift in attention. Although this intervention specifically aims at helping clients not to feel distressed after waking up, it frequently turns out that the negative self-focus demonstrated by the client's reaction to waking is reflected in negative self-focus and over-evaluation in other salient areas of the client's life.

Behavioural work: adding the missing qualitative dimension

When building up the activity levels of depressed clients, Beck et al. (1979) make the useful distinction between 'mastery' (M) and 'pleasure' (P) orientated activities. 'Pleasure' may be seen in terms of the dimensions of getting absorbed in vital life interests. 'Loss of pleasure' is also one of the criteria for depression in *DSM-IV-TR* (American Psychological Association, 2000). When people are depressed, it often seems as though pleasure is drained out of their lives. I will use the terms 'achievement' (A) and 'enjoyment' (E) for mastery and pleasure. These terms seem to chime more easily with clients in the UK. Beck realised that depressed clients may not enjoy activities that they had enjoyed previously but that they might mechanically complete them against the grain. The addition of the 'achievement' rating allows them to award themselves points for persevering, an important aspect of 'recovery behaviour'. Thus ratings for achievement (A) and enjoyment (E) can be added to the client's Activity Schedule. An example from part of one client's Activity Schedule is shown in Table 5.4.

Wendy's Schedule (Table 5.4) illustrates a number of important points. It is clear that inactivity is associated with a lack of achievement, low self-efficacy and little enjoyment. These factors were reinforced by many negative thoughts:

Table 5.4   Wendy's Activity Schedule with achievement and enjoyment ratings

	Monday	Tuesday	Wednesday
0600–0700	Wake, breakfast (A=1; E=1)	Sleep (A=0; E=2)	Wake (A=0; E=0)
0700–0800	Resting (A=0; E=1)	Breakfast (A=1; E=2)	Breakfast (A=1; E=1)
0800–0900	Watching TV (A=0; E=1)	Getting ready (A=2; E=0)	Resting (A=0; E=0)
0900–1000	Watching TV (A=0; E=1)	Getting ready (A=2; E=0)	Watching TV (A=0; E=1)
1000–1100	Went to shop (A=1; E=2)	Sue came for coffee (A=2; E=6)	Housework (A=3; E=2)
1100–1200	Resting (A=0; E=0)	Took Sue to material shop (A=5; E=7)	Resting (A=0; E=0)

'I just can't do anything these days', 'I just spend hours being pathetic', etc. The corollary is also true: almost any positive activity that Wendy could manage made her feel better. In addition, the activity that really stood out as enjoyable was hosting Tuesday's visit of her friend, Sue, especially going out with her to look at materials. Sue and Wendy were textile artists and the fact that Sue still valued her opinion on materials was vital in boosting both the achievement and enjoyment ratings for this event.

Pleasure predicting

Pessimism is another major criterion for depression in *DSM-IV-TR*. It is good to tackle pessimism quite early in therapy because it has the potential to undermine the whole therapeutic enterprise with beliefs such as 'Nothing will help me', 'Therapy could work for others but not me' and 'There's no point in trying.' Sometimes the client's more specific pessimistic predictions – typically beliefs like 'I won't enjoy doing that now I am depressed' – will undermine the client's efforts to build up activity levels. The technique of **pleasure predicting** is an effective intervention to counter this. When confronted by pessimism, the therapist can go back to the pragmatic CBT default position: 'Well, that's possible but shall we see?'

It is realistic to think that depression can make it hard to enjoy things but depression can also make it hard to think that you will enjoy things when you might. Understanding this fact can lead to setting up a behavioural experiment such as that for Wendy described below:

> **WENDY** had wanted to cancel Sue's visit when it came up in a review of her upcoming week. She made a string of pessimistic predictions: 'Sue will be bored with me now I am like this', 'Sue is only coming out of kindness' and 'I'll be too worried to enjoy myself.' The therapist encouraged her not to cancel but to see how things would actually turn out. Wendy made a prediction of how she thought she would enjoy the visit (E=3) and then subsequently compared it with the 6 and 7 that actually ensued. She was able to understand and see that her pessimistic predictions could be wrong. Another interesting aspect that emerged from this review was that Wendy had spent almost two hours getting ready for the visit, trying on numerous clothes to be 'smart enough' for Sue. It turned out that Sue had been in her attic before the visit and Wendy was actually quite amused by how 'dowdy' she looked.

Bennett-Levy (2003) has suggested that behavioural experiments are often the most valued part of therapy for many clients. Whereas completing thought records can be experienced as 'a tedious but logical process… [that] help me to slow down and put things into perspective' (Bennett-Levy, 2003), behavioural experiments can be more emotionally convincing: 'doing is believing'. Because clients often report 'procrastination' as a major problem, experiments that can be done during sessions can prove especially powerful because 'there is no time like the present'. Sanders & Wills (2003) discuss a number of behavioural experiments conducted outside the therapy room (for example, going to a zoo to overcome bird phobia). These activities may also have the benefit of developing other sides of the therapeutic relationship, where the client and therapist can experience each other in ways a little outside the 'business as usual' of the therapy room. Clients often report appreciating these activities but they are also challenging and sometimes throw up unusual difficulties. One such incident occurred when a client I was with became very upset in a public place. This was a great embarrassment to him. I have found that it is helpful to plan how to handle such eventualities in advance.

Behavioural experiments should be collaboratively and clearly devised: the more precisely the client's negative belief is defined and the clearer the hypothesis about the way the belief will be tested is, the more effective behavioural experiments are likely to be. For example, a student client, Julie, believed herself to be 'inadequate' and 'worthless'. A key sign to her that she was inadequate was that she was fearful about various assessments on her course. She considered that she was much more fearful than others. She agreed to test this belief by casually asking other students how they felt about various assessments. She was amazed that not only did most other students share her fears but that some expressed them more strongly. This news forced her to review her opinion of the degree of her own inadequacy based on this criterion. In this case, the therapist had experience of teaching students in Higher Education and had good reason to suspect that the results might run this way. Therapists often, however, have to walk the line between encouraging open experiments and shielding clients from experiences that are likely to be negative. Even so, it is often helpful to plan how the therapist and client will react to an experiment that goes badly wrong.

Figure 5.1 shows a format devised by Bennett-Levy et al. (2004) and this text remains the 'bible' for helping therapists to devise behavioural experiments over a wide range of situations.

Graded task assignment (increasing quality in behavioural tasks step by step)

The CB therapist most usually aims to increase both the quantity and quality of the client's behavioural patterns. Just returning to previous functioning can seem a very big step, however, and just as we would phase a person who had been off sick back into work, so the client can plan to return to more usual functioning at a slow but steady rate. Beck et al. (1979) tell the illustrative tale of a hospital patient who said she could hardly pursue her previously favourite hobby of reading. The therapist suggested that she found the shortest book in the ward library and read some if it to him. After several demurrals, she agreed to read just one line. In the event, she read the whole paragraph and by the time the therapist had returned to her some hours later she had finished the book. The basic principles at work here are those of breaking things down into manageable units and letting success feed on success. There is an element of shaping behaviour towards desired

Date	Situation	Prediction: How will I know if my prediction comes true?	Experiment to test prediction	Outcome?	What I learned
Monday	Standing outside the supermarket	I'm feeling so bad I am going to pass out. Unless I get out of here fast then I may be very ill (90%).	Stay in the supermarket. Stop trying to do anything to control the anxiety and see what happens.	I felt quite uncomfortable but I did not pass out, or even need to sit down. I stayed there and was pleased with myself. The bad feelings went away after a few minutes. Found some nice new ice cream!	Stay with it, things are not as bad as they feel. Anxiety won't make me pass out. I enjoy things and feel good if I don't avoid and run away. Buy this ice cream again!

FIGURE 5.1 *Behavioural experiments diary (Bennett-Levy et al., 2004)*

ends by getting somewhere close to the right target and then moving by degrees as close to the final goal as possible. I often say to clients that as long as they keep moving towards the goal, even by small steps, they will keep improving.

These gradual steps can also work with rebuilding relationships after absence or illness. The importance of the interpersonal aspects of behaviour is often fundamental: maintaining friendships, meeting new people and taking the initiative when appropriate are the meat and drink of proactive social behaviour but may seem distant to clients immobilised by depression, stress or fear. So a natural, step-by-step framework of approach to reconnecting with people might be:

1. Re-contacting already established friends.
2. Taking small initiatives with established friends.
3. Taking larger initiatives with established friends.
4. Finding out about places where new friends might be contacted.
5. Taking small initiatives with new friends.
6. Taking larger initiatives with new friends.

The CB therapist can negotiate this kind of framework with the client as a series of small, low-risk steps. Such tasks may need especially careful consideration if their success is dependent on the reaction to others. It can therefore be helpful to get the client to think about whether he could cope with getting unfriendly responses to the above steps. Not everyone can handle being rejected by 99 out of 100 requests for a date, as Albert Ellis reports of the task he undertook to cure his shyness, though it is a marvellous example of robust self-concept (Dryden, 1991). Thinking about the worst that could happen often seems to put a safety net in place underneath the client, one that inhibits how far he can fall if things go wrong. The same principle of building up behaviour step by step is also used in 'exposure' therapy for fears and phobias, though in a somewhat different way that we will consider shortly.

Developing rewarding behaviours

Williams et al. (1997) make the point that depressed people do have real problems in interactions with others. These stem from the fact that when depressed they may become unrewarding social companions and may be prone to breaking various social norms regarding self-disclosure and conversational give and take. Other people may be quite sympathetic at first, but, sooner or later, tend to feel they have had enough. How quickly this stage is reached is particularly crucial for the future of the relationships between sufferers, spouses and partners. There has been some debate over whether depressed people lack social skills in this regard. This does not really seem to be the case. Rather, depressed people seem to need extra social skills, more than average, to deal with the difficulty that their own unrewarding behaviour can create. Humorous cynicism may be an example of such advanced social skills.

Evidence shows that if depressed people do not reward those around them sufficiently, they are doing no more than mirroring their own processes of failing to reward themselves sufficiently. Managing the rewards of one's behaviour to oneself is one dimension of a series of self-control strategies that seem helpful in the recovery from depression (Lewinsohn & Gotlib, 1995). Other strategies are self-monitoring and self-evaluation. The word 'reward' in the context of behavioural work often brings to mind the obliging white rat running through mazes. Humans, on the other hand, feel most rewarded by social reinforcers such as smiles, recognition and attention from others, though several colleagues and clients from continental Europe have told me that the English 'polite' versions of these qualities can cloak varying degrees of sincerity. Therapy is a useful forum where these issues can be mapped, practised and where real-world interactions can be monitored. I sometimes say to clients that I feel like a boxing coach in their corner. I towel them down, give them a swig of water and tell them to try a left hook in the next round. Most clients seem to like having support 'in their corner'. The following example from my casebook features a discussion about how the client can rehearse being more rewarding in his behaviour towards people who can help him:

CASEY was an expatriate American tradesman. He was an ex-hippy and regarded himself as 'still crazy after all these years'. He suffered from depression twinned with an explosive temper, which was frequently expressed towards difficult customers. This led him to alienate his customers to the point that he was running out of orders.

Therapist: So, Casey, this week you were going to tell me how you got on with discussing the possible work with Kareem.

Casey: Oh, hell, that was a screw up... I mean I'd reached what I thought was a pretty solid agreement with him... I knew when I could do it and gave him a price that was good for him and very tight for me... and then the next day he called to say that he was thinking of doing it another way and could I do this, that and the other... I knew what it was... he'd told Flora [his wife] and she'd come up with all her horseshit... and he was too polite to put her right... they are a freakin' nightmare, those two... so I told him that he and Flora should freakin' well sort themselves out...

Therapist: Okay then, so it's kind of back to square one...frustrating for you. But I'm wondering if that could have gone any other way... you know, we've talked before about giving people feedback they can 'swallow'.[1]... It is great that you can be forthright and we discussed how Brits may not be good at that... but that's what you've got to deal with... Do you reckon you gave Kareem feedback he could chew?

Casey: You got me there, Doc!

To some extent, the therapist is helping Casey to learn to oil social interactions with more genuine kindness and consideration. Such consideration may sometimes need to be turned towards the self in the development of what Paul Gilbert (2005) has termed 'compassionate mind'. This is a quality of inner warmth and healing towards the self and towards others, and can be cultivated to promote recovery.

It would be a shame, however, if therapists restricted themselves to only paying attention to the social dimension of rewards. Other types of 'reward' have been shown to be effective, including money rewards for cutting down on addictions (Petry, 2000). Clients can also learn self-reward to help in habit-breaking (see the section on 'constructing a personal reward system' in Butler & Hope, 2006).

When assessing why problems exist or how they may be ameliorated, it is good to consider Cicero's question, *Cui bono? (Who really benefits?).*[2] There are subtle, almost hidden rewards for some behaviours and if clients are benefiting, sometimes only in the short term (to long-term detriment), they will tend to keep those behaviours going until their perception of the benefit changes.

Strengthening coping behaviours

It is generally more helpful for therapists to stress that clients can strengthen aspects of their existing coping strategies than to talk of remedying behavioural deficits. It is quite rare for clients not to have some aspects of most coping strategies, though we know these may well be distorted or weakened by current problems and symptoms. This section will focus on the processes of helping clients to strengthen their assertiveness skills, learn to relax and use visualisation. The thoughts on visualisation will link naturally to the section on facing up to fears.

Assertive behaviours

> **GARY** had worked in the 'ideas department' of a multinational company but had lost his job when a crisis had led to redundancies. Gary felt that he had missed out because he had ceased to be a 'player' in the company hierarchy. He saw this as being due to the fact that he had always lacked the assertiveness skills that would guarantee a proper hearing for his ideas. This problem had come up during other periods of his life, such as in school, where he had been academically brilliant but unpopular with both other pupils and most of the staff. He also felt that his brother was favoured over him at home, although in later review it became apparent that this was due to the fact that the brother had many problems and had absorbed much parental attention. Now Gary had much repressed anger – almost as if he didn't really expect to get a fair hearing. At times when he needed to firmly state his views and preferences, he tended to be either passive aggressive or ostentatiously hurt.

What was missing from Gary's response was the assertive response, so that developing assertive responses therefore became a therapeutic goal. Gary began by monitoring situations that upset him in his everyday life. These included situations like not being respectfully served in shops and restaurants as well as in more pressing professional situations. They were nearly all linked to a lack of

Table 5.5   Assertive Situations hierarchy

Assertiveness task	Difficulty rating
1. Telling the boss I can't do something	100
2. Telling peers I can't do something	80
3. Asking the boss for extra resources	75
4. Telling peers I want extra resources	65

assertiveness. Client and therapist built a list of office situations in which assertiveness was difficult. These situations were arranged in a 'hierarchy' of ascending difficulty. The therapist can help by ensuring that all aspects of these situations have been considered and by asking the client to estimate the difficulty of each situation by rating each one out of 100, where 100 equals the most difficult any situation can be (see Table 5.5).

The idea that he had a right to state what he felt and what he wanted to happen was a real revelation to Gary, as was the allied idea that this did not necessarily mean that what he wanted to happen would happen. He learned how to take satisfaction in being able to state what he wanted and realised that what lay beyond that was frequently in the power of other people. We were able to role-play situations like shops and business encounters in the therapy sessions. During these role-plays Gary was able to rehearse assertive responses such as the 'broken record' (repetition of what you want regardless of what the other person says) and the empathic assertion ('Martha, I understand that this is really important to you but when you spoke to me just now, I felt that you weren't really thinking about how this might be hurtful for me and I'd really like you to acknowledge that'). This 'New Gary' was now more confident in himself but some of his workmates still thought they were dealing with 'Old Gary'. It was obviously time to introduce his colleagues to the new brand. For him, there was a 'visualisation exposure' element to rehearsing more assertive responses to his new work colleagues: he could now 'see' how he and they would be in the testing situation.

Therapy with Gary was proceeding reasonably well and we discussed the interesting question of whether the assertiveness was truly in what you say or in the way you say it. It happened that I had a supervision session just after this and my supervisor commented that it might be helpful for Gary to consider being more kind to his 'grumpy self'. We discussed this idea in the next session and it seemed to hit the nail on the head for him. He was never going to turn into the very interpersonally sensitive person implied in the measured tone of empathic assertiveness, but he could learn to be his grumpy self in a lighter-handed and more ironic way. He continued developing assertive responses but also let his grumpy side win out over his lighter way at times – especially in the more testing work situations. One colleague responded positively by saying 'Good for you' when he grumpily refused to contribute to an office charity effort and another laughed out loud when, to retrieve a mistake, he said 'I bet I irritated the hell out of you then, didn't I?'

Suggestion: Assertiveness

Form: Therapy trio or duo

Aim: Practise giving rationales for building new behaviours and constructing hierarchies of testing situations.

Instructions: After giving a rationale for building a new behaviour to the client, devise a hierarchy of four or five situations in which you would like to act in a more assertive way. Help the client to draw up a description of the 'old plan' for dealing with these situations and a 'new plan' for how they could be handled differently. Take brief feedback from all the participants in the exercise.

Relaxation

Stress is a pervasive problem in modern life. Many clients report that they have never really learnt how to relax. Indeed, for some clients, relaxation is defined as doing activities such as watching TV and gardening. Teaching some relaxation techniques can be helpful because they add an extra dimension to the client's range of positive and coping behaviours. Relaxation techniques also help in a more general way to heal some of the damage that the nervous system takes from extended periods of anxiety and depression. Part of the problem with stress reactions comes from the fact that the nervous system adjusts to operating at higher levels of arousal and thus becomes more easily primed to react. Relaxation techniques can help the client to combat these reactions by encouraging the body to operate at lower levels of arousal. Some of the methods used in CBT are:

- **Mindfulness:** The introduction of 'mindfulness' into CBT (Segal et al., 2002) has developed a more elaborated and deeper response to this problem. Mindfulness training stresses that therapists themselves must be practising mindfulness in order to be most helpful to clients in this area. Mindfulness is often practised in groups but can also be adapted for individual sessions (Fennell, 2004).
- **Progressive muscle relaxation:** This works by focusing attention on different parts of the body in a sequential fashion at the same time as tensing and relaxing muscles.
- **Breathing:** Breathing techniques use the different methods for deep breathing and holding breaths in particular sequences.
- **Visualisation:** Visualisation sessions often begin with some of the other methods described above so that the client gets into a relaxed state. The client is then encouraged to imagine various types of image that may relate to her problem issues or therapeutic goals.

There are obviously different contexts in which relaxation can be pursued, including the use of tapes and CDs. It is also useful to be able to cover relaxation in individual sessions. There are various methods that can be used. Some additional notes on practising relaxation and a list of other relaxation resources have been posted on the SAGE website accompanying this book. Sometimes clients will report that they can relax with the therapist during sessions but not at home. It is worth exploring exactly what kind of relaxation the client is doing at home. Are they giving it appropriate time and space, for example? It may also be worth offering to make a tape of the therapist conducting the relaxation as sometimes clients react negatively to voices that they do not know. It is useful for the therapist to facilitate discussion on how the client might want to incorporate relaxation into her life. Some relaxation sequences can last up to one hour and need to be practised pretty regularly (Segal et al., 2002). With in-session practice, clients can often develop much shorter versions, a few minutes even, and these become something that the client can do when faced with a particularly stressful moment at work, for example.

Another helpful method for this type of situation is visualisation. Here the client can be helped, in a state of relaxation, to call to mind a peaceful situation. Present tense, first-person language is used to intensify the feeling of being back in the remembered incident. This is a coping strategy that has general utility but can also be part of exposure therapy to feared situations or memories. Some processing therapies recommend helping clients to imagine a safe place that they can bring to mind if processing has to be suspended because they have become very upset (Shapiro, 2001). In my view, it is good to discuss this with clients because knowing how you will deal with sudden stress may well play a role in preventing it from occurring in the first place.

Whatever relaxation methods are used, it is important to collaborate with the client, offer a rationale and give the client as many choices as possible. Clients can react unexpectedly, fearing they will be hypnotised or they will betray their nervousness by laughing. These fears can result in the exercise actually making the client feel more tense. A simple way of using relaxation in sessions is for therapist and client to do an exercise together and then discuss how it might be done at home. Sometimes it is helpful to have relaxation techniques available to allow a calmer discussion of a subject that is likely to raise an overwhelming reaction. Therapists should, however, be wary of any use of relaxation that might reinforce client 'safety behaviours'. Some clients think, for example, that they can only survive a panic attack by using relaxation. This would not be helpful for the process of CBT interventions with panic because treatment is designed to show the client that panic is probably caused by their catastrophic reactions to something that is unlikely to prove harmful (Clark, 1996).

Facing up to feared situations and intrusive thoughts and images

CBT approaches are always designed to impact on specific problems and so tend to vary according to the problem. We began this chapter by looking at behavioural activation, which is used predominantly with depressed clients. The final skill area we will look at is exposure, which is used predominantly to overcome various anxiety problems.

Early behavioural therapy worked on the notion that a fear or anxiety response might be extinguished if it was paired with an incompatible but rewarding response, such as relaxation. This insight, reciprocal inhibition, was operationalised as the procedure of **systematic desensitisation**: the client is exposed to a feared situation, either for real or in the imagination ('*in vivo*' or 'imaginal'), while practising the relaxation response at the same time (Wolpe, 1958). This proved to be a successful treatment. Another tradition that was imported into CBT from behaviour therapy was that of the scientific and empirical evaluation of therapy (Rachman, 1997). Ongoing evaluation of systematic desensitisation showed that the relaxation element did not add to the overall effectiveness of the exposure element. Since those findings, CBT has naturally focused more on the exposure element of the treatment (Kendall & Hammen, 1998).

Exposure treatment puts together many of the elements we have seen in use with other methods: detailed descriptions of feared situations; a construction of a graduated hierarchy of such situations, measured in SUD (subjective units of distress) ratings. This is usually best achieved by getting the person to face the actual situations themselves. If this is not possible for various reasons,[3] it may be possible to work with simulations of the situations or by getting clients to imagine the situations as vividly as possible. It is usually helpful to do some of the exposure in therapy sessions, though the therapist may look to get the client into self-practice as soon as is reasonably possible. Sometimes it can be helpful for therapist and client to work together outside the therapy room. For me, this has involved expeditions to supermarkets, civic amenity sites and driving on roads and motorways. (One skill that might be mentioned here is that of checking with your professional indemnity insurers!) Some of my colleagues have also entered zoos and aeroplanes with clients. Devising appropriate plans can involve therapist creativity:

KAREN suffered from emetophobia: a constant fear that she would be sick or that she would witness someone else being sick during or shortly after mealtimes. As the work went on she was able to identify a number of food types that particularly increased her fear of being sick. These were incorporated into a hierarchy, part of which is shown below. We worked through this in and between therapy sessions. In therapy sessions, Karen was encouraged to reveal her thoughts and feelings during this process as well report on her SUD ratings. It was possible to do cognitive restructuring with some of her thoughts. During this time, her phobia was reduced considerably and she was able to learn coping strategies for times when it persisted. One of the things that came out of this was that the food that most repelled her was minestrone cuppa soup (MCS). This was one of the few occasions when my preparation for therapy involved cooking. I myself was forced to admit that the minestrone cuppa soup looked incredibly like sick itself. Karen also obtained a video of people being sick from an emetophobia self-help organisation. We used this for a separate hierarchy concerning the fear of others being sick. The main aspect of this hierarchy was to watch the video for slowly increasing periods of time.

Hierarchy (Difficulty ratings out of 10, where 10 is intensely difficult, in brackets):

1. Spooning out rice with chopped ham (4).
2. Touching & smelling rice with chopped ham (5).

3. Eating rice with chopped ham (6).
4. Pouring MCS into a bowl (8).
5. Touching and smelling MCS (8.5).
6. Spitting MCS out of the mouth (9.5).

A different type of exposure is described in the scenario with a client, Jana:

   JANA was an immigrant from Eastern Europe and had been involved in a car crash some three years before. She had quite severe PTSD symptoms, which included an inability to drive. This was a great inconvenience to her and led to problems with finding jobs. Her hierarchy was:

1. Sitting in the driver's seat of a stationary car (with breathing, relaxation and describing thoughts and feelings) with therapist present (3).
2. Driving around the block with the therapist present (7).
3. Driving a longer distance with the therapist (7.5).
4. Driving a longer distance without the therapist (7.5).
5. Driving to the scene of the accident with the therapist (9).
6. Driving to the scene of the accident without the therapist (9).
7. Driving by herself to final therapy session (9).

The hierarchy was achieved without too much difficulty. One interesting thing that emerged from the work was that the car she had crashed had great symbolic value to her, marking the success of leaving her own country for a new one. In PTSD work, processing the meaning of the trauma is often very helpful so that no matter how technical and behavioural this may sound, emotional and meaning level work were also taking place.

There seem to be no universal rules that govern therapist behaviour during exposure exercises. Clients tell me that they prefer it when the therapist keeps up a fairly sparse, low-key conversation. I find that asking about thoughts and feelings, as well as asking for ongoing SUD ratings seems a natural and useful thing for the therapist to do, although one should be wary not to enter any new elements into the situation that have not been pre-agreed. Unexpected therapist behaviour may throw the client right off track. It is important to stay with the exposure situation until the SUD ratings have been at least halved or, ideally, come right down to minimal levels. I have been, however, in rare situations when this was not possible. It is sometimes suggested that the therapist plans extra long (one and half or even two hours) sessions to take account of complications arising from the client becoming over aroused. This may be increasingly hard to do as demand for CBT increases – therapists now usually have tight schedules themselves. In practice, I have found that the client can nearly always suggest a fall-back plan if asked beforehand. One client I worked with decided that if she was upset, she would call work and tell them she was unwell and then have some quiet hours at home. Fall-back plans to deal with unduly intense reactions to exposure exercises have worked well. The aim, after all, is to move the client towards self-practice as soon as is practical.

Clinical hints and troubleshooting

Sometimes as you have read about these interventions, you may have asked yourself 'Where is the skill here? Isn't this just a question of giving the right form and explanation to the client?' It is a good question. My answer might surprise some. It is because these skills are potentially so mechanical that the importance of a therapeutic delivery of them is so important. We referred earlier to the myth that a CB style is cold and impersonal. There has been a wealth of evidence, from Sloane et al. (1975) to Keijsers et al. (2000), that CB therapists can be just as warm and interpersonally skilled as other therapists. It may be that CB therapists even find this stance easier than other types of therapist because the concepts they work with are more user-friendly and collaborative than is the case elsewhere. Using preset formats potentially *frees up* therapists to let the therapy run itself and be able to concentrate on the interpersonal relationship that runs alongside the use of technique.

So what are the interpersonal aspects that we are talking about? Firstly, we need to make sure that the client really does understand what he is being asked to do and why he is being asked to do it. The explanation needs to be matched to the client learning style and level of understanding. For example, with scientists we can talk about the scientific dimensions of CBT, while with clients who had a bad time at school, we can make the experience as unlike school as possible. Here again the need for collaboration shows itself as the therapist works to fit the style of CB therapy to the needs of the client – rather than working the other way round – forcing the client to fit the therapy model. Procedures like exposure can be demanding for the client and the therapist needs to be able to stand firm if questioned about their usefulness. The therapist may also need to guard against being 'talked out', that is allowing time to drift so that the task cannot be embarked upon. The trick seems to be to strike the right balance between support, understanding and challenge (Egan, 2002). This is usually just a little bit beyond the client's present comfort zone. I agree with Egan (2002) that therapists tend to underestimate the degree of challenge that clients can usually take. Listening carefully and empathically to clients paradoxically enhances the ability to challenge when necessary: hearing what they think they can take and what is really motivational to them. There is often a fear of not doing the exercise right. It is important to convey that it is not about getting it right or wrong, but about learning. It is also important for the therapist to be fallible.

Clients with anxiety problems frequently seek reassurance from those around them. CB therapists have tended to see this as a type of 'safety behaviour' and as one to be gently challenged (Salkovskis, 1996a). It can, however, seem severe to refuse reassurance, so perhaps the tone to be striven for is one of regretful and limited reassurance.

It is also useful for therapists to know that exposure therapy does not always work. A small minority of clients react badly to it and some of them experience setbacks, sometimes showing a marked deterioration in mood. It is therefore helpful to alert clients to this possibility and devise both a strategy for dealing with the setback and for trying an alternative approach to the problem. My experience has been that such clients may benefit from a short 'holiday' from exposure.

Often a different, perhaps gentler, hierarchy of steps can be devised so that they can have another attempt, and, having learnt from the previous experience, gain more success a second time.

Suggestion: Facing up to a fear

Form: Therapy duo or trio (including an observer)

Aim: Practice giving rationales for facing up to fears on a graduated basis and in constructing a graduated hierarchy to shape a new response.

Instructions: Give the client a rationale to explain why a graduated, step-by-step approach can be helpful in facing up to fears and then help the client to identify an area in which he has some kind of phobia or fear. End by asking the client if he can nominate a date by when he will have completed the first step. Take brief feedback from all the participants in the exercise.

PRACTICE TIP: Intentionality (self-efficacy plus)

One of the ways that cognitive therapy and behaviour therapy have been able to have such a beneficial alliance has been the increased understanding of the cognitive element of behaviour. As we do things, we tend to have thoughts about what we are doing and these thoughts influence the way the behaviour develops. The first great statement about this came from Albert Bandura, who showed that behavioural performance was greatly influenced by the belief we held in ourselves as being able to perform that behaviour well. This he termed 'self-efficacy'. A similar concept with reference to both client and therapist skills in therapy has been that of 'intentionality' (Ivey et al., 1997). Intentionality in this sense refers to a deliberate choice from a real and viable range of options followed by committed attempts to enact. Rather as in the practice tip for the last chapter, intentionality can be elusive and capricious, and yet the more we are able to 'see ourselves' doing something, the more likely it is that we will do it. The section below makes a suggestion about trying to maximise the chances that a specific homework assignment will be carried out. The suggestion is specific to a particular homework task but the principle is transferable to almost any intentional behaviour of client or therapist.

Enhancing scheduling tasks with intentional statements

Homework assignments require motivation and may sometimes not be completed by clients. It can sometimes help clients to visualise themselves doing the homework task. This idea is also expressed by Gary Emery (1999) in relation to using Activity Schedules to forward plan more active days. It seems to help clients to actually complete these activities if they write them down as sentences, say them and/or visualise them. Things seen in our mind's eye are more likely to come to fruition. For example, the client may produce the forward plan shown in Figure 5.2 for a particular day:

The client is then encouraged to construct the pattern for the day into a brief narrative and then speak it aloud. This can be a nice way to finish a session – on a self-efficacious and intentional note.

0600–0800	Get up, breakfast, get dressed
0800–1000	Check weather forecast, get bus to Chepstow
1000–1200	Meet Sam in pub car park and walk Offa's Dyke Path to Tintern
1200–1400	Pub lunch and walk back
1400–1600	Finish walk, bus back to Bristol
1600–1800	Have tea and rest
1800–2000	Work on Chapter 5 of my dissertation
2000–2200	Watch TV and get to bed
2200–2400	Sound asleep!
INTENTIONAL STATEMENT: I am going to have fun as well as doing work on Tuesday. I'll get up and going early. I will meet Sam for a walk and pub lunch but get back to Bristol in time to do some work on my dissertation before getting to bed in good time for a refreshing sleep after my exertions.	

FIGURE 5.2   *Example of a forward plan for a particular day*

Further reading and resources

Bennett-Levy, J. et al. (2004) *The Oxford guide to behavioural experiments*. Oxford: Oxford University Press.

Bourne, E. (1995) *The anxiety and phobia workbook*. Oakland, CA: New Harbinger, especially Chapter 4 on relaxation.

Emery, G. (1999) *Overcoming depression: client's manual*. Oakland, CA: New Harbinger.

Hersen, M. (ed.) (2002) *Clinical behavior therapy: adults and children*. New York: Wiley.

Patterson, R. (2000) *The assertiveness workbook*. Oakland, CA: New Harbinger.

The Oxford Cognitive Therapy Centre (www.octc.org.uk): For relaxation manuals and tapes, and training in CBT methods.

Notes

1   If they cannot chew and digest your feedback, they may spit it out. I thank my colleague, Amelia Lyons, for this concept.

2   Cicero used the term and concept in his defence of Milo, described in Cicero, M.T. (1975) *Murder trials*. Harmondsworth: Penguin.

3   One of my clients was phobic about flying to New York and very unreasonably (I thought) was not prepared to take me along as her guide in an '*in vivo*' exposure treatment! She got to New York none the less.

6

SKILLS FOR WORKING WITH EMOTIONS IN CBT

I did a series of workshops with Dr Beck a few years ago. He and I have private jokes that we sometimes play out when we do presentations with each other. We did one workshop in the morning and he said, 'Affect is the royal road to cognition.' He was talking about how you can't do cognitive therapy without affect being present. ... Later, in the evening, we were talking to a group that was largely psychoanalytic and he said, 'Cognition is the royal road to affect.' I just looked at him and smiled as he turned the message round to fit his audience, but in fact, both were true. Affect and cognition are wedded to each other, so that you can use affect to help figure out and guide you to cognition, you can also use cognition to help figure out and guide you to affect.
Christine Padesky (1994)

In 1997, Diana Sanders and I argued that, contrary to what critics said, CBT did pay proper attention to emotion (Wills & Sanders, 1997). Over 10 years and almost 700 clients later, I still stand by this assertion but, in retrospect, I consider that there were some aspects of our argument that were a little under-developed. I now think that CB therapists need to work harder on identifying and working with emotions, including their own, than I then thought. I am now also more aware of problems that can arise when CB therapists are not prepared to do this work. Fortunately, considerable resources are now available to us for achieving this aim. Some of these resources come from outside CBT. Concepts from emotion-focused therapy, for example, can be helpfully integrated into a more emotionally grounded version of CBT (Leahy, 2003). From within CBT, there has also been a resurgence of interest in working with emotions. This includes incorporating meta-cognitive and mindful attention to help accept anxious and other feelings (Wells, 2000), emotional processing in trauma work

(Scott & Stradling, 2000) and validation and self-soothing of extreme negative emotions (Linehan, 1993).

This chapter will begin by discussing the nature and function of 'healthy' and 'unhealthy' emotions (Greenberg, 2002). This will include discussion of the somewhat complicated relationship between thinking and feeling. It will particularly advocate the 'two minds' model of mental functioning: an approach that is now commonly shared by quite a number of different therapeutic models, as ideas about this seem to be converging. Building on the assumptions that one of the main functions of emotion is to give people information about the current state of their being in the world, the chapter will then discuss how therapists can work with both functional and problematic manifestations of such emotions. Various researchers have established a small number of 'primary emotions' – sadness, anger, fear and shame – that seem to occur most regularly as problems in therapy. Whereas CBT sometimes gives the impression that it wants to eliminate negative feelings, the chapter explores the notion that such emotions will often need to be accepted in the first place before any change work can begin. Mindfully paying attention to uncomfortable emotions can be helpful in this regard. Sometimes, however, negative emotions may need to be 'processed'. There are different formats for doing this, but here I describe a generic form of cognitive-emotional processing. Such methods have been particularly helpful in working with traumatic and shame-based emotions and examples will be drawn from such situations. Finally, extreme emotional reactions are prevalent in certain client problems areas and can be hard for both clients and therapists to handle. Methods of emotional regulation and self-soothing have been shown to be effective with extreme emotions, especially when twinned with validation of clients and, implicitly, validation of their emotions. In these situations, it is particularly helpful to see emotions as being driven by desperate attempts to fulfil unmet needs.

The nature and functions of emotion

Emotion is a form of information that tells people that there is something happening inside them or in their environment that needs to be attended to. Anxiety, for example, draws attention to possible threats in the environment and therefore has at least some survival value. In this sense even negative emotions are functional and it can be important for the therapist to help the client foster acceptance of the emotion as a first step. As argued in the previous chapter, attempts to suppress emotions may well only reinforce them. Emotional reactions seem to occur much faster than more deliberate cognitive processes, though it is hard to explain certain emotional reactions if it is not assumed that there is at least some fleeting evaluative, probably non-conscious, cognitive element. Emotions are also motivating; they often have built-in behavioural reactions: 'action dispositions'. We tend to pull away from things because we experience them as bad and move towards them because we see them as good. These reactions can happen so quickly, however, that we are only able to identify the sequence in retrospect. To some extent, what we say about our emotions may never quite fully express the visceral feeling of them. It seems most reasonable to assume some kind of reciprocal interaction between

1. Can you put a name to what you are feeling?
2. What thoughts seem to run along with that feeling?
3. What does the emotion seem to be saying to you?
4. Where in your body can you feel the emotion?
5. Does the feeling remind you of anything – memories, images or metaphors?
6. What is happening to the feeling as you notice it? Is it moving? Is it intensifying or calming down?
7. What does the emotion tell you that you need?
8. As you feel the emotion, do you want to interrupt it? Stop it? Avoid it?

FIGURE 6.1   *Helpful questions in identifying emotions*

emotions and thoughts. When emotions and cognitions are acting in harmony, humans can react instinctively sometimes and more reflectively at other times.

Emotions seem to play a key role in helping humans to identify their needs. Hunger is a good example. Physiological processes are deeply involved, triggering many different bodily reactions as well as psychological ones. The feeling of hunger is also highly effective in mobilising the appropriate action of seeking food. Similarly, anxiety seems to activate awareness of danger and the need to act to ensure safety.

The speed of emotional reaction can, however, sometimes mean that accuracy of the perception of need is sacrificed to the speed of the judgement. Anxiety sufferers typically become hyper-vigilant for signs of danger and begin to over-interpret possible environmental signals as clear and present danger. This takes us back to the need for balance in cognitive-emotional processing, as discussed in Chapter 4. Ideally, the cognitive system realistically appraises the risk as it is picked up on the emotional radar. The person may or may not then decide that the situation is dangerous enough to justify action of some kind. If the threat has not been registered in the first place, then the cognitive system would not have the chance to process it in a slower and more deliberate way. Not only can the emotional system and the reasoning system go out of balance, they can sometimes act independently of one another. Furthermore, memories may be encoded in body emotions out of conscious awareness so that, in Bessel van der Kolk's (1994) memorable phrase, 'the body keeps the score' in trauma. In PTSD, the body may be tricked into reacting as if the trauma were happening now even though the mind knows it isn't.

It should be evident by this stage of the book that CB therapists are always keen to welcome into their technical repertoire good questions that can help to open out and/or focus on any significant area of psychological functioning. Good questions for exploring emotions are shown in Figure 6.1.

The answers to these questions would help us to know what kind of **emotional schemes** a client might have. Greenberg (2002) describes emotional schemes as being a Gestalt mental organisation that contains various visceral, emotional and cognitive elements, including 'meta-emotional' information, feelings and rules about emotions themselves. This is a concept very similar to recent descriptions of schema and modes laid out by Aaron Beck (Beck, 1996). Greenberg (2002) distinguishes between 'primary' and 'secondary' emotions. The primary emotion is a basic feeling, whereas the secondary emotion might hide or suppress the primary one. A classic example is the twin emotions of hurt and anger. People, especially men, often express their hurt through anger. Indirect expression of emotion can be problematic as it can mean that the primary emotion may never be worked through or processed. As was mentioned with anxiety, the first therapeutic step is therefore often to acknowledge the presence of the primary emotion of hurt.

Cognition and emotion

From time to time, a debate arises over whether cognition has a primary influence over emotion or vice versa. Although it is possible still to find some early statements in CBT that imply cognitive primacy in emotional problems, a more widely held view now is that expressed by Beck et al. (1985: 86):

> In essence, far from being a cause of anxiety disorders, cognitive processes constitute a major mechanism by which the organism adapts itself to the environment. When a variety of factors interfere with the organism's smooth operation, it becomes the mechanism through which anxiety disorders ... are produced.

Debate limited to the simple idea of a linear model of how cognition and emotion relate to each other will be unproductive. As implied in the above quotation, a more helpful approach is that of a network model in which cognitive, emotional and other processes run alongside and are intertwined with each other. The common-sense notion of 'heart and head' seems to fit quite well with many current notions of psychological functioning. Padesky & Mooney (1998) use the terminology 'experiential mind' and 'analytical mind' to refer to the present-time emotional and fast style of processing as opposed to the more reflective and slower processing style respectively. These 'minds' can work in tandem and occasionally in opposition to each other. We all know the latter experience of conflict from situations where one might say 'My heart said yes but my head said no' (or vice versa). Similar distinctions are made by Teasdale (1996), Epstein (1998) and Greenberg (2002). Epstein and Greenberg discuss 'emotional intelligence' which, for them, is characterised by both systems working well and in harmony with each other. CB theorists have tended to show how the clear use of cognitive strategies helps clients access their analytical minds when they are overwhelmed by emotion. Current humanistic theorists have tended to move from the unreserved trust in emotions that characterised the earlier stage of their evolution to a basic trust in emotions when considered with emotional and cognitive understanding using 'reflexivity' (Greenberg, 2002). Rennie (1998: 3) defines reflexivity as 'our ability to think about ourselves, to think about our thinking, to feel about our feelings, to treat ourselves as objects of our attention, and to use what we find there as a point of departure in deciding what to do next'.

Approaches to working with emotions

Emotions are very varied so that any blanket prescription of how to work with them should be viewed with suspicion. Earlier we noted how functional and adaptive emotions can be, even ones such as anxiety that we tend of think as negative. We know from clients, however, how easily emotions can slip from being adaptive to maladaptive. A client can seem wistfully sad and gently melancholic about a loss to her life one day, only to suddenly appear suicidal a few days later. The emotion has taken on a different tone and quality and needs to be dealt with differently. Many clients show strong emotional, and cognitive, avoidance as part of their symptom pattern. Sometimes their anger seems to be a secondary emotion, covering a primary emotion of hurt or sadness. Sometimes emotions can appear instrumental and designed to articulate a need in an indirect way, as when some people cry to get other people to respond more to them. All these situations represent different aspects of emotional functioning. The following steps are therefore often helpful to the therapist:

- Identify what the client's current emotions are.
- Decide if the emotion being dealt with is healthy or unhealthy.
- If healthy, what kind of healthy processing might be useful?
- If unhealthy, is it primary, secondary or instrumental?
- If primary, might emotional regulation, cognitive restructuring, emotional regulation or changing emotion with emotion help?
- If secondary or instrumental, what other strategies might be helpful?

We have already described questions for asking about emotions. Most therapists have ready skills in this area but not all clients can identify their feelings well and accurately, sometimes because they lack 'feeling words' for an emotional vocabulary. For these situations, an **emotion log** (Leahy, 2003) can be very helpful. A basic version of such a log is shown in the following suggestion.

Suggestion: Identifying feelings

Some clients really do struggle to name feelings and to differentiate between different types and intensities of feeling. Various exercises have been devised to help clients to develop a 'vocabulary of feelings'. A very simple diary for recording feelings can sometimes be helpful in this regard. The one below invites you merely to record whether you can remember experiencing any of these feelings at any point over the last few days. It can be elaborated for a multiplicity of purposes.

	Day before yesterday	Yesterday	Today
Anxious			
Guilty			
Angry			
Sad			
Fearful			
Excited			
Happy			
Proud			

The log may help you to identify some of your emotional patterns and reflect on how well you define and understand your everyday emotions.

The distinction between healthy and unhealthy emotions can be seen in the following descriptions:

> **Healthy emotions** may be negative but tend to have a sense of freshness and newness. They are less related to 'old stuff' and seem to be clearly expressed and to be pushing the client in a certain direction. They do not interfere with the client getting help.
>
> **Unhealthy emotions** are negative but are old and familiar, relating to previous history. They feel 'stuck' and are often hazily expressed. They show destructive effects, including inhibiting the client from getting proper help.

If emotions are identified as healthy, then clients can generally be encouraged to accept and welcome them in: to let the emotions come. The therapist may not need to be too active in this process. If healthy emotions are flowing, then they are often self-correcting. As the emotions move, the client seems to naturally reach out for new, more healing meanings nested within them. The client can be encouraged to give the process proper time so that he can stay with and dwell on the feeling. The therapist can help to clarify points of meaning, perhaps reaching back to thoughts and beliefs identified in the formulation. If emotions are unhealthy, then a more deliberate strategy may be needed: cognitive restructuring, described in Chapters 5 and 7, or more active cognitive-emotional processing or emotional regulation, described below. With secondary and instrumental emotions, the therapeutic task is to get at the underlying primary emotion, for example the woman who covers hurt with anger should be encouraged to acknowledge and work with her hurt and the man who cries to get sympathy can be encouraged to acknowledge his actual needs and work out how to ask in a more appropriate way for them to be met.

The development of mindfulness has been one of the most exciting developments in CBT. At first look, a synchronicity between science-based CBT and mindfulness, strongly related to Buddhism, is a surprise. Yet the link has been there since the early days. Aaron Beck is a regular meditator and has had a recent intriguing dialogue with the Dalai Lama.[1] The wider range of strategies linked to mindfulness is dealt with elsewhere (Baer, 2006), but here we will examine a highly practical application: helping clients to deal with anxiety. This involves using the AWARE strategy devised by Beck et al. (1985) in a particular way. The AWARE strategy is a five-step process that involves:

1. Accepting the anxiety.
2. Watching the anxiety.
3. Acting with the anxiety.
4. Repeating steps 1–3.
5. Expecting the best.

The reader is recommended to read the full version of the strategy in Beck et al. (1985: 323–4). Looking carefully at the steps, we can see, however, that the client is being invited into a revolutionary new relationship with her anxiety. Anxiety has been in all likelihood regarded as a highly harmful negative state to be avoided and suppressed at all costs. We know also that, paradoxically, this avoidant and suppressing approach actually often empowers the anxiety. So instead of avoiding and/or suppressing the anxiety, the client is invited to accept, welcome and say hello to the anxiety. This is opening the person up to what the feeling has to teach her. Once the anxiety has been accepted, it should be 'watched' and acted with rather than harried and suppressed: a case perhaps of 'Feel the fear and do it anyway' (Jeffers, 1991). This also involves the client in a different relationship with the anxiety, shifting from the 'worried observer' to the 'detached observer'. The final step adds a nice cognitive finale to the procedure, giving the message that it is best to expect the best because what you fear most rarely happens.

The AWARE strategy can be used in various ways. It can, for example, be used as a behavioural experiment to test the effects of staying with the emotion of anxiety rather than trying to make it go away. Clients often think that the emotion will get out of control if they do not suppress it. Ironically, suppression and avoidance seem more often to make anxiety rebound in an even stronger form. Another use of the AWARE strategy is for clients to follow it by themselves at home. Many of my clients have found it very helpful to use it in this way. I usually introduce it in session by asking the client to close his eyes and get into a relaxed state, usually by progressive muscle relaxation (see Chapter 5). I then read out the AWARE strategy script in a gentle voice. This often has a great impact on clients and they are able to practise it at home without undue problems. It is helpful to keep coming back to the strategy and occasionally to re-use it in session, especially if an anxiety attack spontaneously arises during the session. Some clients have reported that the AWARE strategy has been one of the mainstay tactics for dealing with anxiety attacks and has also helped them develop a more mindful approach to their anxiety symptoms.

Making CBT more emotionally grounded

An aspect of CBT that sometimes prevents people from accessing its more helpful methods is the association with the psychiatric sector where emotions such as anxiety and depression are seen as symptoms to be eliminated rather than as having some kind of basis in emotions that are healthy. Behaviourists have, however, been the doughtiest opponents of psychiatric labelling (Rachman, 1997). Although much CBT is now done outside the psychiatric sector, the language associated with it can still cause problems.

When CB therapists discuss 'emotions' with other therapists, sometimes they are not talking about the same thing. Some CB therapists have argued against the accusation that CBT ignores feelings by saying that the emotions were always there because CBT dealt with problems like anxiety and depression. This argument misses the point that such emotional symptoms represent only a narrow and problematic range of emotions and have perhaps drawn us away from the tradition of regarding emotions as 'healing forces'. Other problems have arisen in the approach of CBT to emotions in that there is a danger that the emphasis on cognition in CBT may lead to incomplete treatment of emotion. If the client does not clearly identify the feeling, any transformation may prove superficial or premature. For example, a client may fear others making negative evaluations of him in a particular situation. He might then do a thought record and become convinced that people in that situation were not making such evaluations. The anxiety may, however, mask a deeper fear of evaluation itself and this may relate to shame-inducing experiences. The anxiety might also mask anger at the unfairness of evaluation or of being thrust by a third party into some situations without proper preparations. Thus the cognitive change could merely represent a change of words (semantic change) within an emotional scheme but may leave that scheme carrying the same negative meaning and emotional charge. The bad feeling has had the edge taken from it but is still as unbearable as ever. This type of change has been described as 'defensive restructuring'.

This point has been addressed within CBT theory. Ellis, for example, speaks of the need for 'elegant change' (deeper philosophical change) as opposed to change of the inferences on the periphery of deeper cognitive change (Dryden, 1991). Deeper philosophical change should allow the client to live a fuller life with as little need for defensiveness as possible. CB therapists can overcome these problems by learning to stay with and dwell in both their own feelings and those of their clients. One exercise that can help in this is the 'focusing' exercise, first devised by Gendlin (1998). This adapted version of the exercise invites us to come down from our heads into our hearts and yet to check back with our heads. I hope this doesn't sound too touchy-feely to some of my CBT colleagues. I actually come from Birkenhead.[2]

Suggestion: Focusing

1 Find some space, both physical and mental. Listen to the sound of your breath. Whenever your mind wanders, and that's what minds do, simply come back to the sound of your breath. Sit comfortably, breathe steadily from your diaphragm and relax.

2 Scan your body all over. Get the general feel of your body and then begin to notice different parts of it. Are there knots of feeling? What are they telling you? Gradually come to focus on what is your major concern as you sit there right now.

3 See if you can put words to what you are feeling – give it a clear descriptive word. If it is hard to find words, go back to the body sensations and ask them what they are saying. Keep going back between the sensation and the words that are forming. Sometimes this will come to a crescendo feeling of 'Yes that is it.'

4 Keep checking if the words are right. Let the words and the meaning flow and change if that is what they seem to want to do.

5 Keep receiving the sensation and feeling words and phrases. Let them flow and keep telling you what you are feeling and what you need.

6 Let the experience come to a close. Is it okay to close now? Afterwards check (especially with clients) was it really okay to close? What will you do if these feelings crop up again before we next meet (safety procedure)?

Cognitive-emotional processing

Focusing relates strongly to the rather old therapeutic concept that suggests that client issues should not only be identified and worked with but also should be 'worked through'. The expression 'working through' is a commonplace one in psychotherapeutic discourse yet is also perhaps one that may have a variety of meanings for different things. The various strands of meaning connected with 'working through' seem to be:

- identifying difficult feelings/painful ideas,
- holding the feeling/idea in open awareness,
- allowing the feeling/idea to develop into a new form,
- reflecting on the changing meaning of the feeling/idea,
- staying with the development of the new feeling/idea until it accommodates into a new gestalt of feeling and/or meaning.

Some other terms used in psychotherapeutic discourse for all or part of this pattern of psychological development have been 'accepting feelings into awareness', 'emotional reprocessing' and 'cognitive reprocessing'. I consider that they can be operationalised in CBT in what might be called 'cognitive-emotional processing', which is a set of therapeutic manoeuvres that has some similarities with Eye Movement Desensitization and Reprocessing (EMDR). I will illustrate cognitive-emotional reprocessing with an actual case example concerning a client, Bez, with PTSD, and will highlight relevant therapist skills in each step of the process.

Identifying emotions that may need to be processed

We have described some methods for identifying feelings earlier. The main method is by using basic counselling techniques and the skills of listening and empathic reflection. Careful listening allows the therapist to hear that certain words are 'feeling words' and are discernible because they are delivered in a different register from more factual discourse. Certain expressions seem to hang in the air because they are redolent with meaning and emotion. Sometimes this is heard in a change of tone or accent in the voice; at other times it can be detected by the presence of an unusual emphasis, phrase or metaphor. Simple reflection is often a good way of testing whether what you think you have heard as significant is indeed so.

For CB therapists there is also a second layer of empathic listening that comes from training the ear to hear cognitive patterns that we know are linked with certain types of emotion. This might be thought of as advanced accurate cognitive empathy. It comes from knowing, for example, that anxiety will be linked to the kind of thoughts that will overestimate danger and underestimate the client's capacity to cope with danger (Sanders & Wills, 2003). We dealt earlier with the difficulty that arises when a client seems unable to identify or name feelings. Another difficulty that can arise has been called the 'think/feel confusion' dilemma. This dilemma is partly a linguistic one in that saying things such as 'I feel like I am

Table 6.1   Thoughts and feelings chart

When I have a thought like...	It makes me feel...
I am not good at anything	sad
I have lost everything	depressed
I will get left out	anxious
I will be harmed by this	fearful
I will go mad	worried
he deliberately blanked me	angry
nothing goes right for me	frustrated
I have done the wrong thing	guilty

going to fail the test' has become current English usage. 'I am going to fail the test' is, however, a thought: a prediction in fact. 'I feel' probably points to a feeling of anxiety. 'I feel anxious because I think I am going to fail the test' makes complete sense but is a bit long-winded.

This is a dilemma for CB therapists because although you know what the client means, you are keen that he should be able to identify the thought and the feeling. Linking thoughts and feelings is therapeutically helpful because the client will be able to use this linkage to work on changing his feelings by changing his thinking. The language is easily understood so that it can seem pedantic to get the client to restate it. Confusion between what is emotion and what is thought, however, may hamper his ability to work with thoughts and feelings and to do thought records. The best way to clarify this point may be to help the client use written exercises such as thought records and direct where you think various statements go best, backed up by occasional but consistent explanations of the thought/feeling link. Sometimes a thought/feeling link chart such as that shown in Table 6.1 can facilitate this.

Accepting traumatic emotion/s into open awareness

BEZ was working for an international charity that sought to supply emergency aid in war zones. He could function well when he was in these war zones but, once back home, he suffered from intense anxiety, violent tempers and depression. Earlier he had served as a soldier and had been involved in military operations against guerrillas and civic unrest. The head of the charity recognised PTSD-type symptoms, placed an embargo on further service abroad and persuaded him to go for therapy. Because serving abroad meant everything to Bez, he was a reluctant client at first and, like many PTSD sufferers, showed strong tendencies to avoid thinking or feeling anything much about his problems and symptoms. He thought he couldn't be having PTSD symptoms because he coped with war zones so well.

1. Identify the excluded feeling.
2. Discuss the possible reasons for exclusion, e.g., family rules about emotion, etc.
3. Discuss the pros and cons of allowing the emotion in.
4. Ask clients if they are willing to try feeling it – 'to see what happens' – but make it clear that clients can come out of the feeling by simply asking to refocus on something else.
5. Encourage clients to stay with the feeling without evaluating it.
6. Ask clients to indicate when they have 'had enough' and finish accordingly.
7. Review the experience and reconsider any emotional rules identified in step 2.

FIGURE 6.2   *Bringing excluded feelings into open awareness*

The therapist now helps Bez to bring his emotions into open awareness, by getting him into a relaxed state by using relaxation routines and by instituting a 'safe place' procedure. A similar procedure was described in Chapter 5 in relation to exposure therapy: a procedure with some similarities of purpose to that described here. The therapist can then introduce the idea of bringing troublesome emotions (especially anxiety) into awareness. The therapist should stress that the aim is to make this a non-fearful and mindful sense of awareness with as little evaluation as possible. Bez described arriving at this sense of new awareness of his emotional hurts by saying:

> I began to realise that I had these wounds (moving his hand over his chest) all over my body. The wounds were not physical but they were deep and open and painful. I'd been trying to ignore them but now I was looking at them and thinking, 'My God, I have been wounded. I need to set about some healing.'

Clients are invited to allow the emotions to come and then to 'just watch' and/ or 'just notice' them. The emotions should be monitored, again just noticing that they are rising or falling in strength. The client may stay in this process for as long as it is tolerable: usually it *is* tolerable because holding the emotions in this way often results in them starting to subside naturally. If they do not start receding, the therapist should take the client to the 'safe place' that he has been asked to imagine before starting and/ or simply end the procedure and talk about low-key matters until the client begins to resettle. Therapist and client should review the experience of the session – whatever way the session has gone. If successful, they can plan to use it again and/or the client can try to develop it as home practice. If not successful, they can discuss whether it is worth trying again and, if so, what amendments might be helpfully included in a revised version.

> **BEZ** was able to develop this way of letting his anxiety in and then watching it with detached mindfulness, at least during therapy sessions. He did report ongoing problems outside sessions and also began to talk about traumatic experiences in and before his soldiering days.

At this point the focus of therapeutic work switched from being a form of anxiety management to a more specific form of cognitive-emotional reprocessing.

Holding the experience/feeling and allowing it to unfold (reprocessing)

> **BEZ** described a combat experience when his best soldier buddy was killed in an ambush. As he described the events, a remarkable and rather scary transformation came over him. His voice became a strained and hoarse whisper. He was sweating heavily and shaking violently so that water appeared to be cascading from his head like a fountain. The therapist fortunately understood that he was processing traumatic memories and indeed was in some senses back there in the combat zone.

Literature on the 'emotional processing of fear' (Foa & Kozak, 1986) says that this kind of processing seems to be most healing when there is reliving (that is., of the original experience) plus cognitive restructuring. Descriptions of the pioneering work of Dr Rivers with First World War shell-shock victims read along uncannily similar lines (Slobodin, 1997).[3] This reprocessing work can enable the client to feel something like the feeling of fear of the real situation and simultaneously to access new information regarding the situation of fear, for example, that the situation was, or at least is now, more benign than it feels. It is also, however, recognised that the restimulated feeling of fear can reach such intensity that it blocks processing and healing. Hence the therapist emphasises a secure therapeutic relationship and uses the 'safe place' procedure. As the client views these traumatic events, there may be a cinematic dimension to the processing. Some clients have described watching traumatic images as if they were from a film being projected on to the walls of the room they were in. The therapist can encourage this feeling because it usually aids processing, but at the same time can ask good questions – such as 'What can you see?', 'Who is there and what are they doing?' and 'What does the image seem to mean?' – that can promote information (cognitive) processing. The therapist can ask the client to explore the meaning of the events he is reliving and can get the client to identify core beliefs that they seem to symbolise (Ehlers & Clark, 2000; Shapiro, 2001). In this case, Bez identified the beliefs 'The world is full evil men' and 'I too am an evil man.' In this case, the first belief is directly understandable, whereas the second points to some as yet unknown area of experience and possibly relating to another area of trauma.

At this moment, Bez must have been experiencing feelings of such intensity that they could have blocked effective processing. The proof of the pudding is, however, in the eating and at the end of this session Bez reported himself to be exhausted but relieved. Yet he reported subsequently that he was still experiencing considerable problematic symptoms between sessions. These on-going symptoms pointed to the possibility of another area of as yet undisclosed trauma.

Reporting on their early experiences of working with trauma and abreaction, Breuer and Freud (Breuer et al., 1982) developed the 'talking cure' but also referred to it as 'chimney sweeping': the clearing of blocked mental passages in order that experience should flow naturally. The analogy is a good one and is matched in current EMDR terminology by the term 'channel clearing'. The idea of channel clearing implicitly holds that there are usually several, often related, channels of trauma that may need to be cleared. In CBT, we would conceptu-alise these different channels as having different meanings and different links to networks of feeling, beliefs, sensations and behaviours. Trauma stories in their raw unprocessed state are characterised by fragmentation and haziness (Brewin, 2003). Increasing clarity and coherence of the story are associated with healing. It seems that traumas often nestle within each other and so uncover-ing and reprocessing trauma may turn out to be like peeling off several layers. Sometimes this peeling back reveals new and unexpected layers of meaning and thus it was with Bez.

> **BEZ** came back after the session duing which he had felt intense emotions and told me that he had reached the conclusion that the death of his friend was not the original cause of his trauma but that there was 'something else'. He was initially very reluctant to say what this was but eventually he revealed that he had lost his soldierly discipline on the following evening and fired a plastic bullet directly into a crowd of rioting demonstrators. The 'rules of engagement' were that soldiers should shoot into the ground so that the plastic bullets would not kill. (They could kill if shot directly at people.)

Reflecting on the changing meaning of the traumatic event

Over a number of weeks therapist and client kept returning to this memory of the event of that traumatic night of the riot. The therapist began by getting the client to relax and visit his safe place and would then ask if he felt ready to return to the night of the traumatic event. The traumatic event had now shifted to the night after Bez's friend had been killed: the night that he shot into the crowd of demonstrators. The central point in the re-telling of the story was always the moment when he shot into the crowd but now the memories surrounding that moment gradually returned in greater and greater detail. This seems to be a normal and healthy aspect of re-telling and filling out the trauma story.

> **BEZ** now began to remember a lot more about events surrounding the event: the situation in the country at that time (the early days of the civil war), the people involved and the training they had (or, more accurately, not had) to deal with the type of situation they were in. He began to see that he and his 'badness' were less central to events than as he had been viewing them: as a soldier, he was part of a much larger social-political system with many points of badness and goodness on all sides. He also began to talk more about his school years and adolescence and how, he now realised, he had become a soldier 'quite unthinkingly'. He was still very unhappy and greatly troubled by all this, but both he and the therapist felt that this was a bad memory that had been stuck but that was now developing and moving. Bez said, 'It's very strange, you know, it is still horrible but it feels as if some fresh air is getting in there now.'

Staying with it until a major shift (accommodation) comes

Sometimes therapist and client need to persist in staying with traumatic events that may need to be processed more completely. Therapists might feel that healing is developing but can never be quite sure when the decisive corner will be turned. There is something about working with PTSD that adds an extra dimension of unpredictability.

> **BEZ** kept coming to therapy and going over the same trauma story and seemingly the same old ground. The therapist was becoming a little unsure whether any further progress could be made, though Bez himself remained solidly sure that it would. Then, in a session, he remembered a small detail about the operation that evening. As he was climbing into the troop carrier that took them down to the area of the riot, an officer had stopped them, looked in the vehicle and said, 'This is our chance to get our own back.' Bez was quite sure that the comment referred to the death of his friend on the evening before and that it amounted to a semi-official encouragement to hurt or even kill a rioter when they went out on the patrol.

The therapist felt sure that an important point had been reached: the knowledge that Bez had been part of a political-military system responding to social turbulence had general and impersonal relevance to Bez, whereas the officer's intervention was very personal and especially significant in that the command structure of armed forces generally requires soldiers to follow orders from officers. He could now begin to forgive himself and to see himself as a 'small man in a big conflict' and a man who was 'not wholly evil' but subject to the same terrible dilemmas and pressures as are other men in these situations. As a mark of respect to him, I should add that he did not regard this as an excuse. In fact, he also remembered that a non-commissioned officer, a man he greatly respected, had seen him fire the rubber bullet into the crowd and had given him a severe dressing down and added 'never mind what the officer had said'. Nonetheless, the tectonic plates of meaning had shifted and this was signalled by the fact that Bez now moved on to various other traumas that had occurred when he was a member of a violent gang during his adolescence. He never returned to combat experiences – the chimney had been finally swept clean of them. A few weeks later, Bez ended therapy because he was about to be sent off by the charity organisation to another war zone. We conducted some follow-up therapy by email. The fact that he was going to a war zone again was significant because his boss had vowed not to send him abroad again until he was coping with home much better. The last that I heard from him was that he was continuing to be well and was finally planning to marry and cease his foreign travels.

Imagery and shame

When the therapist asked Bez to name the most difficult emotion that he felt during the worst of processing his trauma, he named it as 'shame'. Shame is a frequently reported feeling in therapy, especially when various types of trauma and childhood abuse come up. CB therapists are increasingly addressing emotions other than those in the *DSM*. Paul Gilbert, for example, has developed a thorough-going conceptualisation of shame from a cognitive perspective (Gilbert, 2006). Shame often seems to have a strongly visceral sense of being contemptuously looked on by others as being bad, flawed, inferior and inadequate. Clients often need to undergo some kind of 'de-shaming' process and, additionally, to develop an increased sense of internal empathy: what Gilbert has called the 'compassionate self'. Some clients may be particularly ready to engage with their emotions via imagery, often an ideal medium within which to work with shame. The therapist can help the client to recreate a vivid and emotionally felt scene. This might be a historical event but might also be an imaginary scene that contains the key meaning elements involved in the client's shame. This 'scene' might automatically begin to 'process', as we described in the earlier section, but sometimes the painful images just keep 'looping'[4] and it then may be helpful to give the process some forward momentum out of the loop by introducing 'imagery rescripting' (see Suggestion box below).

OWEN always felt on the outside of the peer group when he was at school. Partly in retaliation to this, he had developed into what he called a 'shy and nerdy boy'. Unfortunately, his classmates reacted to this by calling him 'Nonce', which he did not really understand other than the fact that it was a severe put down. He was increasingly ostracised and this culminated in an incident when he was surrounded by classmates chanting 'Nonce, Nonce, Nonce' at him. He had never been able to face this jibe without showing hurt and now saw that he was powerless to stop it. It would only stop when the group decided it had hurt him enough. A particularly hurtful point was that even the one or two friends he had in the group had joined in the chanting.

Years later, in therapy for persistent obsessional worry, this scene kept coming to Owen's mind and he and the therapist decided that it might contain some

(Continued)

(Continued)

kind of unprocessed shame that might be contributing to his current anxiety. The therapist led him into an imagery exercise in which, by speaking in the first person and the present tense, he was able to reconstruct the experience in startling clarity. The image, however, remained stubbornly unchanged and his distress remained high. We therefore began to rescript the scene by seeing it as part of a television programme in which a commentator reconsidered the various motives of the actors involved and went on to find out what had happened to them since. In brief, the friend who had 'betrayed' Owen explained how he had been scared not to join in with the chanting and how he had tried to make it up to Owen in various ways afterwards. Owen could now remember various actual ways in which this friend had signalled to him that 'he didn't really mean it'. It also turned out that the ring-leader of the group, who had come from a difficult background, had developed various problems, including alcohol addiction, in more recent years. Owen occasionally saw this man and recognised that an unspoken understanding of these facts flowed between them.

Owen subsequently reported that the imagery rescripting had been very meaningful to him and that it had, along with other parts of the therapy, helped him to gradually get on top of his recurrent anxiety symptoms.

Suggestion

Identify an embarrassing or shameful situation you have been in. Stay with the feelings associated with this event. What was the loss of face that you suffered here? Is there a critical voice somewhere? Speak back to it from a grounded sense of self. If this was an actual event, try to reconstruct it as vividly as possible. Go for detail: What was the weather like? What were you wearing? Who was there? What were they doing? How might you like to change this scene? Would you like to bring someone in to help? What do you need? Bring it in. We can be as creative as we wish to be when using imagery. As the scene changes, does the feeling change? Does the meaning of what is taking place change? If so, and the change is helpful, how can you wrap this up and put it in a place that you can draw strength from?

Trauma and shame are intense emotions. So too is the feeling that goes with abandonment. Sometimes clients need to be able to soothe such emotions so that they can tolerate them long enough to undertake reprocessing work.

Self-soothing and extreme emotions

Extreme mood swings are one of the features of borderline personality disorder (BPD). There is a similar tendency to swing in relationships between 'idealisation' and 'devilisation' of the other. Clients with borderline symptoms may approach a potential partner in a very intimate way, only to pull sharply away as they begin to wonder if they are getting too close. This is confusing and difficult for the other person to read and they may decide that the relationship is not worth their effort and reject the client, thus confirming her 'abandonment schema'. As many of these clients have experienced abusive childhoods, they often have both 'emotional deprivation' schema and 'mistrust' schema. These schemas act as antagonists, on the one hand, driving the client to move closer to others, but, on the other, to keep a wary distance. (These types of schemas will be described further in Chapter 7).

The elements of this formula are difficult to reconcile and are almost guaranteed to keep the client in a constant state of high and undulating emotion. Although I have described this as a feature of BPD, I have found that many clients display this kind of pattern without justifying a full diagnosis. In any case, strategies that help clients deal with these situations as they arise will be very helpful to many clients. Linehan (1993) has described an overall approach to BPD as 'dialectic behaviour therapy' (DBT). It is not appropriate to attempt a full description of this model here, but we can profitably draw on two of her key strategies that impact on extreme emotional swings: validation and self-soothing.

One of the reasons why validation is so important to trauma survivors is that they have frequently been in very invalidating environments. Linehan (1993) sees her validation concept as being 'dialectical' in that it tries to be neither wholly change orientated nor acceptance orientated. If the therapist stresses the need for change, then the client is partly invalidated in that the client is not accepted as she is. On the other hand, an approach that is overly accepting may be taken as saying that it is okay for the client to stay as she is: this may be seen as not taking seriously the client's pain in living. To some extent the therapist's attitude should oscillate between these two attitudes, though helpful middle ground can be found by stressing that the client's responses to her situation *do* make sense of her life situation as it is now. It can also be helpful to acknowledge the kernel of truth in the client's extreme responses to her current life situation. Such clients may also have an uncanny ability to pick up negative therapist responses. Since working with them can be difficult, it may be just as well for therapists to acknowledge the kernel of truth in these observations too.

Accepting strong emotional responses that may swing from one extreme to another can begin to defuse the client's cycle of avoidant and/or emotionally suppressing reactions, and the inevitable empowerment of the negative emotions that results from such strategies. The client can then begin to practise 'distress tolerance' strategies: distraction, self-soothing, improving the moment and focusing on the pros and cons of staying the same and changing (Linehan, 1993). Here we will focus on self-soothing skills. References on the other skills are included in the further reading section at the end of the chapter.

The skills of self-soothing are essentially about comforting oneself as well as nurturing and being kind to the self. It is important to note that some clients may have had very little previous experience of being soothed and comforted in ways such as a mother might use 'kissing it better' to soothe a child's bruised leg. Kohut (1977) gives a convincing account of how parental soothing gradually builds up knowledge of how wounds, internal and external, can be healed and soothed (Kahn, 1991). Soothing is a very visceral matter. Touch has especially powerful healing effects. The smell of baking can carry the experience of 'someone is baking me a cake' and the meaning 'the baker cares for me, or likes me or thinks I'm special'. Self-soothing techniques therefore often use the following sensory modalities (listed with examples):

SMELL: Experience the smell of baking.
TOUCH: Stroke a friendly animal. Put on some clothes that feel good next to your skin.
HEARING: Listen to some soothing music, music that you associate with good times. If you are near some flowing water, that sound can be soothing.
TASTE: Now eat that cake or some other sensuous and textured food.
VISION: Look out over a favourite view or appreciate a favourite painting.

The idea is to enter into another sensory-emotional modality, moving away from the pain of extreme negative emotions into a more sensual and comforting modality. When working with clients, the therapist can sense that they are moving into a painful area and sometimes it can be helpful to acknowledge this and ask them if they really want to go there. It may be appropriate to move closer to them with a gentle presence and ask them to make eye contact and return to the present moment. This is an immediate response that is only possible in the present moment of the session. The list above shows similar redirection techniques that do not need a therapist or a therapy session. This list is obviously just one set of examples and the therapist should help clients to generate lists of self-soothing activities that they feel could help them. It is also wise to anticipate reactions that might be quite idiosyncratic. For example, some clients might make a cake and then go into self-critical mode if it does not seem as tasty as the ideal. Some clients may really feel that they do not deserve to feel soothed or to feel pleasure, sometimes because of family or personal rules that have said this. The general principle is that it is good to generate lots of different responses so that if one does not work, clients can simply go on down the list until they find one that does.

The meta-message is that there *are* things that you can do to overcome these feelings that make you feel so helpless. They won't always work perfectly every single time, but at least you will have things to try – forewarned is forearmed. It is also important for therapists to keep reviewing and reflecting on the experience of using self-soothing. Humanistic therapists have argued that 'changing emotion by emotion' is more effective than changing emotion by cognition (Greenberg, 2002). I personally have an open mind on this question, though I suspect that different strokes will work with different folks. In any event, as we are evidenced-based practitioners, we should be open to whatever might work best with our clients.

> ## Suggestion
>
> Go to the list of self-soothing suggestions above and construct such a list for your-self. Try to pick out a range of things that you think it might help to do if you end up feeling low or upset this week. Try to give at least one of these soothing techniques a try over the next few days and, when you do it, try to do it as mindfully as possi-ble. Review the experience with a colleague and ask about their experiences of 'changing emotion with emotion'.

Conclusion

This chapter has made the case that, in order to be effective, CB therapists have to develop emotional intelligence and apply it to their therapeutic interventions. Sometimes this can involve finding ways of working round the client's, even one's own, emotional avoidance, sometimes helping the client to find and really feel the core feeling and sometimes helping the client to manage emotions when they seem overwhelming. This does not involve abandoning any cognitive or behav-ioural methods but ensuring that all such interventions are emotionally grounded. Although the importance of emotions has always been stressed in CBT, there are some points where it is quite easy for the CB therapist to stray into premature closure of emotions. The best way for CB therapists to avoid these pitfalls is to commit to more reflexivity in relation to their own emotions and to build an emotionally grounded version of CBT from there.

Just as people cannot live by bread alone, so too can they not live by emotion alone, or by reason alone Greenberg (2002: 29).

PRACTICE TIP: Dealing with a client's requests for reassurance about anxiety

In Chapter 3, we explored the notion that specific client behaviours and emotions are likely to 'pull' certain types of response from therapists. Such behaviours and emotions may even have evolved from the need to reach others in a particular way. Because of the success of CBT in many of the anxiety disorders (Sanders & Wills, 2003), CB therapists are often asked to work with clients with anxiety problems. One of the main criteria for most of the anxiety disorders is 'avoidance', and this may be behavioural avoidance (for example, avoiding going to parties because one has felt uncomfortable at them previously), emotional avoidance (suppressing any feeling or anxiety)[5] or cog-nitive avoidance (refusing to even think about things connected with anxiety). Safety behaviours and reassurance-seeking can also be seen as avoidance. Anxiety sufferers tend to develop reassuring-seeking behaviours with people who are important to them (they reason that if a favoured person says it will be okay, then it probably will be) so that sooner or later an anxious client is quite likely to seek reassurance from the therapist. In one way, this seems quite natural and it seems only human to say that things probably will be okay. Reassuring therapist responses work up to a point but they can also easily slip over into the unhelpful. The usual signs of this happening are:

- the therapist notices that this is a repeating pattern and there are signs of it becoming a self-perpetuating one,
- the therapist starts to feel constricted by the requests or inauthentic about her responses. There may be an anxiety that the client will implode if there is no reassurance or that the relationship will not hold.

The best way to think about reponding to these requests may be to:

- use immediacy to raise your feeling about the pattern that may be running directly with the client,
- initiate a problem-solving process on how clients can develop self-reassuring and/or self-soothing processes.

One of my clients recognised that her way of dealing with her anxieties about her teaching sessions was to ask her partner to reassure her that the sessions had gone well. On reviewing this process, she realised that nothing he could say could reassure her in any real way – because he wasn't present at the teaching session. Furthermore, it put pressure on their relationship because it required him to make an inauthentic response. She decided there and then never to do this again and reported afterwards that that was the auspicious moment when she began to put her social anxiety behind her.

Further reading

Greenberg, L.S. (2002) *Emotion-focused therapy: coaching clients to work through their feelings*. Washington, DC: American Psychological Association Press.
Leahy, R.L. (2003) *Cognitive therapy technique*. New York: Guilford Press, especially Chapter 8 on emotion-processing techniques.
Linehan, M.M. (1993) *Dialectical behaviour therapy for borderline personality disorder: client manual*. New York: Guilford Press, especially the section on emotional regulation techniques.

Notes

1   A DVD of this event entitled 'A Meeting of Minds: Aaron T. Beck and His Holiness the 14th Dalai Lama in Conversation' (2005) is available via bokvideo@cognitivterapi.se.
2   The same town as Lily Savage, not a place where touchy-feely is a dominant paradigm!
3   Also described in Pat Barker's brilliant novel, *Regeneration* (Barker, 1992).
4   More research is needed on why certain people seem to 'loop' during processing. One cause of looping that I have encountered is ongoing pain. As one client put it to me, 'How can I come to terms with this when the pain is with me every single day'.
5   Unfortunately successful suppression often has a 'rebound effect' that makes the feeling stronger than ever.

7

SKILLS FOR WORKING WITH ENDURING NEGATIVE PATTERNS

Lord Stevens ... will say his inquiry[1] was justified because 'it will put an end to conspiracy theories'. I wish him luck, but I have studied Holocaust denial and its modern equivalent, the denial of the Serb massacres of the Bosnian Muslims, and learnt that no amount of evidence can shake true believers out of their fantasies.

Nick Cohn, 'There's no telling some people', Observer, 4 June 2006

When we traced out longitudinal formulations in Chapter 2, we saw that there was a different type of cognition – an early maladaptive schema – at the top of the diagram. In CBT, the term 'early maladaptive schema' has evolved to mean a cognitive structure, usually derived from early experiences that carry highly general and rather primitive meanings. These meanings may be expressed in the form of core beliefs. When these schemas are negative, they are often highly resistant to change. CBT strategies for changing negative schemas use similar methods to those used for changing negative automatic thoughts (NATs) and assumptions but also new methods have evolved. This chapter will begin by elucidating certain aspects of schemas that are necessary to bear in mind when we are working to change or modify them. It will then discuss some of the main skills needed to identify early maladaptive schemas, including the skills of using imagery. The chapter will describe methods of schema change and modification. The interpersonal theme of Chapter 3 will be revisited as we consider how early maladaptive schemas can affect the therapeutic relationship. Some of these affects may be negative and yet, if firmly grasped, they can be turned to therapeutic good. Methods for working with the negative content of early maladaptive schemas will also be described, including the use of continua, historical tests of a schema, psychodrama and role-play (Padesky & Greenberger, 1995).

There has been a debate in CBT about whether it is useful to use the term 'personality disorders'. This is a complicated matter but in general I prefer to use the term 'schema-driven issues'. I think that CBT has played a useful part in helping to defuse some of the negative stereotypes connected with personality disorders by focusing on core beliefs that are linked to problematic personality patterns (Beck et al., 1990). Understanding these schematic beliefs not only makes sense of various personality styles, but may help establish targets for change (for a fuller account of these issues, see Sanders & Wills, 2005). Some writers about schema-focused work have drawn a distinction between 'standard cognitive therapy' and 'schema-focused therapy', with the latter involving longer-term work and different running orders for interventions[2] (Young et al., 2003). At present, I have an agnostic stance towards the usefulness of this distinction. In my own practice, I have found it possible to use schema-focused methods in both short- and long-term work and I have not found it particularly helpful to think in terms of two different types of ordering of interventions. I have, however, found it useful to vary different types of interventions in relation to the idiosyncratic needs of individual clients. My feeling is that American therapists are more ready to use the term 'personality disorder' than are European therapists, and this may lead them to see more need for variation in the delivery of CBT. I state my position as 'agnostic', however, based on the limited evidence of my own practice and the practice of those I have supervised and taught. There are some therapeutic contexts – especially of clients who have been hospitalised for long periods – of which I have little experience.

The nature of early maladaptive schemas in CBT

The word 'schema' may have been first used in a psychological context by Bartlett (1932) in his work on memory. He used his famous example of a story called 'The war of the ghosts' to show that memory worked on the basis of straight recall *and* story reconstruction based on previous memory structures, 'schema'. Beck et al. (1979) used the schema concept to theorise how certain clients would have a vulnerability to think in a 'depressogenic way', involving the 'cognitive triad' of negative thoughts about the self, the world and the future. This tendency did not show itself all the time but could be triggered, especially when already in a negative mood. Although this is a highly plausible concept, it is only fair to say that it has been hard to demonstrate it experimentally and there is a 'chicken and egg' quality about the idea that the 'cause' of depression is only evident once depression has begun. As in other parts of CBT, work on cognitive and schematic processes is helping us to build a more sophisticated version of what is already a useful clinical concept (Wells, 2000). It is probably wisest to regard the early maladaptive schema concept as a very useful clinical metaphor. I also agree with Ian James' (2001) cautions about schema-focused work in that it seems to induce in some neophyte therapists a truly alarming tendency to engage in 'amateur psychoanalysis'. There is much in schema work to be excited about, but there is also much to be modest and cautious about.

In the original formulations of cognitive therapy, the term 'schema' covered both what we now think of as 'assumptions' and 'core beliefs'. Now although terminology is not completely universal, most CB therapists describe early maladaptive schemas as being an overall structure that contains unconditional core beliefs (for example, 'I am bad') and conditional beliefs or assumptions (e.g., 'If I can please people, then people may think I'm okay'). Both these beliefs may, for example, occur within a 'worthlessness' schema (Young et al., 2003). There is an increasing understanding that early maladaptive schemas are network reaction patterns that result in vague, gut and visceral feelings about the self. This is probably because they evolved during early experience, sometimes before the client had much vocabulary to describe them. They have therefore been recorded in consciousness as physical feelings.

CHRISSY found that she got a depressed feeling when she was caught in the rain and cold while shopping. I knew that she had an abusive childhood and asked her if there was anything in her memories that might trigger her into a feeling about being wet. She went into a very strong early memory about being locked outside her parents' bedroom in a cold house. Her parents would some-times lock themselves away for hours, she thought, to have sex. On this day, she had a very wet nappy and soon became sore in the cold. She had wept in pain and called to her parents to attend to her but they just laughed. She was never completely sure that the memory was germane to her feeling of depres-sion in wet weather now, but we merely noted that the feeling was very simi-lar. Ongoing work with Chrissy focused on helping her to learn to regulate her emotional mood swings more, partly by developing more self-soothing skills (Linehan, 1993). This was longer-term work and, though she made some progress, Chrissy was not able to maintain a commitment to it beyond a couple of months.

In time, such raw experiences may be retained in the form of core beliefs, that is, with a characteristically dichotomous nature – and may be related to the black-and-white thinking associated with the language of early childhood. Early maladaptive schemas can therefore be particularly difficult to change. There seem to be various schema maintenance processes that strengthen this resis-tance to change. Negative schemas may operate in a homeostatic way, for exam-ple, by distorting positive data so that they do not have to change.[3] Positive data seem to bounce off early maladaptive schemas and are not therefore noticed or stored by the client. Data that do enter the early maladaptive schema tend to be distorted along the same lines as the cognitive distortions described in Chapter 4.

We need to think of *weakening* early maladaptive schemas, as a first step, while at the same time building up more functional, alternative schemas. Once these new structures start to build, even if in only a small way, there is then an address at which positive data can be delivered and stored. It is important that an alter-native schema builds up into a relative robust structure that can keep on devel-oping. Because they have been encoded at very deep levels, however, we need to prepare clients for the likelihood that negative schemas will never completely be left behind. It is more useful to think in terms of developing a different relation-ship with such schemas.

> GLENDA told me about various very upsetting childhood experiences that resulted in her being sent away from the family home by her stepmother. This treatment was in marked contrast to that afforded to her more attractive, older sister. Glenda said that she had come to believe that 'I am not as good as other people' and that, further, she believed this belief would never be 'rooted out'. Later in the session, she said that she had to fight her desire to be a perfect mother in order to be a 'good enough' mother.
>
> Therapist: You know, earlier you said that your belief in your inferiority couldn't be eradicated. In a sense, I agree with you about that. It might be hard to completely shake it off but I wonder if you may be able to develop a different relationship with it?
>
> Glenda: How do you mean?
>
> Therapist: Well, did you perhaps develop a different relationship to the idea that you should be a perfect mother?
>
> Glenda: Oh, well, I suppose I did. Obviously, I wanted to be the best kind of mother I could be but wanting to be perfect just put me on edge all the time.
>
> Therapist: But it is not like that now. How did you pull that one off?
>
> Glenda: Mmm... (Silence) I suppose that I just got more able to wear motherhood lightly or something like that.
>
> Therapist: So might it be possible to wear not feeling as good as others more lightly?

Therapists may experience more resistance from clients undertaking schema work. Clients may be hooked into playing along with them and may need to have a strategy for consciously weaning off schematic behaviour. A negative early maladaptive schema may be compared to a relationship with an old acquaintance that always seems to have a negative hold over us. At some point we realise that we don't get anything out of this relationship but we can't always stop them from popping up in our lives every now and again. They will keep trying to exert the old negative hold over us but we can inhibit them from doing that by, firstly, not engaging with them any more than we have to, and, secondly, by giving less weight to the old negative jibes. If possible, we may even be able to get on the front foot and give them a bit of their own back.

Working with negative assumptions (conditional beliefs)

One way of thinking about negative assumptions, or 'rules of living' as they are also called in CBT, is to see them as compensation devices to help people cope with their negative core beliefs. Thinking things like 'I am bad' and 'Other people will not help' and 'The world is a hostile place' are themselves bleak beliefs to have to live with. If people really believe them, then only a minimally satisfying life may be possible. Even within these bleak landscapes, however, the human spirit will often reach for hope so that it would be natural for people to start to think 'Okay, I may be a bad person, but perhaps there is a way that I can at least get other people to see me as at least okay and, if I succeed in this, perhaps I may even be okay in some kind of way.' Mary, mentioned previously, in her desperation came to believe that she was not as good as other people (worthlessness schema) yet, in some part of her mind, she also knew that in many ways she did seem at least equal to some others. The problem was that, as hard as she tried (too hard probably), she couldn't seem to get the feedback from other people that would have confirmed this small suspicion that she was as good as at least some of them. Nevertheless, she kept coming back to the hope that, one fine day, she might achieve this and the effort was bolstered by a conditional belief, or assumption, that 'If I keep trying really, really hard to please people, one day some of them will give me some positive feedback.' Later we were able to try some behavioural experiments to test her negative belief that, if she were to act more confidently, she would only be put down. Not only did this not prove to be the case but, paradoxically, acting in a more confident and playful manner resulted in positive feedback (see Chapter 3).

Identification of assumptions via the downward-arrow technique

When working with a client's negative automatic thoughts, a therapist may often wonder exactly *why* they make the client feel quite so bad. The answer to that question may well be that something even more disturbing lurks underneath the negative thought and that thing is usually an unhelpful assumption. The method for identifying unhelpful assumptions is through the 'downward-arrow technique' (Burns, 1999a, 1999b). This method essentially takes the above question in the therapist's mind and keeps asking it in an iterative manner until the client's thoughts reach 'the bottom of the ladder'. The following case example comes from work with a 30-year-old client, Bruce, who was referred for social anxiety problems. Bruce was born with a congenital defect that meant that his teeth didn't grow properly. They all had to be removed and replaced by false teeth when he was 9 years old. Bruce felt very conscious of this defect, as he called it, and was always fearful that people would find out. He tried to cover this up and initially did not even tell the therapist about it, despite the fact that it was a major driver for his social anxiety. He had come to therapy after a relationship (which he was hopeful would develop) had broken up out of the blue. He had received a 'Dear John' letter in which his girlfriend told him that she was sorry but she no longer felt the same about him.

Therapist: So when you were feeling so fed up and thinking about your girlfriend, what was going through your mind?

Bruce: I was thinking that she has really seen me, you know, seen me for what I am and she couldn't possibly want me.

Therapist: Right so she has seen you for what you are and does not want you? What was so very bad about that?

Bruce: You're joking! I wanted her and she didn't want me.

Therapist: Yes, I can see that is bad but what is so very bad about it that makes you depressed?

Bruce: It is just another example of someone not wanting me. It looks like no one will ever want me.

Therapist: And if no one will ever want you, what then?

Bruce: I'll be on my own for ever. And that will prove I'm defective.

So here, Bruce's unhelpful assumption is that 'I am defective and will always be left alone.' As well as getting this out, therapy moved forward because Bruce made clear his self-feeling of being 'defective', an unusual word and one that points towards a 'defectiveness schema' (Young et al., 2003). The therapist reflected the word back to Bruce and this finally led Bruce to tell the therapist about his false teeth – a big step forward for him.

Using flashcards to undermine unhelpful assumptions

The activation of unhelpful assumptions is often a main element in triggering psychological problems. Looking at most longitudinal formulations,[4] it can be seen that the part of the map in which events cue off unhelpful assumptions is like a long thin passage between the historical 'old stuff' associated with schematic memories and the current symptoms' reactions. Being long and thin, it is a good place to block the reaction. Therapy flashcards can assist by taking the insight generated by the 'downward-arrow' process and using it as a device to step back from and defuse the triggered reaction. Bruce and I built the flashcard in Figure 7.1 from the identification of an assumption about physical 'defectiveness' rooted in the early experience of shame.

The flashcard aims to help the client by supplying some cognitive material that will help him to step back from the immediate experience of distress – 'It is

---

FLASHCARD

I sometimes have the assumption that: *If people see my defectiveness, they will reject me.*

It is understandable that I have this assumption because: *I have had a physical problem since I was a boy. The fact that I can hide my problem means that I can 'play safe'. My mum and dad encouraged me to play safe in life.*

This works against me because: *I get very nervous in the company of strangers, especially women. It makes it hard for me to approach relationships with confidence. Nervousness also seems to be spreading to more and more things.*

The assumption is wrong because: *Most of the people who know about my problem don't seem that bothered about it and seem open to my other qualities.*

The way forward for me now is: *To understand that people who would reject me for that reason are probably better not being part of my life anyway. It would be good for me to be more proactive in telling people about my problem and also in putting my real self over to them in more confident and active ways.*

FIGURE 7.1 *Example of flashcard: Bruce*

understandable that I feel this way but it is not wholly right' – and enable him to react more reflexively – 'I am entitled to feel some sadness about this, but it doesn't say everything about me and my life and it doesn't help me to go and seek after my goals after I have allowed myself some moments of distress.'

Suggestion: Practising the downward arrow and developing a flashcard

Most of us can identify an assumption that is not so very functional in our lives. (If you have trouble finding one for yourself, try 'I must not fail as a therapist.') Try using the downward-arrow technique on this assumption, either by yourself or with a partner, to get to the 'bottom of the ladder'. What would be so bad about failing as a therapist, for example? You may also wish to try developing a flashcard for the same assumption. If working with a partner, it might be helpful to review how the sensitive use of the downward arrow felt. It does sometimes feel a bit relentless. Think about what makes it okay and not okay to pursue.

Working to change assumptions: developing new adaptive standards and assumptions

Rules that have been followed habitually for many years may be hard to renounce until a newer more adaptive rule is in place. Therapists can facilitate this process by initiating a debate that opens out the client's previous strategy:

Therapist: Bruce, I'm wondering: can we take this issue about having to hide your weaknesses and open it up to more scrutiny? You know, at present, you have this pretty omnipresent anxiety that if people see who you really are – that you have false teeth – they are not going to want to be friends with you. This problem is at its sharpest with girlfriends, who you fear may not be attracted to you, but it is also a problem with male friends. You said that you sometimes go along with what they want in case they start to make fun of you.

Bruce: That's right. I don't know why I cannot stand up for myself at times like that, I just seem to get self-conscious and it is easier to let other people make the running.

Therapist: So that's one thing, isn't it? It would make sense to have a rule about how you show yourself to others depending on exactly who they are and what you want to do with them: in other words, a more varied rule.

Bruce: To some extent I do that. Some of my friends know about my problem – they have found out somehow or other. Like when I was out drinking with Tony and I was sick and my bloody teeth came out (laughing). He was alright actually, he just picked them up and said, 'Here, your teeth came out, mate' and handed them back smart style. As far as I know, he never said anything to anyone else. Tony is good as gold though.

Therapist: So some people can know and it's alright, but you're not sure about others knowing?

Bruce:	Yeah, I mean it's one thing a mate knowing but I would find that so difficult if it was a girlfriend. I never told Jean anything about any of that.
Therapist:	What do you think might have happened if you'd told her?
Bruce:	Well, the worst would have been that she finished with me and that happened anyway...

In this dialogue, some potentially new elements about developing a more flexible rule are emerging:

- It might be possible to take the initiative with some people.
- There might be good and bad ways of revealing himself.
- Acting first might help to bring things to a head sometimes.
- Taking the initiative might help Bruce feel more in control.
- He may not be able to control the fact of having false teeth, but he can control how he does and doesn't tell people about it.

Therapeutic discussions over matters like this tend to go on over several months and sometimes are helpfully combined with behavioural experiments: what happens if you tell someone about your false teeth on a first date?

Working with early maladaptive schemas: schema-driven interpersonal problems

In Chapter 3, we introduced the idea of how the client's interpersonal style can become involved in the therapy and how this was heavily influenced by the fact that so many of the key cognitions in CBT were interpersonal by nature. This process becomes intensified in the schema work because, firstly, the client's issues tend to be more deeply entrenched and problematic as they relate to long-held patterns laid down in early experience, and, secondly, therapy is more long-term, involving more ups and downs, and therefore imposes more strains on the therapeutic relationship. If you think that your therapist will eventually get tired of you and your problem, you may, for instance, devise little 'transference tests' to see how she reacts to minor frustrations. These things may well frustrate the therapist so that the client's strategy becomes a self-fulfilling prophecy. Young et al. (2003) describe these strategies as 'schema maintenance' strategies because they so obviously work to keep early maladaptive schemas in place in the long term. Other schema strategies that serve the same function are schema avoidance (keeping away from things that may trigger early maladaptive schemas and thereby never learning to deal with them) and 'schema compensation' (over-developing a strategy that serves to camouflage the early maladaptive schema: the 'boasting' that seems to cover low self-regard and to which people may react with the thought 'Methinks he doth protest too much'). All these schema mechanisms may be experienced by the therapist as client resistance. In fact, they most probably represent the early maladaptive schemas' survival strategies (Leahy, 2001).

For the purpose of this chapter, we will focus on two key aspects of these schematic factors that impinge on the therapeutic relationship in CBT: the way core beliefs and early maladaptive schemas may show themselves in difficult client reactions and how these can particularly impact on the structured nature of CBT. Clients may sometimes be irked by the business-like nature of CBT. When difficulties arise in CBT it can feel to the therapist as if an unreasonable delay is taking place that can lead to a sense of irritation. One way of conceptualising these problems is that they are connected to transference and counter-transference problems. Although most strongly associated with psychodynamic therapy, these concepts can also be put to use in CBT.

The concepts of transference and counter-transference have been somewhat more widely conceived in relation to CBT than in classical psychoanalytic theory. A therapist can, however, remind the client of another person from their past, but more generally may provide an intense example of a type of relationship that has troubled clients before. Several clients that I have worked with have displayed narcissistic traits and this personality style appears to relate to beliefs about being special and being entitled to special privileges (Beck et al., 1990). Many observers have also noted that the inflated self-presentation of such clients may also be underlain by a much more fragile and self-critical self-concept and sometimes the client may flip from one of these modes to another in a session. This can be extremely confusing for people in the client's life, even to his therapist.

A narcissistic personality style may also interfere with initial contracting and agenda-setting, that is, they make even getting started difficult. Some clients with 'entitlement schema' (Young et al., 2003) may question whether the therapist is 'right' for them. This may conceal a suspicion that the therapist is not good enough to treat them and they may insist on spending a good deal of time discussing this early in the therapy. At this point, a therapist may become aware of her own schemas being activated by this rather provocative behaviour from the client. It is very easy, but counter-productive, for the therapist to be drawn into 'retaliation'. In one way, it is justified for the therapist to think 'He should make his mind up – this is just wasting my time.' It may even be quite healthy to allow oneself to express this reaction in private or in supervision. The therapist must, however, remember that the reason that the client is in therapy is to solve problems like this. If therapy was all about easy alliances and positive work, therapists would need less training and would deserve only low pay. The therapist should try to slow down his reaction and feel empathy for the client.

The formulation should prove helpful to the therapist: if the client really truly believes that he is 'special', then it does make sense to consider if any other person is special enough to work with him. It is perhaps natural for people to think how well equipped any professional is to work with them, though it is culturally unusual to express this thought. Therapists can find much help from the way Beck et al. (1990) have charted various schematic beliefs, including some description of their function alternatives.

Avoidant schemas can also get in the way of agenda-setting, especially as therapy moves towards a mode focused on working on specific problems. If the client has followed a strategy of 'keeping a low profile' so that she has avoided many testing life situations, then putting these situations on the agenda might seem quite alarming, especially if there is some kind of inference that this therapist may require you to try to do something to change these patterns. A therapist can use 'immediacy', as described in Chapter 3, to put these things on the agenda – 'I notice that as we begin to focus on things, you kind of go a bit missing in the discussion: I am wondering if I have that right, and, if so, is it something we should try to tackle together?' This intervention moves the strain between therapist and client back to collaboration, though the therapist should be aware that clients may be genuinely unaware that they are avoiding the issue.

The client with a dependence schema may confuse the therapist by being overly ready to take the therapist's advice, do the homework and report that progress is being made. These reports could reflect genuinely accurate reports on what is going on, but they could also be tinged with the client's need to please the therapist and stay in a safe dependent position, perhaps avoiding getting an imagined 'sacking' for being 'a bad client'. The dependent schema may not definitively show itself until the end of therapy approaches: when suddenly the client will be triggered into major distress and relapse. As ever, the therapist needs to be aware that his own schemas may be triggered here. It is not unknown, and perhaps not unnatural, that therapists may enjoy being meaningful helpers to vulnerable clients and so may also have mixed feelings about ending. With some clients, they may even feel relieved when the end of therapy has finally loomed into sight. Both therapist and client can, however, come to realise that ending therapy is an opportunity to rehearse and complete a 'good ending' and thus give their respective schemas a gentle tug to open them to encompass a wider range of situations in future.

The main skill required of the therapist in handling these situations is that of self-awareness and understanding, coupled with an appropriate use of supervision. It may, for example, be that the therapist's schemas are antagonistic to the client's schemas (Leahy, 2007). There is an element of 'physician, heal thyself' involved in understanding our own schematic concepts, and using cognitive methods to review the negative thoughts raised in transferential situations. The way incidents are handled in therapy should also resonate with the way we use CBT methods. Therapy cannot usually stop to allow relationship repairs to be made nor should therapist and client be engaged in endless navel-gazing – they do have work to do. Therapeutic effort should be ongoing and the methods used should be congruent with the interpersonal style established in the therapeutic relationship.

Working with schema content: continua

We concluded our thoughts about handling transferential situations by suggesting that it would be therapeutic to help clients to open their negative early maladaptive schemas to other adaptive possibilities. This is because early maladaptive schemas are rigid and dichotomous. To weaken their negative influence we need to do things that will start to break down their dichotomous nature. The continuum technique is designed to do just that. As elsewhere in CBT, the technique is a simple one but can be adapted to different ends and purposes. Here it will be explored in relation to use with highly dichotomous self-schemas. Other types of use are described in Padesky & Greenberger (1995). I follow several different versions of this technique with the same client situation:

HAMID was brought up as a member of a minority religion in a Middle Eastern country. His religion was facing persecution at the time of his childhood – a situation that eventually resulted in his family fleeing their country. During the period of persecution his parents had been very concerned for his safety and only let him go out of the house in very restricted circumstances. The one and only time he ever disobeyed his parents about going out, he was caught out by a really unlucky quirk of fate. Now, years later, seemingly successfully living and working in the UK, he had a severe bout of depression and believed that he was 'useless' and 'could not cope with life'. He spent much of his day ruminating on these thoughts and refusing to go out.

I suggested to Hamid that we should test out his negative core belief 'I am useless' using a continuum. The process begins by drawing a simple line and putting 0% usefulness on one end of the line and 100% usefulness on the other. It is recommended that therapists test out the evidence for the positive attribute of 'usefulness' rather than 'uselessness' because, as well as attempting to weaken the negative early maladaptive schema, we are also trying to build up an alternative, more functional schema. It is, however, important to begin by defining terms because until we understand what the client actually means by 'useless' and 'useful' we will not be able to pursue the question in the right kind of way.

It is also important to note that this kind of work is usually more effective when the therapist already knows the client well. The therapist can then use this information to help the client see things from different perspectives. The therapist here, for example, knew that Hamid was married. In the past Hamid and his wife had got on well but now things between them were very strained. He had a good job in a technical role with a big firm. He had done quite well in the job but tended to hide his light under a bushel, especially the fact that his technical skills were greater than some of the people he worked with. He had been off work for two weeks and felt really badly about this.

I began by asking Hamid to place himself on the continuum and he placed himself near to the 0% marker, as shown in Figure 7.2. I asked him also how he would have placed himself as he was functioning before he was depressed. He placed himself just over the 50% marker. This was good because it showed that the way he felt about himself varied and was affected by his depression. Earlier, when helping him to use thought records, Hamid had learnt something about the way depression has a negative effect on the way clients think about things. The next step was to get him to place other people on his line. I wasn't totally sure about the wisdom of asking about his wife but it seemed unavoidable and he placed her close to his own very negative position, as shown in Figure 7.2.

0% USEFULNESS		50%	100% USEFULNESS
HAMID	HAMID'S WIFE (HIS VIEW)	HAMID BEFORE DEPRESSED	HAMID'S WIFE (SELF VIEW)

FIGURE 7.2   *Example of a continuum: Hamid*

0% USEFULNESS		50%	100% USEFULNESS
HAMID	HAMID'S WIFE (HIS VIEW)	HAMID BEFORE DEPRESSED	HAMID'S WIFE (SELF VIEW)

0% GOOD TECHNICAL SKILLS			100% GOOD TECHNICAL SKILLS
HAMID'S PEER COLLEAGUES	HAMID	HAMID'S WIFE	HARRY (HAMID'S BOSS)

% GOOD EARNER			100% GOOD EARNER
HAMID'S WIFE IN UK	HAMID'S PEERS	HAMID'S WIFE IN MIDDLE EAST	HAMID HARRY

0% GOOD WITH CUSTOMERS			100% GOOD WITH CUSTOMERS
HAMID	HAMID'S PEERS	HARRY	HAMID'S WIFE

FIGURE 7.3   *Continuum: Hamid (developed)*

He expressed a lot of anger towards his wife as he placed her near to himself. Hamid was angry because his wife kept telling him what he should do about his illness and he added 'Well she thinks she's up here (pointing to 100% end) but what she says is stupid and she is really down here (pointing at the other end)'.

So far it can be noted that we have managed to establish that, whatever uselessness and usefulness are, they are things that do vary, both between different people and within the same people at different times. The narrow range of meanings in the belief is already beginning to 'stretch' so that it can take in wider and more adaptive meanings. In order for further stretching to be as effective as possible, it is essential now to begin to define the terms 'usefulness' and 'uselessness' more. This can be done by asking the client: 'What are the things that make up "usefulness", would you say?' and 'What does someone have to do to be up there?'

When asked this question, Hamid pointed to the example of his boss at work, Harry. The therapist then asked him which of Harry's characteristics were 'useful'. Hamid pointed to his technical skills, the way he made money for the company and the way he handled customers. This was interesting because I knew that Hamid had quite a favourable view of his own technical skills. We were subsequently able to place quite a few of the staff from his office on the continuum in a way that was favourable to him (see Figure 7.3).

The therapist now asked Hamid how he would place his wife on this dimension. His wife had been a skilled linguist in her own country but had not been able to find such work in this country and was working in a shop. Hamid was quick to 'defend' her by insisting that she should be rated as highly as him with regard to these criteria. This was also useful because it took discussion outside the heated atmosphere of his office and also reminded us of the important fact that people's worth is not entirely related to the rewards they receive. At this point, the therapist noticed that Hamid was very engaged in the task and had brightened up considerably. It was interesting that, given his earlier criticism of his wife, Hamid was now arguing strongly in her favour. He pointed out that his wife had been unlucky in her life because her parents had held her back but that she had strong personal qualities and had fought to make the best of things. At this point, the therapist asked if 'personal

0% USEFULNESS		50%	100% USEFULNESS
HAMID	HAMID'S WIFE (HIS VIEW)	HAMID BEFORE DEPRESSED	HAMID'S WIFE (SELF VIEW)

0% TECHNICAL SKILLS			100% GOOD TECHNICAL SKILLS
HAMID'S PEER COLLEAGUES	HAMID	HAMID'S WIFE	HARRY (HAMID'S BOSS)

0% EARNER			100% EARNER
HAMID'S WIFE IN UK	HAMID'S PEERS	HAMID'S WIFE IN MIDDLE EAST	HAMID HARRY

0% EFFECTIVE WITH CUSTOMERS			100% EFFECTIVE WITH CUSTOMERS
HAMID	HAMID'S PEERS	HARRY	HAMID'S WIFE

0% PERSONAL QUALITIES			100% PERSONAL QUALITIES
HAMID'S PEERS	HARRY HAMID	HAMID'S WIFE	

FIGURE 7.4   *Continuum: Hamid (final version)*

qualities' such as resilience, interpersonal skills and friendliness should also be considered in relation to 'usefulness' – the therapist remembered also that Hamid had made some negative comments on Harry in relation to these qualities.

It can now be seen in Figure 7.4 that the continuum was starting to look very different from the original rather dichotomous version. The material in the continuum gave rise to further discussion over several more sessions and all these discussions confirmed what was suggested by the original continuum diagram: that Hamid's belief that he was 'useless' was a dichotomous early maladaptive schema that obscured infinitely more truth than it revealed. It would be nice to conclude that this kind of discussion naturally comes to a satisfying therapeutic conclusion. Continuum work can, however, develop in various ways. Sometimes it benefits from continual practice and repetition, but at other times it may halt altogether, seeming still incomplete but yet may spontaneously re-emerge later in therapy. This may be because we are meeting our old friend *'aporia'* (in this case, 'schematic cognitive dissonance') again. The shifting plates of meaning are so fundamental that it is much less likely that we will have a decisive 'Ah-ha' experience resulting in a nice tidy conclusion.

Suggestion: Trying continua

By yourself or with a partner, try out the basic continuum method on an important (core) belief that you hold. For this purpose, the belief can be positive or negative. You are mainly trying to get the 'feel' of the exercise here. You may use the type of continuum shown in Figure 7.4, though it is important to extend it to as many definition criteria as seems appropriate to you. If you are working with a positive belief, you may find yourself resistant to 'stretching' it. This may lead to an interesting discussion about whether we treat positive and negative beliefs differently.[5]

Historical test of a schema

Schematic beliefs are likely to be rooted in client history – often early history. They may have been consolidated and reinforced over a long period and so it is helpful to consider their development, especially if other information has historically and cumulatively bounced off – that is, not been allowed entrance over many years. The technique called 'historical test of schema' tries to recapture some of this lost evidence and use it to foster the development of a new positive schema or core belief. This can be done as a written self-help exercise (Greenberger & Padesky, 1995) but, in my experience, can be more powerful as part of reprocessing negative past experiences in session. The extract on p. 141 from such a session is taken from a practice DVD developed by the author and some colleagues (Simmons & Wills, 2006). The client, Jan, whom we have encountered earlier in the book (see p. 56), has been working on social anxiety and has identified a core belief that 'People will not help me.' The task of the session is to review life experiences to see how far they reflect evidence for and against this core belief.

Greenberger and Padesky (1995) suggest that therapist and client collaboratively collect evidence that supports a new alternative core belief: in this case, 'People will help me.' The example in Table 7.1 shows the results of the therapist and client examining Jan's experiences of being helped and not helped along a time line from her early life to the present day. Once again the narrow range of meanings in the schema will have to be stretched to accommodate the evidence that is far more diverse than the core belief would predict.

Reviewing early emotional experiences like this in session may well induce strong emotions in the client in the current moment. These emotions may then

Table 7.1 Example of historical test of a schema (Jan)

	People who helped	People who didn't help
Age 0–9	Mum helped with school work sometimes	Mum over-correcting my school work
Age 10–19	Some teachers (netball)	Girls who made fun of my northern accent
	French teacher's husband	Mum over-correcting my school work
	Made some friends after Paris	Some teachers. Three girls in Paris
Age 20–29	My daughter	My first husband
	My son	
Age 30–39	Some customers in South Africa	South Africans who would only speak Afrikaans
	My second husband	
	University course tutors	
Age 40–49	Some bosses	Some bosses
	Dr H	
	My therapist	

be processed along those lines suggested in the previous chapter. Sometimes such therapeutic exchanges can simultaneously process negative experience and build up new alternative more positive meanings. This is what happens in the following extract, which, of necessity, is heavily edited:

> The therapist invites Jan to pick out a point on the time line where issues of whether people would help or not present themselves.

> **Jan:** The incident that most readily comes to mind happened on a school trip in Paris when I was 12... four of us were allowed to go off shopping... the other three ran off and left me, on my own... in Paris!!! [...]
>
> **Therapist:** So what do you think about that now?
>
> **Jan:** Well, first of all, the teachers were negligent... but I can't understand why I let that happen to me... I didn't really fit with these girls... I have the sense that I was pretty much on my own... I knew deep down that they wouldn't like me, no matter what I did... It was never dealt with... there was laughter behind my back. If it hadn't have been for the French teacher's husband, I'd probably still be there...
>
> **Therapist:** So let's think about him for a moment.
>
> **Jan:** He was a nice man... but he was switched on to the fact I was missing. He was my hero, I suppose.
>
> **Therapist:** Right, but there was someone who would help.
>
> **Jan:** That's a point... When I got home, I burst into tears... and my mum went storming into the school, but that didn't help. She was fighting my battles for me instead of giving me the tools to fight for myself... and, of course, it just made things worse for me... It didn't stop the teasing.
>
> **Therapist:** Right, so that's interesting too, isn't it? Here was another person who thought they were helping but in this case, they weren't... So it looks like 'helping' is quite a complicated thing. Sometimes people don't seem to help, sometimes people do seem to help and sometimes they think they're helping when they aren't?

> Later... after exploration of this and other life line experiences:

> **Therapist:** So what might be another way of putting this thing about whether people help?
>
> **Jan:** I guess... some people have helped me. I can't expect everyone to help but I can expect some to... I'm not any less likely than anyone else to be helped... There's nothing different about me that makes me less able to be helped than others.

For most of the time in this dialogue, Jan was actively processing these emotionally felt experiences. The therapist gently encouraged her to go on processing with the reasonable hope that it was likely that positive new information would arise and that bringing this into the schema would start to modify the early maladaptive schema's negative biases. In a sense, the therapist can only get in the way of this processing and so should focus on encouraging the client's continued engagement and make occasional comments and summaries. In this case, Jan was very keen to write down all these experiences and the new angles on 'helping' that emerged, and this cued nicely into another intervention described by Padesky for building up alternative positive beliefs: the positive diary.

Suggestion: Trying a historical test

You can try this again by yourself or with a partner. As in the previous suggestion, it can be used with either a positive or negative core belief. You may want to use the same one as in the previous suggestion or start with a new one. Using simple schema questionnaires[6] with trainee counsellors showed that they had some action in four or five schema areas on average ('self-sacrifice' and 'unrelenting standards' were the favourites!). Allow yourself to be creative with the format. The orthodox format is shown in Table 7.1 but some people may be more familiar with 'time line' methods. I have even used art therapy methods to draw a life picture and one of my clients took this a stage further by animating hers! In review and/or discussion after the exercise, consider how you felt during it. Evoking emotion is a major factor in this method. Many clients have reported 'mixed feelings' to me about this. On the one hand, there may be the residual feelings of 'bad stuff' memories but, on the other, there is also often a good feeling that comes from 'getting things in perspective'.

Positive diaries

Keeping a positive diary is essentially a way of building up a source of evidence to confirm that alternative positive beliefs are realistic and not 'pie in the sky'. This is important because some of the problematic mechanisms of the way negative schemas work are that, firstly, they bounce positive experiences away and, secondly, even when positive experiences are somewhat available, they are distorted, forgotten or discounted. It is helpful for the therapist to be collaborative, merely putting the rationale for the idea and then encouraging the client to organise the task and the completion of it in a way that fits in with her preferences and general life patterns. I am always interested to notice how clients approach the task. One client showed me a very tattered small notebook that she used for her diary. When I asked her about this, she explained that she did not really think she was worthy of a nice-looking larger notebook. After much prompting she eventually agreed that she was worth something better. It may be worth watching what the client does about this and holding the possibility of upgrading the standard of the notebook to fit the task. Alternatively, the therapist can suggest a nice notebook from the start.

Sometimes, when events may need to be processed, it can be helpful to use more actively evocative techniques such as psychodramatic role-play, described in the next section.

The use of psychodramatic and role-play techniques when working with schemas

We have highlighted the fact that a client's schema-driven problems have often been around for many years. One thing that might arise from this is the fact that, unlike in less complex problems, the client may have no memory of functioning without early maladaptive schemas being constantly activated. By coming into therapy therefore, they may be embarking on a journey to somewhere that exists only in theory. This may seem a risky enterprise to them. In such situations, clients have often become emotionally and cognitively avoidant as a way of dealing with the constant triggering of intense emotion. We have discussed the need to evoke emotion in various contexts in Chapter 6. In the context of working with schema-driven problems, emotion can be helpfully evoked by various psychodramatic and role-play techniques. Whereas continua and positive diaries can be used in an ongoing way to stretch constricted early maladaptive schemas to accommodate wider ranges of meaning, these role-play techniques should probably be used more sparingly. By using role-plays, therapist and client can engage with schemas in a fuller context. The issues that emerge from such work can then be the basis for much ongoing follow-up work.

Like drama and theatre themselves, psychodrama and role-play are capable of being expanded in many creative directions. Historically, drama therapy has been more associated with humanistic and psychodynamic therapies, but the so far rather modest forays of CBT in that direction could be developed much further (Jennings, 1990). For the purpose of this chapter, I will focus on what is probably the most commonly practised style of psychodramatic role-play in CBT: the re-enactment of evocative childhood experiences and the replaying of certain aspects of those experiences from a different perspective.

The client may be invited to re-enact such a scene to facilitate coming to terms with various historical events or the people in them. It may also be hoped that these experiences can be processed or 'worked through' in some way that has eluded the client thus far. Various skills already discussed can be used in this new context: encouraging first person/present-tense language, or exploring emotional experience and the cognitive content of core beliefs and thoughts connected with the scene. The following example comes from the previously presented case history of Mary, the eldest child of a large farming family who believed that she 'just didn't measure up'.

> **MARY** felt nervous about entering into an historical role-play but had felt so bad for so long that she was keen to try something that might 'help to break the chains', as she put it. She turned out to be quite adept at entering fully into such work – she described herself as 'an actress manqué'. Thinking of her core belief about not measuring up, she took herself back to a childhood scene in which, aged 10, she had been left in charge of a young brother. He wanted to go to play in one of the fields behind the farmhouse. It was a cold winter's day and Mary realised that she was feeling very unwell. It turned out that she had a temperature. Her brother, however, kicked up a terrible fuss and, to placate him, she agreed to walk down to the field for a few minutes. As she walked down, she began to feel more ill and knew that she had to get back to the house before she fainted. At this point, her little brother ran away from her and she couldn't find him and felt too unwell to go on searching. She went back to the house, hoping to find someone who could resume the search for her brother but alas no one was at home. She fell asleep in front of the fire. She awoke to find her mother holding her soaking wet brother
>
> *(Continued)*

(Continued)

(he'd fallen in a pond). She was ranting and raving at Mary, saying she was use-less and that her brother could have drowned. As she told this story, Mary shook with emotion as she remembered the shame that she had felt. The therapist had never before seen her so out of control. As she was able to talk a bit about the shame she felt, she established a little more composure and then felt able to pro-ceed to reconstruct the scene. The therapist asked Mary what she, as that 10-year-old girl in that scene, needed. She said she needed support and help to stand up to her parents' bullying. She felt that, even in imagination, she couldn't do it for her-self, but could imagine being supported by a favourite aunt, who told the parents that she was 'very ill and only 10' and that they should thank the Lord for their son's safety and be ashamed of themselves for bullying Mary. As the final moments of this scene were replayed, Mary finally was able to echo some of the things that her imaginary aunt was saying and to say them directly to her parents. Mary shouted out – in a way that was out of control and yet normal – for the one and only time in the therapy. This was part of a wider set of new things that Mary was trying at this time, but she herself reported that it was a significant part of 'coming to a new sense of herself'.

After this session, Mary continued working on her core beliefs. She decided that she did not want to undertake long-term therapy and, after some 15 sessions or so, had reached the point where she amended her belief to 'I do measure up, even if I can't convince as many people as I'd like to of that fact', and felt that she had done enough work for now to get her back on the road. At three months' follow-up she reported that a new zest for work and life had maintained itself and, although she still had problems from time to time, she felt she had 'turned the corner'.

Schema mode work and schema debate

Role-plays have always been part of cognitive therapy (Beck et al., 1979) and, as Judith Beck (1995) notes, they can be used for a wide variety of purposes. They are particularly good at getting at 'both sides of the argument' in internal debates. Although early maladaptive schemas are very powerful, they are usually in compe-tition with other more functional schemas that the client holds. Role-play can there-fore be used to facilitate and work through these debates. Therapist and client can play different roles in these debates and may also alternate or switch roles. The ther-apist can sometimes get the client to access both sides of the role-play. As cognitive therapy began to address the deeper issues connected with personality difficulties, role-plays began to take on aspects of psychodrama (Beck et al., 1990). Role-play can be used to re-enact family scenarios to bring out and work with schematic core beliefs – as shown in the previous dialogue. Sometimes this work can be combined with encouraging interaction between the schematic and anti-schematic material. Young et al. (2003: 272) have described '… schema mode work … [where] … each part of the self can be labelled as a mode, and the two modes can then conduct dialogues and negotiate with each other'. Young et al. (2003) detail types of interac-tion that can occur between different parental and child modes. The following abbreviated dialogue integrates several aspects of schematic role-play but perhaps comes closest to a dialogue between 'vulnerable child' and 'healthy adult'. We return to Mary and her compulsive attempts to please people. She seems to have internalised the critical parent we saw in action in the previous extract:

Client: [Describing her parents favouring her brother and sisters] ... I didn't warrant the treatment that others did ...

Therapist: You have a broad smile on your face as you say this and yet it sounds painful.

Client: It is ... it is ... how else can I deal with it! [**Later**] ...

Therapist: Do you link your having to please people to these events?

Client: I can see that I have been looking for other mothers ... my mother used to say, 'Do this for me or I won't love you' ... she manipulated things so my brothers and sisters got all the cream ... it was honestly them and me ... but I was told it was *my* fault ... I was the scapegoat ...

Therapist: So how do you think you thought about all this as a child?

Client: Well I thought that I didn't measure up to the others and I'll have to work harder and harder and harder ... My parents thought that the others were better than me ... so I was thinking that there must be something about me that was not right ... It still comes out at work like that sometimes too ...

Therapist: Okay so that's the Child Mary's way of thinking about that and it comes out at work sometimes, what about the Adult Mary?

Mary: I am still nurturing her of course! But I can see that the old stuff results in me working my butt off for recognition and in actual fact I am just putting their backs up ... not only that but they are after their own recognition, they are not particularly interested in mine.

We can see that two clear modes of thinking, each with a kernel of truth, have emerged and that synthesising these modes would be helpful and likely to lead, if well-facilitated, to negotiated resolution between them. Mary went on to describe how a previous therapist 'buried her alive' by stressing her responsibility for her family situation. We can't know what was actually said but the previous therapist may have been trying to empower the client by stressing her responsibility for her own life but in this case had, almost certainly unwittingly, allied with the critical parent and had overloaded the dialogue between the different modes.

A final caveat about schema mode work is needed – remember that schemas are best thought of as metaphors and should not 'be reified' – made into 'things'. There seem to be so many modes – such as 'inner child', 'true self', 'inner critic' – in the literature of popular psychology that it can sometimes seem like it is getting pretty crowded in there! We really are whole people and though it can help to think of parts of us in negotiation for heuristic purposes, it is often useful to end such exercises by reminding ourselves that these parts really do go together.

Conclusion

As mentioned already, there are different intensities for working with schema-driven problems. This chapter has focused mainly on a set of basic techniques for working with assumptions, core beliefs and early maladaptive schemas as part of everyday clinical practice. There are therapists who advocate a more thoroughgoing version of schema work as a format of therapy, distinct from CBT: schema-focused therapy (Young et al., 2003) and cognitive-behaviour therapy for personality disorders (Beck et al., 1990) and borderline personality disorder (Layden et al., 1993; Linehan, 1993). It is still unclear which range of clients need these more specialist versions of CBT. From my own practice, and that of those colleagues whose work I know well, I would say that there is a significant number of clients who benefit from work that addresses schema-driven problems. This kind of work can be integrated with more symptom-based CBT without undue difficulty. Schema-focused work can also be effective as relatively short-term interventions with clients, though it is important to recognise that a minority of clients will need longer-term work (Cummings & Satyama, 1995).

PRACTICE TIP: Tapping into core process material by imaging historically significant scenes in the client's life

When I was training as a CB therapist one of my fellow trainees told me about a client who had a problem with a constant self-critical voice. The client said that it was like having a parrot lodged permanently on his shoulder whispering negative thoughts into his ear. The therapist had played[5] with this idea by giving the 'parrot' a personality. The client chose to call the parrot 'Kilroy' so that the therapist might start off the session by asking 'How is Kilroy today?' This idea stuck in my mind and I have quite often told the story of Kilroy to my clients. They seem to like it. The idea of Kilroy opened my eyes to the possibility of using imagery as part of CBT. The point is that imagery can capture whole passages of meaning in easy-to-understand but well-packed visual representations.

There is an enormous variety of ways that one can use imagery in CBT. It is one of those territories that has not been fenced in by definitive statements so that there is still plenty of room for creativity – and one might think that is appropriate for a creative form.

In the practice DVD produced by Mike Simmons and I (Simmons & Wills, 2006), there is a section of a therapy session where the client, Jan, is talking in her own critical voice. The therapist tells her about Kilroy and then asks if the critical voice has any particular quality. This launches her off into a series of memories about her mum and about various incidents in early adolescence where she had experienced some 'spiky' exchanges with her. As she goes further into these memories, it is clear that at least some part of her mind is 'back there'. They are not, however, engaged in re-experiencing therapy at that moment so the therapist calls her back to the present and asks her what she wants to do about that voice. She turns towards her shoulder, presumably prompted by the image of Kilroy, and brushes off her 'parrot-mother'. She tells her to 'buzz off back to her knitting' because she and the therapist are busy talking about important things. A few simple sentences – but packed with meaning about past, present and future.

Further reading

Greenberger, D. & Padesky, C. (1995) *Mind over mood.* New York: Guilford Press.

Layden, M.A., Newman, C.F., Freeman, A. & Morse, S.B. (1993) *Cognitive therapy of borderline personality disorder.* Boston, MA: Allyn & Bacon.

Padesky, C. & Greenberger, D. (1995) *The clinician's guide to mind over mood.* New York: Guilford Press.

Young, J.S. et al. (2003) *Schema focused therapy: a practitioner's guide.* New York: Guilford Press.

Notes

1   The Stevens Inquiry was into the death of Diana, Princess of Wales.
2   For example, standard cognitive therapy usually begins with interventions aimed at symptom relief, schema-focused therapy usually does not (Young et al., 2003).
3   George Kelly (1963) suggests that healthy personal constructs should be flexible enough to accommodate new data.
4   See website materials accompanying this book for a set of formulations.
5   The 'depressive realism' hypothesis has conjectured that mental health may depend on having a slightly positive 'spin' on life (see Brewin, 1988).
6   See Young & Klosko (1998). Young also has longer questionnaires (see Young et al., 2003). I use schema questionnaires only occasionally with clients and find the shorter one less overwhelming for them.
7   Thanks to Damian Gardner for sharing this concept.

8

DEVELOPING CBT: A PERSPECTIVE OF ENGAGEMENT AND LIFE-LONG LEARNING

I have just celebrated the thirty-fifth anniversary of my work as a therapist – I feel that I might be getting the hang of it now.

Letter from the author to Brain Hunter, January 2006

Es tu CBT? (Voulez-vous CBT avec moi?)

During training, CB therapists may have to consider to what extent they can sign up for the concepts and methods of CBT. How well, for example, do these concepts and methods fit with their current attitudes and values. One of the key aspects of CBT that seems to distinguish whether trainees are able to take to it appears to be the degree to which they are able to feel reasonably comfortable with implementing structure. For some, structuring the process can carry connotations of being 'directive' and of forcing one's expertise on clients. Such attitudes can inhibit trainees from fully implementing CBT. How this attitude impacts on fully implementing CBT may determine whether the model becomes 'the major thing I do' or 'one of the things I do' (Wills, 2006b).[1]

This chapter is concerned with this longer-term development of CB therapists and of the way they practise the model. The evolution of CBT has been strongly influenced by the fact that much of it has taken place within psychiatric settings. This has been a mixed blessing in that, on the one hand, there has been a solid base on which to build practice (and psychiatry itself needed more psychological treatment options) but, on the other, psychiatry has negative associations, especially in the public perception. Negative feeling against psychiatry partly results from a failure to appreciate how it has developed in more recent years. CB therapists could do more to bridge the gap by developing more services outside hospital-based settings. This would allow us to communicate more directly with both the client population and with our fellow mental health professions, who seem to regard CBT with increasingly ambivalent feelings (Sanders & Wills, 2003). It would also be helpful if the wider field could try to overcome some of their prejudices and think about what they can learn from CB therapists. After all, as I hope this book shows, CB theorists and practitioners have shown a willingness to learn from them.

In order to thrive and prosper in a challenging post-training environment, CB therapists will need to strengthen their skills, especially in applying CBT to the diverse needs of our varied clients. This task must be undertaken alongside deepening and strengthening the understanding of both the science and the art of CBT. These skills will need to be developed in the context of implementing CB therapy with clients, some of whom may have stronger feelings of resistance than many CBT texts show. This chapter will consider developing the skills, science and art involved in being a CB therapist. It will also consider the various practice and socio-political settings in which a CB therapist is likely to be practising. It will explore ways of coping with life in this demanding profession. A particular importance will be given to joining the CBT community, but also to using that base to relate to other parts of the profession, such as enjoying the fellowship of like-minded souls and communicating with and learning from others. The emphasis will be on longer-term development because learning any form of therapy is very much a case of life-long learning.

Developing a deeper understanding of CBT science

There is a veritable research industry constantly working to solidify and extend the theoretical and practical bases of CBT. The annual conferences of the British Association for Behavioural and Cognitive Psychotherapies (BABCP), the European Association for Behavioural and Cognitive Therapies (EABCT) or the World Congress of Cognitive Therapy usually comprise 40 or more grouped seminars each presenting a number of research papers on defined clinical areas such as phobias, body dysmorphia or working with adolescents, etc. The presenters within these groups are often not clinicians but are pure researchers looking at a very precise but limited area of psychopathological reaction or treatment response. They may also be clinician researchers looking at broad theoretical questions or general treatment responses. On the one hand, the basis in research is reassuring but may also promote a nagging feeling that there is always some new piece of research to assimilate before seeing your next client. Much of the research is now becoming so specialist and complicated that is hard for people doing everyday practice to understand. I remember sitting in one presentation recently and thinking 'This feels like it is a 12-year debate of which I've missed the first 11 years and 364 days!'

Christine Padesky makes the slightly tongue-in-cheek point that learning cognitive therapy when she did, in the late 1970s, was easy because there was only one cognitive therapy book and one application to learn: depression. Now there are many applications, all with accompanying literatures and treatment protocols. I have found that it takes about two years to become really competent in using a treatment protocol. There are about 20 common problems that occur in non-specialist therapy practice so that, by this reckoning, most therapists would be approaching retirement age as they became competent.

One option for handling the problem of the multiplicity of potentially useful knowledge is to become more of a specialist so that you can master a limited area more quickly. While training as an alcohol counsellor, an alcohol specialist told me that once one had seen around 50 clients, one had seen most of the significant variations of drinking problems, a quantitative formula that lines up with the two-year estimate above quite well. A possible limitation with this solution is the well-attested fact that clients tend to have more than one problem (co-morbidity) and what appears to be the presenting problem may often be concealing something else that is more fundamental. The therapist, has the option of referring on to another therapist, but referring on may be difficult if any kind of bond has developed between you and the client while this problem clarification takes place.

Specialist practice as a solution is not, however, available or congenial to all. Most therapists working in big organisations such as the National Health Service need to be 'happy generalists', learning about the nature of problems as they go along. I was socialised into a positive attitude towards being a generalist partly by working in a primary care setting and having constantly to learn about quite rare medical conditions. In such settings, many therapists have learnt that clients do not always expect therapists to be experts. In fact they often seem to value the sense that the therapist is learning along with them – as long as therapists show an appetite to learn and are honest about what they do and do not know.

A therapist's level of knowledge is one of the factors related to expertise and influence. Research into the role of 'therapist influence' in therapy has produced some interesting results (Heesacker & Mejia-Millan, 1996). A quality of quiet expertise in the therapist works well but if expertise is over-projected, it may have a negative effect. The attitudes of patient collaboration and learning along with the client seem best to ensure that the client is not alienated by experiencing the therapist as an overbearing 'expert'.

To some extent, of course, certain aspects of CBT formulation and practice do go across the board so that one does not have to 're-invent the wheel' each time you meet a new client or open up a new problem area. I can, however, foresee a time when CB practice might become so complicated by endlessly developing applications and yet more 'radical new approaches' that there will be a danger of fragmentation and a sense of loss of the comparative simplicity and parsimony of the original model. Wells (2006) has made a positive contribution in counteracting this trend towards over-elaboration by developing a format for formulating across all the anxiety disorders. I suspect that aids to maintain parsimony, such as that proposed by Wells, will become more and more necessary as CBT continues to develop. There is also a danger that developing an over-complicated version of CBT will take us further away from recognising that all therapy models have common processes. The recognition of common processes helps us to dovetail into the rest of the therapy world and this in turn helps us to participate in the development of a united therapy profession dedicated to the mission of serving the needs of clients. Such a unified profession unfortunately still looks some way off and, in the meantime, CBT practitioners will still need to make decisions about whether to specialise and/or the range of clients that is reasonable for them to take on.

Developing the art of CBT: relationship and structure

Advocates of other psychotherapeutic models have often criticised CBT for, among other things, lacking a deeper understanding of the therapeutic relationship. While I think that the therapeutic relationship is sometimes 'mystified' by attributing essentially unknowable spiritual aspects to it, I would say that it is sometimes possible to detect in advocates of CBT the belief that if only we could make our theories yet more powerful, we might just be able to by-pass much of the messiness of human encounters. Most everyday practitioners do not, however, seem to feel this way, and it is heartening that there is much more of a tradition of interest in interpersonally informed encounter developing in more recent CBT literature on the therapeutic relationship (Sanders & Wills, 1999; Bennett-Levy & Thwaites, 2007; Gilbert & Leahy, 2007). A therapist who is interpersonally sensitive is likely to make more subtle use of the CBT structure.

Beutler et al. (1994) consider the role of 'therapist variables' and cite some interesting evidence (of particular interest to CB therapists) regarding clients' responses to being structured by therapists. CBT practitioners see structure as being a central principle in the practice of their therapy. Beutler et al. (1994) suggest that some clients respond well to structure but others show a distinct discomfort or even antipathy to it. This concurs with my experience of using CBT and poses a central dilemma to CBT practitioners in their ongoing work. I have already suggested that, when confronted with resistant clients, it may be helpful to look to the client's individual formulation (see Chapter 2). Have clients been intrusively overstructured by parents or teachers at some point in their histories, for example? I think it is also possible to wear the CBT structure lightly and, when confronted with client discomfort with structure, 'structure lite' may be the preferred therapeutic stance until you are clear about how to pitch the degree of structure based on the revealed idiosyncratic needs of the client. It may also be necessary to be flexible: to renegotiate and modify the structure at times.

The need for flexibility was presented to me while I was writing an earlier part of this book. I had a late morning call from a client, Nathan. He is a man in his fifties who had a very sharp emotional reaction when a long-standing relationship ended. He was intensely angry at the former partner and felt a depressed disgust about himself. He sounded very distressed on the telephone and urgently asked me for my next available appointment – formally quite a few days off. I was behind with my writing schedule and had set aside that day for writing, but something that I heard in his voice led me to arrange an appointment for that day. He came clutching a letter and thrust it into my hand. We sat together in silence while I read the letter. It was a letter written to his sister and read very much like a suicide note. On the previous evening he had had a difficult conversation with his former partner and then called his sister for help. His sister suggested that he pull himself together and Nathan experienced this as a very hurtful rejection.

Nathan had been a client who had not entirely taken to CBT. There was a contextual factor in his attitude to CBT in that he felt that it was his partner who had the problem and he found it difficult to adjust to the idea of working on himself to cope with her. He'd had a 'hippy' childhood, had gone to a 'free school' and often found himself feeling constrained by 'structure'. During previous sessions,

I'd responded to this feedback by taking several steps back and by holding the therapeutic tiller with a very light hand. He had quickly developed a strong sense of trust in me: in his words, 'You just feel like someone who isn't going to lay a trip on me.' I remember recognising his discomfort and irritation as we worked on a thought record and my saying something like 'Here's you feeling really shitty and there's this idiot trying to get you to write down your negative thoughts!' He smiled. What I said might be considered as what Young et al. (2003) describe as a form of empathic confrontation. Yet Young et al. seem to want the cognitive point of view to prevail: they define 'empathic confrontation' as 'the therapist empathises with the reasons for patients having the beliefs they do – namely, that their beliefs are based on early childhood experiences – while simultaneously confronting the fact that their beliefs are inaccurate' (Young et al., 2003: 92). In this situation, some part of me could agree with Nathan on the sheer effrontery of surveying his 'negative' thoughts. If I had no desire to prevail, I *did* want to persist on the basis that I knew the activity of recording thoughts had helped people in some situations similar to his and so might be worth a go.

Nevertheless, the situation that morning was critical. We sat in silence for quite some time[2] and Nathan continued to show great distress. He held on to my arm and we sat, waiting for words, if words were needed, to come. This was the 'fertile void' described in Chapter 3. Gradually words came and we talked about his suicidal thoughts and weighed the balance between living and dying. His mood slowly lifted and we were able to make some plans for future meetings and further therapy work. Was I doing CBT during this session? An observer would have found it difficult to discern much overt CBT structure in what was occurring. An observer able to discern the underlying structure of our discussion might, however, have noticed that the therapist's line of interaction followed the logic and structure for dealing with suicidal thoughts suggested in the brilliant chapter on suicidal thoughts from Beck et al. (1979).

The situation with Nathan was not an everyday occurrence and yet it demonstrates the need to shape the therapy to the idiosyncratic needs of the client. It is helpful in my view to be familiar with therapy protocols and structures because they offer ideas about what *might* be done in various phases of therapy. We might even argue that such steps *should* be done except where there were indications to the contrary. We cannot, however, argue that they *must always* be done, regardless of considerations for the individual client. This is the range of positions over which the discussion about the need for structure and the usefulness of protocols is debated. Few, I suspect, would argue for the latter position by asserting that there was *never* any need to divert from a prescribed path. By admitting *sometimes* that there is a need for such diversions, we admit the need for *art* and *artfulness* in CBT. We might, of course, then argue about the scope and range of the need for artfulness. In CBT, this debate is hindered by the fact that the main effort of research has so far been in outcome studies. It would now be helpful to take a leaf from the wider school of therapy and undertake more process research using qualitative research methods. Such research would, for example, examine how CBT practitioners might react when confronted with a client who is unhappy with being structured by the therapist. How does the client deal with being structured? How does the therapist deal with clients dealing with being structured? What happens next? What kind of negotiation leads to positive resolution of these impasses? It may well be that the answers will point to the need for a therapist artfulness that is highly idiosyncratic, yet artists may often find it helpful to learn from each other's idiosyncratic art.

Finding a good balance between the science and art of pratice is the main pursuit of continuing development and lifelong learning.

Developing practice: continuing professional development and supervision

Continuing development

Ashworth et al. (1999) followed trainees from cognitive therapy training courses and found that many, especially those returning to large organisations such as the NHS, quickly become faced with the dilemma of being promoted away from the practice area. Such promotions may result from the fact that training opportunities in CBT have been limited until recently, so that training has focused on 'mature' professionals from such areas as the NHS. In November 2006, Lord Richard Layard launched an initiative to persuade the UK government to train up to 10,000 extra therapists to deliver more psychological therapy, especially CBT, to NHS patients (Linklater, 2006). If training on this scale does become available, loss of therapists through promotion would be less of a problem. Ashworth et al.'s (1999) findings, however, also point to the reality of post-training atrophy (the gradual withering away of a newly acquired skill), in this case due to promotion. Other causes of the atrophy can be:

- a return to old ways,
- a lack of support for that skill in the organisation or environment,
- a lack of adequate supervision.

We have already discussed how CBT trainees who have previously followed other therapeutic models or traditions react to training. The training experience usually provides a feeling of being in a 'learning community', in which people similar to oneself are going through similar experiences and trying to achieve similar things. There is formal support but there are also conversations over coffee breaks and communal jokes. In the case of CBT training these jokes are often about which tutor or trainee has the most repellent maladaptive schemas. Once this 'learning community' is no longer available, it is easy for former trainees to revert to previous ways of doing things. In this case returning to previous therapeutic styles and interventions. This can be an especially powerful tendency as you begin to encounter problems in implementing CBT or problems that you have not used CBT with as yet.

When newly trained therapists start to address these problems, they tend to turn to colleagues in or near their present organisations or contexts of working. If such colleagues are not immediately available, one way of contacting such people is via a professional organisation such as BABCP and its regional branches. It is true, however, that CBT practitioners can still be quite thin on the ground in some areas, and many practitioners still have to travel to get regular 'doses' of updating, which is of course a required part of the continuing professional development aspect of the accreditation systems for both BABCP and the British Association for Counselling and Psychotherapy (BACP).

Ongoing re-accreditation and development

Systems of accreditation tend to organise round the principle that there is a considerable effort to vet clinicians for their initial registration and this vetting is subsequently followed up by regular periodic checks that the accredited person is staying true to the values, aims and levels of competence required by the accrediting body. One key element of these checks is that the accredited therapist is continuing to receive appropriate supervision. Another is that therapists are continuing to develop the competence that they established by training and accreditation. It is recognised that this is done in a variety of ways:

- By attending courses, conferences and workshops.
- Through research.
- By writing.
- By reading relevant journals and books.
- By undertaking experiential learning or therapy.

Systems usually require that this continuing professional development involves some kind of mix of these nourishing activities though the individual therapist's right to select the right kind of individual blend of activities is usually respected.

Developing the giving and receiving of supervision

Supervision is another aspect of necessary updating and professional nourishment. Supervision has always been a strong tradition within all parts of the therapy professions in Britain and there have been significant attempts to reinforce and build up the supervision tradition in BABCP in recent years (Townend et al., 2002). The requirements of the BABCP supervision process are very similar those of the British Association for Counselling and Psychotherapy. BABCP has been able to learn much from the pioneering work of the BACP in the fields of the accreditation of supervisors and supervision training (for updated guidelines, see www.babcp.org.uk).

Supervision in CBT has tended to focus on the content of therapy, formulating specific problems and implementing appropriate interventions. As CBT has developed an increasingly sophisticated approach to the therapeutic relationship, there has been an acknowledgement of the need to look at the personal and developmental aspects of the therapists themselves (Bennett-Levy & Thwaites, 2007) and different levels of supervision content (Hawkins & Shohet, 2006).

Good quality supervision is part of an appropriate self-care for therapists and acts as a safety net for clients, although it is not always possible to find such developmental supervision in one's own organisation. CBT practitioners are therefore sometimes obliged to pay and travel for supervision. Independent practitioners are usually faced with the same problems and these can result in considerable expense in terms of time or money. The benefits of supervision may not always become clearly apparent until one hits a real problem with one's practice. Then support and guidance may suddenly become imperative.

Supervision can have some surprising effects on ongoing therapy work. On several occasions I have had the slightly unnerving experience of a client realising that what I have said to them was influenced by discussion with a supervisor. Although I am explicit with clients in telling them that I may discuss them in supervision, it is not usually necessary to go into the specifics (though it is helpful for clients to know that they are not personally identified and the focus of supervision discussion is primarily on therapists and what they are doing). Occasionally though, a client has told me that she could tell that a certain response that I made had been influenced by my discussion with the supervisor. My point is that the supervisor is sometimes like a third presence in the room. Just as a client's absent partner can sometimes assume a presence in the therapy session, so too can the supervisor. Most clients seem to appreciate this safeguard and also like the idea that they are important enough to us to be thought about and discussed outside the therapy hour. Padesky (1996) has written in more detail about the specifics of CBT supervision. Some further reflections on both supervision and training can be found on the SAGE website accompanying this book.

Giving and receiving supervision involves skill by the supervisor and supervisee (Scaife et al., 2001). It is worth noting that CBT supervision has put particular emphasis on recording sessions on tape or disk and this demands the careful selection of extracts from the supervisee. The skill here is to find a useable extract, which should not be too long and which contains representative samples of the client's material, the supervisee's working style and key interactions between them. Ideally, the extract should contain the essence of the dilemma being presented for supervision and not some 'good work' to earn praise. Equally, the supervisor should learn to focus on key moments of what is presented without over-interpreting them – it is an extract after all. The supervisor should strive to be congruent by using guided discovery to help the supervisee articulate the dilemma and, as far as possible, find her own solution to it.

Organising neglected aspects of practice

We have discussed how CBT practitioners often record sessions on tape, disk or increasingly in mp3 format, whether for the client's benefit or for their own. Recordings of sessions can be a very valuable part of supervision. There can be something about hearing the actual exchanges between therapist and client that suddenly makes sense of what has been talked or read about. The fact that a supervisor may listen to a recording adds a new dimension to the agreement on recording between therapist and client. Such agreements should include clarity about how they may be used in supervision. It is recommended that a therapist and client have a written agreement regarding the nature and uses of recording along the following lines:

- how the recordings will be stored,
- the purpose of the recordings,
- who will have access to the recordings,
- what use will be made of recordings,
- when recordings will be erased.

Keeping therapy notes is not an area that has received much attention in the literature so far. Bearing in mind that CBT is regarded as a formulation-driven therapy, it is helpful to consider ways of recording formulations and linking them to ongoing work. Some very useful guidelines for formats used in formulation are available on the website of Aaron Beck's Academy of Cognitive Therapy (www.academyofct.org). The formulations used in this book have been developed along similar lines to this format. It is important to think of ways in which formulations can be appropriately shared with clients. The author has also developed a 'formulation contract', which basically combines the formulation, therapy goals and contract with the client into a simple, single document. An example of such a document is shown in the website materials on formulation that accompany this book.

The formulation contract also specifies how therapy will be reviewed and evaluated. As discussed in an earlier chapter, CBT usually has a built-in evaluative element with the use of standard CBT measures, such as the Beck inventories. Other measures such as CORE (Clinical Outcome in Routine Evaluation) can also be used (Mellor-Clark, 2002). A more qualitative review of progress, in my therapy held every six sessions or so, is a useful addition to the quantitative evaluation of standardised measures. CBT has been tardy in developing qualitative research and there is really no good reason why it should not now try to catch up. Accountability is highly desirable and likely to be increasingly required in all public service fields. It is hard to imagine that accountability to clients can be fully exercised without developing more sophisticated ways of hearing what clients have to say about their experiences of therapy.

Personal development and personal therapy for CBT practitioners

There is an ongoing debate about whether CBT practitioners should follow other therapy models by requiring trainees to undergo therapy themselves. My own view is that it is very valuable for both trainees and therapists to undertake therapy and that they should be encouraged to do so, but I consider that requiring people to undertake it undermines a central ethic of our profession: that in almost all circumstances,[3] people should be free to decide for themselves when they want therapy. Another format for CBT trainees to experience therapy 'from the inside' is the Self-Practice/Self-Reflection method devised by James Bennett-Levy (for a further description of this method, see Bennett-Levy & Thwaites (2007)).

Developing CBT in different arenas and settings

Although the most frequently used format in which CBT is practised is probably still one-to-one therapy, there are also other formats:

- Group therapy/educational group.
- Internet and email therapy.
- CD-Rom and DVD (see www.livinglifetothefull.com).
- Self-help/stepped care approaches.

There is a continuum in group work approaches that stretches from experiential groups at one end to more educational and 'psycho-educational' groups at the other end. Experiential groups tend to have less structure and develop therapeutic foci out of what is happening between group members. CBT group work has been associated more with the structured and educational end of the continuum and may well have a syllabus or predetermined set of topics to cover. A classic example of this may be an anxiety management group, which most usually takes the form of a closed group of around 10–12 members who have been diagnosed with an anxiety disorder. Anxiety management groups often take place within a hospital, health centre or community centre. Clients may be taken through a set of steps similar to that which is learnt in individual CBT: identifying thoughts and feelings, keeping a thought record, using graduated steps to expose oneself to worrying situations and doing behavioural experiments. The benefits of following these steps in a group are that they can be introduced to 8–12 people in the same way as they can be introduced to one person. There is also potential for clients to learn from each other's experiences. There may, however, be less scope for dealing with ongoing 'live' problems such as those that may arise and be worked through in an experiential group. This limitation comes partly from the programme structure but also perhaps from the fact that there has been less interest in CBT group work practice becoming involved in experiential encounters. There is no reason, however, why CBT groups could not also begin to incorporate an experiential dimension. One example of such 'live' CBT work may be American attempts to defuse prisoner–guard 'situations' using CB methods, which apparently often result in quite hot but helpful encounters. The potential for experiential work in CBT groups could be another area that might be illuminated by more process-orientated, qualitative research. Such research might focus on those 'off-the-ball' incidents that must occur in all groups, even the most didactic ones. In doing so, such research might help us if there could be more scope for incorporating more experiential elements into CBT groups.

One very large arena for CBT group work has developed in the probation and other 'offender management' services in the UK, Canada and the USA. These tend to be highly structured programmes, where facilitators are monitored to ensure that they keep to a defined structure. This is to ensure 'programme integrity' but may often result in staff feeling constrained. Participants are overwhelmingly not attending by choice so that it can be hard to use the aspects of the 'therapeutic relationship' that underpin CBT.[4] Nevertheless, the programmes, especially ones that focus on specific areas of offending, do seem to achieve a small reduction in future offending and one must bear in mind that such successes are rare in this inherently difficult area. Strangely, to me, CBT in the criminal justice field seems to have developed in relative isolation from the rest of the CBT community, at least in the UK, and I feel that staff working with offenders would benefit from more contact with people working in other arenas and vice versa. It may be that staff working in difficult areas, such as with offenders, would also benefit from learning CBT skills with other, more voluntary client populations or contexts.

Community justice staff sometimes develop CBT interventions in their individual sessions with clients while exercising their statutory supervision role. Indeed, this is partly encouraged by Home Office approaches to 'targets for effective change', often defined in CBT terms. In these 'Priestley One-to-One' programme sessions it is easier to develop a collaborative relationship. Perhaps this discussion harks back to the specialist–generalist dilemma discussed earlier in this chapter.

Another group of people working in the helping professions that has been involved with CBT work is the social work profession (Sheldon, 1995). Sadly, the therapeutic element of social work has been reduced and there seems to have been a corresponding lowering of the profile of the profession in CBT organisations. The reduction in social workers doing CBT is a shame because social workers have appropriate skills. Indeed, a significant portion of CBT in the USA is delivered by clinical social workers. They are well placed to help deliver the therapy to clients who could benefit. The current system of commissioning work outside social agencies sometimes results in social workers farming work out to people who may be no more competent at it than themselves. It is important to have clear lines of interprofessional communication and that would surely be enhanced when different professions follow similar working methods. No one profession can properly be thought of as 'owning CBT'. Sometimes it appears to me that groups like social workers and probation staff are left by other professional colleagues in a degree of professional isolation, when the work they are doing has many overlaps with psychological therapy. There is a strong case for bringing them in from the cold. Many professions have contributed to the development of CBT and, given the current gap between supply and demand, there should be room for all of them in systems for providing CBT services.

Another professional group that could be engaged in providing CBT services is that of counsellors. I have argued elsewhere that if only leaders in the counselling profession could be more open to CBT, counsellors would be well-placed to provide an especially effective form of CBT, based on sound listening skills.

Developing CBT services: supply and demand

Research continues to show a massive and ongoing demand for counselling and therapy services. Despite the fact that over half of all primary health centres now have onsite counselling, the demand for service provision, especially for CBT, is characterised by long waiting lists. While we all wait to see if the Layard initiative will lead to expansion, thought is increasingly being given to the availability of services at slightly lower levels than one-to-one work. CBT programmes are now available via the internet (www.moodgym.anu. edu.au) and via CD and DVD (www.praxiscbt.com). There have also been schemes to 'prescribe' other CBT materials, including self-help books and other resources (Frude, 2004). Chris Williams and colleagues have been active in promoting brief versions of CBT that can be provided by primary care staff, and these can be built into a 'stepped care' programme in which a client may progress from a minimal intervention, such as being given a self-help leaflet, all the way up to one-to-one therapy or even treatment within a residential therapeutic milieu (Williams, 2003). It would be interesting to have more evidence on how value to clients is added by each step.

Developing the professional identity of CBT

Individual CBT practitioners may choose to immerse themselves yet further in the CBT community or join other professional communities or both or neither. Most will choose to have some sort of association with the CBT community so it may be worth thinking about what the CBT club is and what are the pros and cons of joining it. People vary in their degree of enthusiasm for joining groups and clubs. One of the reasons for joining a club is to meet similar people with whom activities can be shared. Researchers into orientation have shown that, as well as beliefs and behaviours, people who follow similar orientations may possess common personality traits or styles (Arthur, 2001). In organisations within the CBT community we may well come across people a bit like ourselves.

In the Introduction to this book, I referred to the rather farcical attempt to bring different groups of psychotherapists together to devise NVQ criteria. At various points, therapists of the different orientations had to gather together in the same room. One of the ongoing jokes of these meetings were the distinct dress styles adopted by the different groups: the humanistic practitioners were often colourful and vaguely hippyish; the psychodynamic dress sense tended toward the use of tweed; and the CBT practitioners kept things plain and simple. I was amused recently to read an account by Marvin Goldfried of travelling to Esalin in California. Marvin was at that time a behaviourist and dressed in a suit and tie. He decided to explore some humanistic models by going to the well-known Esalin centre in California. He had a two-sided suitcase with clothes suitable for behaviourist meetings on one side and his hippy clothes on the other. He made sure that by the time he arrived in Esalin, he had the appropriate clothes on! Dressing in the right style may seem laughable to many but perhaps suggests that there are dangers in operating too much within one's professional safety zone. Good fences may make good neighbours, as the American poet, Robert Frost, ironically suggests, but so does commerce and mutual visiting. Such free movement of therapeutic goods has sometimes been inhibited by mutual suspicion. The suspicion between different therapists can sometimes be linked to attitudes towards psychiatry. It is intriguing to speculate on how CBT might have developed if it had evolved more outside psychiatric settings. One gets a fascinating glimpse of this 'what if' by reading Beck's book on couples' counselling (Beck, 1988), written on sabbatical leave from the psychiatric setting. REBT, of course, did develop more outside the psychiatric milieu and it is interesting that it is sometimes unfavourably compared to Beck's approach in respect of having a less well-developed research profile.

For my final thought, I return to the theme with which I started this chapter: the helpful role that CB therapists could play in bridging the gap between the psychiatric and non-psychiatric therapy fields. Behaviour therapy was developed so that more psychiatric patients could access non-medical treatments. It is perhaps ironic that this attempt to provide humane treatment to a neglected patient population has resulted in an association of equivalence between CBT and psychiatry in the minds of some therapists. Does this matter? I think it does. Firstly, a positive case needs to be restated for the positive aspects of psychiatry. Peter Sedgwick (1982) was often a lone voice in pointing out that the anti-psychiatrists often failed to distinguish between good-quality and poor-quality psychiatric care and thus helped to open the gates to de-institutionalisation before reasonable alternatives were available – most chaotically in Italy. Secondly, CBT *has* inherited some of the language and assumptions of psychiatry. These have both positive and negative aspects. The use of language links to the diagnostic system as used in publications based on the *DSM* criteria. I have argued that these criteria can be helpful in understanding how different types of symptoms occur together and may point towards clear therapeutic targets and intervention strategies. Diagnostic systems can also be unhelpful when they are held to refer to objective entities as opposed to approximate things. They can also be reductive in that they rarely, if ever, offer any dynamic understanding of psychological problems. In many ways CBT has continued the behaviour therapy tradition of offering more rounded treatment options within the psychiatric system. CBT, however, has much more to offer than being a mere adjunct to psychiatric treatments. We are already making a large and increasing contribution to psychological therapy in the community in schools, colleges and community centres.

We CBT practitioners, however, need to be seen as coming out yet more from our safe psychiatric havens and showing both clients and other professionals engaged in the field that we do truly understand the need to empower clients and the limitations of current psychiatry in achieving that. We need to be able to learn from other perspectives and there are good signs that we are doing this. We need to be open to practitioners of other perspectives, not only for their sakes but also for the sake of influencing them in return. By being open ourselves we are more likely to encourage people to be open to us. We are in a prime position to give psychological therapy significant and humanising content and methods. We also need to stake our claim for influence in the politics of the therapy world, not just because we figure well in outcome research. This evidence is good but we all know that there is an awful lot more that needs to be done in terms of providing a truly responsive system of psychological treatment services. A stronger argument to articulate is that we know that we really do have something good to offer, not only to clients but to other people engaged in the provision of psychological help in all its many guises. The skills of CBT cannot be exercised in the therapy room alone but must also be evident in the way we participate in all the activities that contribute to the provision of humane and effective services for clients.

PRACTICE TIP: Demystification – how to develop a relaxed perspective about giving a conference paper

One of the worst staff training events I ever went to involved supposed 'training' on how to give a conference paper. We novice paper presenters gathered nervously around some conference veterans who proceeded to enlighten us on the hard work that we should undertake to ensure that we were never the victim of one of the many and dire problems that occur when giving a paper. The faces of the conference paper-fodder troops grew more and more wan until we reached the ultimate possible disaster: that someone could stand up and criticise our methodology! I found that something of the contrarian had been slowly building up in me (always a danger with me, I fear!) and I made the following interjection:

I wonder what sort of conferences you guys have been going to? At the ones I go to most people are half asleep most of the time or thinking about who they can have a drink at the bar with in the next break!

Anyway, if someone does stand up and criticise your methodology, or even jokes about your clothes sense, so what? The world, I can confidently predict, will not come to a halt. Many readers will have been to numerous conferences, and I bet few, if any, can recall even one exact criticism of anyone's methodology or much else. It is not just clients who catastrophise, and CB therapists in particular should not shrink from using their own methods to de-catastrophise their own thinking.

Further reading

Linklater, A. (2006) After Freud. *Prospect Magazine*, 123: 36–41. (Also currently available as a free download from the *Prospect* website: www.prospect-magazine.co.uk)

Notes

1 Some further notes on CBT training and supervision are available on the SAGE website accompanying this book.
2 For the value of silence, see the brilliant novel by Sally Vickers (2006), *The Other Side of You*.
3 An interesting debate surrounds the use of CBT methods on probation programmes for offenders.
4 Indeed, typically such programmes may be defined as 'not therapeutic'.

APPENDIX 1: GUIDE TO THE WEBSITE ACCOMPANYING THIS BOOK

There is a website accompanying this book. This can be found on the SAGE website at: www.sagepub.co.uk/wills. It is hoped that the website will facilitate reader responses and will build over time. Materials are organised into four folders:

FOLDER A: A guide to the basic concepts of CBT

- *The nature of cognition and its relationship with emotion and behaviour*
- *Avoidance and safety behaviour*
- *Cognitive specificity*
- *The schema concept*
- *The collaborative therapeutic relationship*

FOLDER B: Examples of CBT formulations

- *Sample formulations of clients mentioned in the text*

FOLDER C: Materials used in CBT practice

- *Thought record*
- *Guide to relaxation*
- *Behavioural experiments diary*
- *Activity scheduling form*
- *A client's guide to using thought records*

FOLDER D: Materials relating to CBT training and supervision

- *Chapter on training and supervision*
- *Using recording in CBT sessions*
- *CBT skill development and training resources*
- *Teaching PowerPoint presentations (covering Chapters 2–7)*

APPENDIX 2: RESOURCES FOR CBT MEASURES

As described within the text, a defining feature of CBT practice has been the use of psychological measures to assess problems and monitor client progress – classically using quantitative measures such as the Beck Depression Inventory (BDI). A plethora of measures have now developed but the situation is complicated by the fact that some measures have been copyrighted and can only be legally obtained from authorised agents. The following brief information has been established as being correct at the time of writing.

Harcourt Assessment (www.harcourtassessment.com)

Therapists need to register so that they can purchase the following measures: Beck Depression Inventory II (BDI); Beck Anxiety Inventory (BAI); Beck Hopelessness Scale (BHS); Beck Obsessive & Compulsive Scale (BO-CS).

NFER-Nelson (www.nfer-nelson.co.uk)

Therapists need to register to purchase: Zigmond & Snaith's (1983) The hospital anxiety and depression scale; Turner & Lee's (1998) *Measures in post-traumatic stress disorder: a practitioner's guide.*

Measures that are currently available in publications

Meta-Cognitions Questionnaire: Anxious Thoughts Inventory (Wells, 1997). Anxiety and depression scales (Greenberger & Padesky, 1995; Burns, 1999b). Penn State Worry Questionnaire (Leahy, 2005). Yale Brown Obsessive Compulsive Scale (Y-BOCS) (Steketee, 1999). Simple schema (life trap) questionnaire (Young & Klosko, 1998).

NB: The measures listed above are only a fraction of available material but serve as a starter guide. There are materials available on the World Wide Web but these require cautious use as some sources are poor quality, illegal and require the disclosure of personal data.

APPENDIX 3: OTHER COGNITIVE METHODS USING COST–BENEFIT ANALYSIS AND PIE CHARTS

It is sometimes said that there are three main ways of challenging negative thoughts:

- Reality testing ('What is the evidence?')
- Pragmatic testing ('Is that thinking justified when it makes you feel that way?)
- Logic testing ('Does that way of thinking really make sense?')

Quite often a CBT practitioner will deploy all of these three ways and then see which seems to be the most helpful to the individual client. Clients obviously have different ways of doing things within their own heads and some ways of challenging thoughts will chime with their internal processes better than others. There is, however, usually no sounder way of finding this out than by 'suck it and see'. It is probably also often a case of 'all hands to the pump' and 'we'll use whatever works'. From my experience with clients, however, I would say that, for most clients, logical challenges often have limited effects. Reality-testing challenges can work well but often they are helpfully reinforced by pragmatic challenges. Pragmatic challenges are often the ones that bring a commitment to thinking about things in a different way, because, the client might say, *they really work against me.* The CBA technique is probably the clearest and most parsimonious of the pragmatic challenges.

Cost–Benefit Analysis (CBA)

CBA has a subtle acceptance of the fact that sometimes the client's negative thinking may have some subtle pay-offs. We can probably all remember that before an exam, many examinees will be heard loudly declaring that they haven't done 'any revision at all!' Isn't it amazing how many then go on to pass? Similarly, some people who declare 'I'm such a failure' may be partly concerned to lower the expectations of others and also avoid later negative labelling by getting in first themselves. CBA helps to acknowledge these 'benefits' yet also to set them against the context of their disadvantages.

Problems with CBA can sometimes arise if clients are not willing to acknowledge that there are any advantages to negative thinking so we end up with a one-sided battle and an unsatisfying victory for the positive rational side. Clients can

Table A.1   CBA for the thought 'I'm such a failure'

Advantages	Disadvantages
I may avoid disappointment	I feel depressed when I say this
I may avoid people expecting too much of me	I will avoid undertaking more challenging tasks and activities
	My self-esteem will suffer
	I may ignore some good aspects of what I can do
	Other people may get fed up with me 'whining'
	Other people may underestimate what I can actually do

sometimes be helped to acknowledge 'benefits' by distinguishing between 'short-term' and 'long-term' cost and benefits. The advantages of negative thinking are heavily weighted towards short-term coping and against longer-term life development. It is probably easier to own a flawed coping mechanism as a way of coping in the short term, until a more positive longer-term strategy can be devised and implemented. Leahy (2001) suggests that the simple CBA above can also be used to review positive alternative thoughts. The CBA is really a form of problem-solving and can be adapted to decision-making. When problems with decisions arise, they frequently involve other people. Therefore it is useful to consider the costs and benefits for others as well as for oneself. The matrix now looks like this:

	Advantages for self	Advantages for others
Decision A (or negative belief)		
Decision B (or positive belief)		

Pie charts

When we discussed cognitive distortions in Chapter 4, we noted that one of the main 'serial offenders' was 'making over-statements'. These types of statement seem to result from negative attention bias – but they also reinforce it. It may well be that there is a form of 'special pleading' going on here. Special pleading is a well-known device to secure advantage by a selective review of the facts of the case. Here they seem to relate to securing disadvantage – unless we consider the case for 'subtle pay-off' made above. The cognitive tactic is usually to get the client to see that their review of relevant factors is restricted and to explore whether a wider consideration of the facts may be helpful.

A flagrant distortion was immediately evident to me when one of my clients blamed herself for the fact that her husband had left her. It turned out that her husband had a gambling addiction and had over the years persuaded her to sign away all their joint

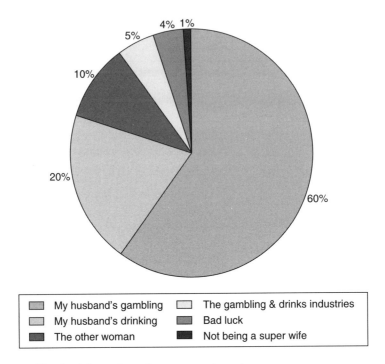

FIGURE A.1   *Pie chart (based on above percentages)*

money and assets to him so that when he went away with another woman, my client lost everything, including the roof over her head. We drew one circle in which she was attributed 100% of the responsibility for the break up – 'If I had been a better wife, he wouldn't have got into gambling in the first place.' Then we listed some other factors that might have been involved so that a new 'pie chart' circle could be drawn. Leahy (2001) is spot on in suggesting adding 'bad luck' to the list – a more potent factor than most of all us allow! The resulting piechart looked like this:

Pie charts can have very powerful effects, but, like all methods, sometimes run into problems. I sometimes feel a bit manipulative when I do this – especially knowing that leaving the client themselves until last virtually guarantees that only a tiny percentage of responsibility will be left by then. In the above example, we had to keep readjusting the previous figures to allow any percentage at all for the last few items. It can also be important for people to retain some responsibility, sometimes as a moral issue but also sometimes to be a player of some account. It strikes me in retrospect that this latter point was particularly true for that client after such a thorough 'disempowerment' by her husband. I wish that I could record that I had registered that at the time – perhaps next time, eh?

Further references

Burns, D.D. (1999b) Ten ways to untwist your thinking. In *The feeling good handbook.* Harmondsworth: Penguin.
Leahy, R.L. (2003) *Cognitive therapy techniques: a practitioner's guide.* New York: Guilford Press, Chapters 2 and 6.

REFERENCES

American Psychological Association (2000) *Diagnostic and statistical manual IV–TR.* Washington, DC: APA.

Arthur, A.R. (2001) Personality, epistemology and psychotherapist choice of theoretical model: a review and analysis. *European Journal of Psychotherapy, Counselling and Health*, 4.1: 45–64.

Ashworth, P., Williams, C. & Blackburn, I.-M. (1999) What becomes of cognitive therapy trainees? A survey of trainees' opinions and current clinical practice after postgraduate cognitive therapy training. *Behavioural and Cognitive Psychotherapy*, 27: 267–77.

Aurelius, Marcus Antoninus (1989) *The meditations.* Harmondsworth: Penguin.

Baer, R. (2006) *Mindfulness-based treatment approaches: clinicians' guide to evidence base and applications.* New York: Academic Press.

Barker, P. (1992) *Regeneration.* Harmondsworth: Penguin.

Bartlett, Sir F. (1932) *Remembering: a study in experimental and social psychology.* Cambridge: Cambridge University Press.

Beck, A.T. (1970) Cognitive therapy: nature and relation to behavior therapy. *Behavior Therapy*, 1: 184–200.

Beck, A.T. (1976) *Cognitive therapy and the emotional disorders.* Harmondsworth: Penguin.

Beck, A.T. (1988) *Love is never enough.* Harmondsworth: Penguin.

Beck, A.T. (1991) Cognitive therapy: a 30-year retrospective. *American Journal of Psychiatry*, 40.4: 368–75.

Beck, A.T. (1996) Beyond belief: a theory of modes, personality and psychotherapy. In P. Salkovskis (ed.), *The frontiers of cognitive therapy.* New York: Guilford Press, pp. 1–25.

Beck, A.T. (2004) Origin, evolution and current state of cognitive therapy: the inside story. Keynote address at the Congress of the European Association of Behavioural and Cognitive Therapies, Manchester, September.

Beck, A.T., Emery, G., with Greenberg, R. (1985) *Anxiety and phobias: a cognitive perspective.* New York: Basic Books.

Beck, A.T., Freeman, A. & Associates (1990) *Cognitive therapy of personality disorders.* New York: Guilford Press.

Beck, A.T., Reinecke, M.A. & Clark, D.A. (2003) *Cognitive therapy through the lifespan.* Cambridge: Cambridge University Press.

Beck, A.T., Rush, A.J., Shaw, B.F. & Emery, G. (1979) *Cognitive therapy of depression.* New York: Guilford Press.

Beck, J. (1995) *Cognitive therapy: basics and beyond*. New York: Guilford Press.

Bennett-Levy, J. (2003) Mechanisms of change in cognitive therapy: the case of automatic thought records and behavioural experiments. *Behavioural and Cognitive Psychotherapy*, 31: 261–77.

Bennett-Levy, J. & Thwaites, R. (2007) Self and self-reflection in the therapeutic relationship: a conceptual map practical strategies for the training, supervision and self-supervision of interpersonal skills. In P. Gilbert & R. Leahy (eds), *The therapeutic relationship in the cognitive-behavioral psychotherapies*. Hove: Routledge, pp. 255–81.

Bennett-Levy, J., Butler, G., Fennell, M., Hackmann, A., Mueller, M. & Westbrook, D. (eds) (2004) *The Oxford guide to behavioural experiments in cognitive therapy*. Oxford: Oxford University Press.

Beutler, L.E., Machado, P.P. & Neufeldt, S.A. (1994) Therapist variables. In A.E. Bergin & S.L. Garfield (eds), *Handbook of psychology and behavior change*. (4th edn). New York: Wiley, pp. 259–69.

Bourne, E. (1995) *The anxiety and phobia workbook*. Oakland, CA: New Harbinger.

Bowlby, J. (1980) *Attachment and loss. Vol. 3: Loss, sadness and depression*. London: Hogarth Press.

Bowlby, J. (1988) *A secure base: clinical applications of attachment theory*. London: Routledge.

Breuer, J., Freud, S. & Strachey, L. (translator) (1982, reissue) *Studies in hysteria*. New York: Basic Books.

Brewin, C.R. (1988) *Cognitive foundations of clinical psychology*. London/Hove: Lawrence Erlbaum Associates.

Brewin, C.R. (2003) *Posttraumatic stress disorder: malady or myth?* New Haven, CT: Yale University Press.

Burns, D.D. (1999a) *Feeling good: the new mood therapy* (rev. edn). New York: Avon Books.

Burns, D.D. (1999b) *The feeling good handbook* (rev. edn). New York: Penguin.

Burns, D.D. & Auerbach, A. (1996) Therapeutic empathy in cognitive-behavioural therapy: does it really make a difference? In P. Salkovskis (ed.), *Frontiers of cognitive therapy*. New York: Guilford Press, pp. 135–64.

Butler, G. & Hope, D. (1995) *Manage your mind*. Oxford: Oxford University Press.

Butler, G. & Hope, D. (2006) *Manage your mind* (2nd edn). Oxford: Oxford University Press.

Carkhuff, R.R. (1987) *The art of helping* (6th edn). Amherst, MA: Human Resource Development Press.

Carlson, R. (1997) *Don't sweat the small stuff... and it's all small stuff*. New York: Hyperion.

Carnegie, D. (1993) *How to stop worrying and start living*. New York: Simon & Schuster.

Casement, P. (1985) *On learning from the patient*. London: Tavistock.

Church of England (2005) *Common worship: daily prayer (services and prayers for the Church of England)*. London: Church House Publishing.

Cicero, M.T. (1975) *Murder trials*. Harmondsworth: Penguin.

Clark, D.M. (1996) Panic disorder: from theory to therapy. In P. Salkovskis (ed.), *The frontiers of cognitive therapy*. New York: Guilford Press, pp. 318–44.

Cummings, N. & Satyama, C. (1995) *Focused psychotherapy: a casebook of brief intermittent psychotherapy*. New York: Brunner/Mazel.

Dryden, W. (1991) *A dialogue with Albert Ellis: against dogmas*. Buckingham: Open University Press.

Dryden, W. (2006) *Getting started with REBT* (2nd edn). London: Taylor & Francis.

Dryden, W. & Trower, P. (1988) *Developments in cognitive psychotherapy*. London: SAGE.

Duckworth, A.L., Steen, T.A. & Seligman, M.E.P. (2005) Positive psychology in clinical practice. *Annual Review of Clinical Psychology*, 1: 629–51.

Eells, T.D. (ed.) (1997) *Handbook of psychotherapy case formulation*. New York: Guilford Press.

Egan, G. (1975) *You and me: the skills in communicating and relating to others*. Monterey, CA: Brooks Cole.

Egan, G. (2002) *Exercises in helping skills: a manual to accompany the 'The Skilled Helper'* (7th edn). Pacific Grove, CA: Brooks Cole.

Ehlers, A. & Clark, D.M. (2000) A cognitive model of posttraumatic stress disorder. *Behaviour Research and Therapy*, 38: 319–45.

Ellis, A. & Dryden, W. (1997) *The practice of rational emotive behaviour therapy* (2nd edn). New York: Springer.

Ellis, A. (1973) *Humanistic psychotherapy: the rational-emotive approach*. New York: Julian Press.

Ellis, A. & Dryden, W. (1987) *The practice of rational emotive behaviour therapy*. New York: Springer.

Emery, G. (1999) *Overcoming depression: therapist's manual*. Oakland, CA: New Harbinger.

Epictetus (1995) *A manual for living (The Enchiridion)*. San Francisco: Harper.

Epstein, S. (1998) *Constructive thinking: the key to emotional intelligence*. Westport, CT: Praeger.

Fennell, M. (1989) Depression. In K. Hawton, P.M. Salkovskis, J. Kirk & D.M. Clark (eds), *Cognitive behaviour therapy for psychiatric problems*. Oxford: Oxford Medical Publications, pp. 169–234.

Fennell, M. (2004) Depression, low self-esteem and mindfulness. *Behaviour Research and Therapy*, 42: 1053–67.

Foa, E. & Kozak, M.J. (1986) Emotional processing of fear: exposure to corrective information. *Psychological Bulletin*, 99: 20–35.

Frude, N.J. (2004) Bibliotherapy as a means of delivering psychological therapy. *Clinical Psychology*, 39: 8–10.

Gendlin, E. (1981) *Focusing*. New York: Everest House.

Gendlin, E. (1998) *Focusing oriented psychotherapy: a manual of experiential method*. New York: Guilford Press.

Gilbert, P. (1992) *Depression: the evolution of helplessness*. New York: Guilford Press.

Gilbert, P. (2005) Compassion and cruelty: a biopsychosocial approach. In P. Gilbert (ed.), *Compassion: conceptualisations, research and use in psychotherapy*. Hove: Brunner-Routledge, pp. 9–75.

Gilbert, P. (2006) A biopsychosocial approach to formulation with a special focus on shame. In N. Tarrier (ed.), *Case formulation in cognitive behavioural therapy: the treatment of challenging and complex cases*. London: Routledge, pp. 81–112.

Gilbert, P. & Leahy, R.L. (2007) *The therapeutic relationship in cognitive behavioural psychotherapies*. London: Routledge.

Girard, R. (1977) *Violence and the sacred*. Baltimore, MD: Johns Hopkins University Press.

Grant, A., Mills, J., Mulhern, R. & Short, N. (2004) *Cognitive behavioural therapy in mental health care*. London: SAGE.

Greenberg, L.S. (2002) *Emotion-focused therapy: coaching clients to work through their feelings*. Washington, DC: American Psychological Association.

Greenberger, D. & Padesky, C. (1995) *Mind over mood.* New York: Guilford Press.

Guidano, V. & Liotti, G. (1983) *Cognitive processes and emotional disorders: a structural approach to psychopathology.* New York: Guilford Press.

Hackmann, A. (1998) Cognitive therapy with panic disorder and agoraphobia. In N. Tarrier (ed.), *Treating complex cases: the cognitive behavioural approach.* Chichester: Wiley, pp. 27–45.

Harris, R. (2006) *Imperium.* London: Arrow Books.

Harvey, A., Watkins, E., Mansell, W. & Shafran, R. (2004) *Cognitive behavioural processes across psychological disorders: a trans-diagnostic approach to research and treatment.* Oxford: Oxford University Press.

Hawkins, P. & Shohet, R. (2006) *Supervision in the helping professions* (3rd edn). Maidenhead: Open University Press.

Hayes, S.C. (1998) Acceptance and Commitment Therapy (ACT). Workshop given at the Annual Conference of the European Association for Behavioural and Cognitive Therapies, Cork, September.

Hayes, S.C., Strohsal, K.D. & Wilson, K.D. (2004) *Acceptance and commitment therapy: an experiential guide.* New York: Guilford Press.

Heesacker, M. & Mejia-Millan, C. (1996) A research programme on attitude change processes and their application to counselling. In W. Dryden (ed.), *Research in counselling and psychotherapy: practical applications.* London: SAGE, pp. 49–78.

Hersen, M. (ed.) (2002) *Clinical behavior therapy: adults and children.* New York: Wiley.

Hobson, R.F. (1985) *Forms of feeling: the heart of psychotherapy.* London: Tavistock.

Hollon, S.D. (2003) Does cognitive therapy have an enduring effect? *Cognitive Therapy and Research*, 27.1: 71–5.

Horney, K. (1951) *Neurosis and human growth: the struggle towards self-realisation.* London: Routledge & Kegan Paul.

Horton, I. (2006) Structuring work with clients. In C. Feltham & I. Horton (eds), *The SAGE handbook of counselling and psychotherapy.* London: SAGE, pp. 118–25.

Inskipp, F. (1986) *Counselling: the trainer's handbook.* Cambridge: National Extension College.

Inskipp, F. (1996) *Skills training for counsellors.* London: Cassell.

Ivey, A.E., Ivey, M.B. & Simek-Morgan, L. (1997) *Counselling and psychotherapy: a multicultural approach.* Boston: Allyn & Bacon.

James, I.A. (2001) Schema therapy: the next generation but should it carry a health warning? *Behavioural and Cognitive Psychotherapy*, 29: 401–7.

Jeffers, S. (1991) *Feel the fear and do it anyway.* London: Arrow Books.

Jennings, S. (1990) *Dramatherapy: theory and practice for teachers and clinicians.* London: Routledge.

Joyce, P. & Sills, C. (2001) *Skills in Gestalt counselling and psychotherapy.* London: SAGE.

Kagan, N. (1975) *Influencing human interaction.* Washington, DC: American Personnel and Guidance Association.

Kahn, M. (1991) *Between therapist and client: the new relationship.* New York: W.H. Freeman.

Kazantzis, N. & Ronan, K.R. (2006) Can between sessions (homework) assignments be considered a common factor in psychotherapy? *Journal of Psychotherapy Integration*, 16.2: 115–27.

Kazantzis, N., Deane, F.P., Ronan, K.R. & L'Abate, L. (eds) (2005) *Using assignments in cognitive behaviour therapy.* New York: Routledge.

Kegan, R. (2006) *The evolving self: problem and process in human relationships.* Cambridge, MA: Harvard University Press.

Keijsers, G.P., Schaap, C.P. & Hoogduin, C.A. (2000) The impact of interpersonal patient and therapist behaviour on outcome in cognitive behaviour therapy: a review of empirical studies. *Behaviour Modification,* 24.2: 264–97.

Kelly, G.A. (1963) *A theory of personality: the psychology of personal constructs.* New York: W.W. Norton.

Kendall, P.C. & Hammen, C. (1998) *Abnormal psychology: understanding human problems.* Boston: Houghton-Mifflin.

Kirk, J. (1989) Cognitive behavioural assessment. In K. Hawton, P.M. Salkovskis, J. Kirk & D.M. Clark (eds), *Cognitive behaviour therapy for psychiatric problems.* Oxford: Oxford Medical Publications, pp. 13–51.

Klein, D.N., Schwarz, J.E., Santiago, N.J., Vivian, D., Vocisano, C., Castenguay, L.G., Arnow, B.A., Blalock, J.A., Markowitz, J.C., Rothbaum, B.O. & McCullough, J.P. Jr. (2003) Therapeutic alliance in depression treatment: controlling for prior change and patient characteristics. *Journal of Consulting and Clinical Psychology,* 71: 997–1006.

Kohut, H. (1977) *The restoration of the self.* New York: International Universities Press.

Kuyken, W. (2006) Evidence-based case formulation: is the emperor clothed? In N. Tarrier (ed.), *Case formulation in cognitive behaviour therapy.* London: Routledge, pp. 12–35.

Layard, R. (2005) *Happiness: lessons from a new science.* Harmondsworth: Penguin.

Layden, M.A., Newman, C.F., Freeman, A. & Morse, S.B. (1993) *Cognitive therapy of borderline personality disorder.* Boston, MA: Allyn & Bacon.

Leahy, R.L. (2001) *Overcoming resistance in cognitive therapy.* New York: Guilford Press.

Leahy, R.L. (2003) *Cognitive therapy techniques.* New York: Guilford Press.

Leahy, R.L. (2005) *The worry cure: stop worrying and start living.* London: Piatkus.

Leahy, R.L. (2007) Schematic mismatch in the therapeutic relationship. In P. Gilbert & R.L. Leahy (eds), *The therapeutic relationship in the cognitive behavioural psychotherapies.* London: Routledge, pp. 225–54.

Lewinsohn, P.M. & Gotlib, I.H. (1995) Behavioral theory and treatment of depression. In E. Beckham & W. Leber (eds), *Handbook of depression.* New York: Guilford Press, pp. 352–75.

Linehan, M.M. (1993) *Cognitive behavioural treatment of borderline personality disorder.* New York: Guilford Press.

Linklater, A. (2006) After Freud. *Prospect Magazine,* 123: 36–41. (Also currently available as a free download from the *Prospect* website: www.prospect-magazine.co.uk).

Liotti, G. (2007) Internal working models of attachment in the therapeutic relationship. In P. Gilbert & R.L. Leahy (eds), *The therapeutic relationship in the cognitive behavioural psychotherapies.* London: Routledge, pp. 143–61.

McGinn, R.K., Young, J.E. & Sanderson, W.C. (1995) When and how to do longer term therapy without feeling guilty. *Cognitive Behavioral Practice,* 2: 187–212.

McMahon, G. (1996) Assessment and case formulation. In C. Feltham & I. Horton (eds), *The SAGE handbook of counselling and psychotherapy.* London: SAGE, pp. 109–18.

Miller, W.R. & Rollnick, S. (2002) *Motivational interviewing.* (2nd edn). New York: Guilford Press.

Milrod, B., Leon, A.C., Busch, F., Rudden, M., Schwalberg, M., Clarkin, J., Aronson, A., Singer, M., Turchin, W., Toby Klass, E., Graf, E., Teres, J.J. & Shears, M.K. (2007) A randomised controlled trial of psychoanalytic psychotherapy for panic disorder. *American Journal of Psychiatry,* 164.2: 265–72.

Moorey, S. & Greer, S. (2002) *Cognitive behaviour therapy for people with cancer.* Oxford: Oxford University Press.

Nelson-Jones, R. (2005) *Practical counselling and helping skills: texts and exercises for the life skills counselling model.* London: SAGE.

Nicholson, J. (2006) *The perfect summer: dancing into the shadow in 1911.* London: John Murray.

Padesky, C. (1993) Socratic questioning: changing minds or guiding discovery? Key note address at the Congress of the European Association for Behavioural and Cognitive Therapies. London, September.

Padesky, C. (1994) *Cognitive therapy for anxiety.* Audiotape. Newport Beach, CA: Center for Cognitive Therapy. www.padesky.com

Padesky, C. (1996) Developing cognitive therapist competency: teaching and supervision models. In P. Salkovskis (ed.), *The frontiers of cognitive therapy.* New York: Guilford Press, pp. 266–92.

Padesky, C. (2004a) *Socratic questioning in cognitive therapy: clinical workshop.* Audiotape. Newport Beach, CA: Center for Cognitive Therapy. www.padesky.com

Padesky, C. (2004b) *Guided discovery – leading and following: Clinical workshop.* Audiotape. Newport Beach, CA: Center for Cognitive Therapy. www.padesky.com

Padesky, C. & Greenberger, D. (1995) *The clinician's guide to mind over mood.* New York: Guilford Press.

Padesky, C. & Mooney, K. (1998) Between two minds: the transformational power of underlying assumptions. Key note address at the Congress of the European Association for Behavioural and Cognitive Therapies, Cork, September.

Papageorgiou, C. & Wells, A. (2003) *Depressive rumination: nature, theory and treatment.* Chichester: Wiley.

Patterson, R. (2000) *The assertiveness workbook.* Oakland, CA: New Harbinger.

Persons, J.B. (1989) *Cognitive therapy: a case formulation approach.* New York: W.W. Norton.

Petry, N.M. (2000) A comprehensive guide to the application of contingency management procedures in clinical work. *Drug and Alcohol Dependence,* 58: 9–25.

Pierson, H. & Hayes, S. (2007) Using acceptance and commitment therapy to empower the therapeutic relationship. In P. Gilbert & R.L. Leahy (eds), *The therapeutic relationship in cognitive behavioural psychotherapies.* London: Routledge, pp. 205–28.

Popper, K.R. (1959) *The logic of scientific discovery.* London: Hutchinson.

Rachman, S. (1997) The evolution of cognitive behaviour therapy. In D.M. Clark & C.G. Fairburn (eds), *Science and practice of cognitive behaviour therapy.* Oxford: Oxford University Press, pp. 27–46.

Rachman, S. (2003) *The treatment of obsessions.* Oxford: Oxford University Press.

Rennie, D. (1998) *Person-centred counselling: an experiential approach.* Thousand Oaks, CA: SAGE.

Rescorla, R.A. (1988) Pavlovian conditioning: it is not what you think it is. *American Psychologist,* 43: 151–60.

Rogers, C.R. (1961) *On becoming a person.* Boston: Houghton Mifflin.

Safran, J.D. & Segal, Z.V. (1990) *Interpersonal processes and cognitive therapy.* New York: Guilford Press.

Salkovskis, P. (ed.) (1996a) *The frontiers of cognitive therapy.* New York: Guilford Press.

Salkovskis, P. (1996b) The cognitive approach to anxiety: threat beliefs, safety-seeking behaviour, and the special case of health anxiety and obsessions. In P. Salkovskis (ed.), *The frontiers of cognitive therapy.* New York: Guilford Press, pp. 48–74.

Sanders, D. & Wills, F. (1999) The therapeutic relationship in cognitive therapy. In C. Feltham (ed.), *The therapeutic relationship in counselling and psychotherapy.* London: SAGE, pp. 120–38.

Sanders, D. & Wills, F. (2003) *Counselling for anxiety problems* (2nd edn). London: SAGE.

Sanders, D. & Wills, F. (2005) *Cognitive therapy: an introduction.* London: SAGE.

Scaife, J., Inskipp, F., Proctor, B., Scaife, J. & Walsh, S. (2001) *Supervision in the mental health professions: a practitioner's guide.* Hove: Brunner-Routledge.

Scott, M. & Stradling, S. (2000) *Counselling for post-traumatic stress disorder.* London: SAGE.

Sedgewick, P. (1982) *Psychopolitics (the politics of health).* London: Pluto Press.

Segal, Z.V., Williams, J.M.G. & Teasdale, J.D. (2002) *Mindfulness based cognitive therapy for depression: a new approach to preventing relapse.* New York: Guilford Press.

Seligman, M.E.P. (2002) *Authentic happiness: using the new positive psychology to release your potential for lasting fulfilment.* New York: Free Press.

Shapiro, F. (2001) *Eye Movement Desensitization and Reprocessing (EMDR): basic principles, protocols and procedures.* New York: Guilford Press.

Sheldon, B. (1995) *Cognitive behaviour therapy: research, practice & philosophy.* London: Routledge.

Simmons, M. & Wills, F. (2006) *CBT skills in practice.* DVD and video. University of Wales Newport.

Sloane, R.B., Staples, F.R., Cristol, A.H. & Yorkston, N.J. (1975) Short term analytically orientated psychotherapy versus behavior therapy. *American Journal of Psychiatry,* 132: 373–7.

Slobodin, R. (1997) *Rivers: the life.* Stroud: Sutton.

Staddon, J. (2001) *The new behaviorism: mind, mechanism & society.* Philadelphia: Psychology Press.

Steketee, G. (1999) *Overcoming obsessive-compulsive disorder: therapist's protocol.* Oakland, CA: New Harbinger.

Tarrier, N. & Calam, R. (2002) New developments in cognitive case formulation – epidemiological, systemic and social context: an integrative approach. *Behavioural and Cognitive Psychotherapy,* 30.2: 311–28.

Teasdale, J. (1996) Clinically relevant theory: integrating clinical insight with cognitive science. In P. Salkovskis (ed.), *The frontiers of cognitive therapy.* New York: Guilford Press, pp. 26–47.

Teasdale, J. (2004) Mindfulness and the third wave of cognitive behavioural therapies. Keynote address at the Congress of the European Association for Behavioural and Cognitive Therapies, Manchester, September.

Townend, M., Ianetta, L.E. & Freeston, M.H. (2002) Clinical supervision in practice: a survey of UK cognitive behaviour psychotherapists accredited by the BABCP [British Association for Behavioural and Cognitive Psychotherapies]. *Behavioural and Cognitive Psychotherapy,* 30: 485–500.

Turner, S.W. & Lee, D. (1998) *Measures in post-traumatic stress disorder: a practitioner's guide.* Windsor: NFER-Nelson.

Van der Kolk, B. (1994) The body keeps the score: the evolving psychobiology of post-traumatic stress disorder. *Harvard Review of Psychiatry,* 1.5: 253–65.

Van Deurzen-Smith, E. (1988) *Existential counselling in practice.* London: SAGE.

Vickers, S. (2006) *The other side of you.* London: Fourth Estate.

Wachtel, P. (1982) *Resistance: psychodynamic and behavioural approaches.* New York: Plenum.

Weishaar, M.E. (1993) *Aaron T. Beck: the SAGE Modern Masters Series*. London: SAGE.

Wells, A. (1997) *Cognitive therapy of anxiety disorders*. Chichester: Wiley.

Wells, A. (2000) *Emotional disorders and metacognition*. Chichester: Wiley.

Wells, A. (2006) Cognitive therapy case formulation in anxiety disorders. In N. Tarrier (ed.), *Case formulation on cognitive behaviour therapy: the treatment of challenging and complex cases*. Hove: Routledge, pp. 52–80.

Wells, A. & Matthews, G. (1994) *Attention and emotion: a clinical perspective*. Hove: Lawrence Erlbaum Associates.

Westbrook, D., Kennerley, H. & Kirk, J. (2007) *An introduction to cognitive behaviour therapy: skills and applications*. London: SAGE.

Williams, C. (2003) *Overcoming anxiety: a five areas approach*. London: Hodder Arnold.

Williams, M.J.G., Watts, F.N., MacLeod, C. & Mathews, A. (1997) *Cognitive processes and the emotional disorders*. Chichester: Wiley.

Williams, M.J.G., Teasdale, J.D., Segal, Z.V. & Kabat-Zinn, J. (2007) *The mindful way through depression*. New York: Guilford Press.

Wills, F. (1998) Changes in therapeutic attitudes during CBT training. Paper given at the Congress of the European Association for Behavioural and Cognitive Therapies, Cork, September.

Wills, F. (2006a) Cognitive therapy: a down to earth and accessible therapy. In C. Sills (ed.), *Contracts in counselling and psychotherapy* (2nd edn). London: SAGE, pp. 41–51.

Wills, F. (2006b) CBT: can counsellors fill the gap? *Healthcare Counselling and Psychotherapy Journal*, 6.2: 6–9.

Wills, F. (2007) Some cognitive distortions occur more frequently than others. Departmental paper, University of Wales Newport, School for Social and Health Sciences, February.

Wills, F. & Sanders, D. (1997) *Cognitive therapy: transforming the image*. London: SAGE.

Winnicott, D.W. (1965) *The maturational processes and the facilitating environment*. London: Hogarth.

Wolpe, J. (1958) *Psychotherapy by reciprocal inhibition*. Stanford, CA: Stanford University Press.

Wright, J.H., Basco, M.R. & Thase, M.E. (2006) *Learning cognitive behavior therapy: an illustrated guide*. Washington, DC: American Psychiatric Publishing, Inc.

Young, J. (1994) *Cognitive therapy for personality disorders: a schema focused approach*. Saratosa, FL: Professional Resources Press.

Young, J. & Klosko, J. (1994) *Reinventing your life*. New York: Plume.

Young, J. & Klosko, J. (1998) *Reinventing your life: how to break free from negative life patterns* (reprint edn). New York: Penguin Puttnam.

Young, J., Klosko, J.S. & Weishaar, M.E. (2003) *Schema therapy: a practitioner's guide*. New York: Guilford Press.

Zigmond, A.S. & Snaith, R.P. (1983) The hospital anxiety and depression scale. *Acta Psychiatrica Scandinavica*, 67: 361–70.

INDEX